MANAGING PRODUCTIVITY IN CONSTRUCTION

For our families

Managing Productivity in Construction

JIT Operations and Measurements

LOW SUI PHENG
National University of Singapore

CHAN YUE MENG
Paul Y. Construction (S) Pte Ltd

Aldershot • Brookfield USA • Hong Kong • Singapore • Sydney

Published by
Ashgate Publishing Limited
Gower House
Croft Road
Aldershot
Hants GU11 3HR
England

Ashgate Publishing Company
Old Post Road
Brookfield
Vermont 05036
USA

British Library Cataloguing in Publication Data

Pheng, Low Sui
　　Managing productivity in construction : JIT operations and
　　measurements
　　1.Construction industry 2.Construction industry - Singapore
　　3.Industrial productivity 4.Industrial productivity -
　　Singapore 5.Just-in-time systems
　　I.Title II.Chan, Yue Meng
　　690'.0685

Library of Congress Catalog Card Number:97-70343

ISBN 1 85972 607 0

Printed and bound by Athenaeum Press, Ltd.,
Gateshead, Tyne & Wear.

Contents

Figures and tables

Preface

The 1991 Strategic Economic Plan of Singapore had alarmingly highlighted the comparatively low productivity in the local construction sector. The 1992 Construction Productivity Taskforce had attributed the low productivity of the local construction industry to its visibly low technology image and acute employment of a large number of foreign workers. Comparing site labour productivity level by using the indicator of "square metre of built-up area per man-day", it has been found that Japan's construction industry is 35 per cent more productive than Singapore's construction industry, while a highly industrialised country like Finland is 75 per cent more productive than Singapore. It is therefore of crucial importance to raise productivity in the local construction sector if Singapore aspires to export her construction services overseas and to join the realms of developed nations by the year 2030.

The feasibility of using the established "Just-In-Time" (JIT) concept from the manufacturing industry to raise productivity in the construction industry was already examined elsewhere. This book seeks to further explore the viable applications of the JIT concept to improve productivity for the "off-site" prefabrication of precast concrete components. To accomplish this objective, an industry-wide exploratory study was conducted in 1993 covering 20 local prefabrication firms in Singapore. In addition to determining the feasibility of JIT application in the local prefabrication industry, this book also develops a viable JIT-based framework to guide the industry towards raising its level of productivity. Because the JIT philosophy has its origin in the manufacturing industry, the first step towards introducing the concept for the construction industry should be targeted at prefabrication in view of the close similiarities between prefabrication and production under factory conditions. Prefabrication is the best avenue for simulating a manufacturing environment in the construction industry.

The findings developed in this study suggest that there is immense potentials for applying the JIT concept to improve productivity in prefabrication for the construction industry. Nevertheless, the eight fundamental principles of the JIT philosophy - namely, attacking fundamental problems; elimination of waste; the "kanban" or "pull" system;

uninterrupted work flow; the total quality control concept; top management commitment and employee involvement; supplier and client relations; and continuous improvements - should be of strategic relevance not only for prefabrication but also for the traditional cast insitu method of construction. For a start, however, the construction industry should first concentrate on the development of a JIT blueprint for prefabrication before extending the concept further to other methods of construction. Before this can be done, practitioners must familiarise themselves with what the JIT concept encompasses and how it can be implemented.

Apart from examining the application of JIT in the construction industry, the other crucial area of importance is founded on the need to establish valid and objective accounting procedures for measuring time waste in construction operations. The measurement of time waste in construction operations can help facilitate managerial control once organisational weaknesses are identified. Following the formulation of a valid accounting procedure for this purpose, three case studies were adopted to test its validity. These case studies were able to demonstrate that JIT waste can indeed be measured. In this connection, the unwavering support of Dr Roland Neo and his colleagues at Neo Corporation as well as the hard work put in by Miss Stephanie Tan Kai Lee in making these case studies possible are hereby gratefully acknowledged. Their inputs have certainly contributed immensely to the advancement of new knowledge in so far as the quantification of JIT waste is concerned.

With the well-being of the construction industry in mind, it is our hope that this book will serve to advance the needs of the industry to help manage, measure and raise productivity in construction.

Low Sui Pheng
Chan Yue Meng

1 Introduction

Background

Over the last two decades, Construction and Works made up, on average, 46 per cent of Gross Fixed Capital Formation in Singapore. This undoubtedly shows the importance of the construction sector's role in the national economy. Despite this significance, the 1991 Strategic Economic Plan had alarmingly highlighted the comparatively low productivity of the local construction sector. As further confirmation of the findings of the 1992 Construction Productivity Taskforce Report, Prime Minister Mr Goh Chok Tong in his 1992 National Day Message, likewise, noted with concern that construction productivity in Singapore is some 53 years behind that of Japan. It is therefore of crucial importance to increase productivity in the construction sector if Singapore aspires to join the realms of developed nations by the year 2030.

The concern for low productivity in the construction sector is both instructive and timely but disturbing. It is instructive and timely because as the age of trade globalization draws imminently near, the construction industry, like many other sectors of the national economy, would need to export its services more aggressively overseas. This is already evident from the substantial investments made by Singapore's construction-related corporations in countries like China, Vietnam, Cambodia and Myanmar. The construction sector's ability to provide a high level of productivity is therefore a significant one if the industry is to compete effectively for projects in overseas countries.

Whilst Singapore's superb infrastructures and amenities like her first-class airport, harbour, road network system and telecommunication facilities are held in high esteem, it is disturbing to note that many have taken these achievements for granted. The truth is that Singapore's economy may not have taken off into maturity so rapidly without the crucial contributions from the construction industry. The construction industry should not, therefore, be taken for granted but a concerted effort should instead be made by everyone concerned to make it more productive and cost competitive. Only then can Singapore's construction entrepreneurs achieve success in their

1

long-term objectives towards regional expansion.

Review of existing literature

A review of past literature has revealed that low construction productivity is not a new issue of concern to the construction industry. General problems which led to low levels of productivity in the construction industry have been examined by numerous researchers over the past two decades. (Bishop, 1975; Maloney, 1983; Sumanth, 1984; Lewis, 1987). These studies have concentrated on factors such as effects of the learning curve and benefits of repetition on the labour force (Thomas, Mathews & Ward, 1986), adverse effects of inclement weather (Grimm & Wagner, 1974), use of plant, equipment and hand held power tools (Cheetham & Hall, 1984; Sozen & Giritli, 1987), and use of computers and artificial intelligence (Christian, 1987; Oglesby, Parker & Howell, 1989); all of which have an impact on construction productivity.

Likewise, specific problems relating to productivity on construction sites were also investigated (Baxendale, 1985). The motivation and training of the workforce has been identified as a crucial factor in the productivity movement. (Thomas, Mathews and Ward, 1986). Where the labour force is concerned, studies have urged management to retain a tight control over workers. Apart from control, training and other forms of incentives have also been shown to be important in motivating the workforce. However, the degree of management control rather than level of financial incentive has shown a strong positive effect on productivity. (Malcolm, et. al., 1987).

The construction industry has been perceived to be a highly complex and fragmented sector of the economy. (Lim and Low, 1992). Empirical approaches have therefore often lend themselves suitably for operationalising productivity in construction activities. The establishment of various norm values or average output rates at different levels of the worker, gangs, subsector and sector has been emphasised. (Suite, 1987). Assessments of actual realised rates for a particular job site against the established norm values should be carried out constantly to assess productivity performance.

Despite the numerous studies on construction productivity, it is surprising to note that not many of these studies have emphasised the need to efficiently control the allocation and management of scarce construction resources to reduce wastage and idle time on construction sites (Malcolm, et. al., 1987). The three major resources in construction - namely, manpower, machinery and materials - have therefore been subjected to much scrutiny as to how their utilisation may be achieved more efficiently.

Productivity in construction has subsequently been examined in the light of the collective incorporation of manpower, machinery and materials on work sites. Where hazardous and other mass rugged activities are encountered in construction, the preferred use of machinery and equipment over manual labour can lead to productivity improvement. However, the use of construction plant and equipment should only be planned and managed to justify their usage with actual corresponding requirements on site. Unless necessary, no plant and equipment should be left idle with excess operating capacities. Likewise, the use of materials should also be planned and managed appropriately to reduce wastage on site. Construction productivity would be affected adversely if the materials required for use are not available in the quantity or quality required when they are needed (Low,1992).

Productivity in the Singapore construction industry

In order to gain an insight of the low level of construction productivity in Singapore's construction sector, it is essential to highlight the findings of the 1992 Construction Productivity Taskforce. The Taskforce is an ad hoc executive committee set up to critically examine and address the low level of construction productivity. The Taskforce was chaired by the Construction Industry Development Board (CIDB) and comprised of professional members from key governmental bodies, statutory boards and the private sector. This section is mainly concerned with the findings of the Taskforce.

The construction sector in Singapore has been perceived by the Taskforce as a low productivity sector primarily because of its visibly low-technology image and acute employment of a large number of foreign workers.

Using value-added per worker (the only indicator for comparison across economic sectors) as the economic indicator to measure construction productivity, it can be seen from Table 1.1 that construction productivity had only increased at an average rate of 3.1 per cent between 1982 to 1991. This was lower than the average of 4.5 per cent for manufacturing and 4.2 per cent for the whole economy. It is thus evident that construction productivity had lagged behind that of manufacturing.

Although value added per worker is the only indicator for comparison across economic sectors, the Taskforce viewed it as a rather limited one when applied to construction. This is due to the following limitations:

1   The severe magnitudes of boom and bust cycles in construction always tend to artificially inflate and deflate the value added respectively.

2   Value added only measures the productivity of one part of the construction process - that of site production which tends to be the least productive part of construction.

3   Material and labour cost increases after contract awards can profoundly alter value added due to depression in the profit margins.

4   It is difficult to use the value added per worker indicator to compare with the construction indicators of other countries.

The Taskforce therefore used an alternative indicator of "square metres of built-up area per manday" based mainly on the physical output per worker. This productivity indicator has been used in some developed countries such as Japan and Finland. The indicator measures the on-site mandays required to put together a unit of completed floor area. The project, or industry, is more productive if less site workers are needed to put up the same amount of

3

Table 1.1
Changes in productivity by sector

(computed based on value added per worker)

Year	Manufacturing	Construction	National Average
1982	-0.7	4.2	1.6
1983	9.1	10.1	5.3
1984	7.2	9.0	6.9
1985	-1.5	5.7	3.1
1986	13.6	-4.3	6.3
1987	3.7	0.8	4.8
1988	2.0	1.6	4.5
1989	3.8	0.1	4.8
1990	4.6	1.4	3.4
1991	3.4	2.8	1.5
Average	4.5	3.1	4.2
1992 (1st Quarter)	-0.9	12.5	1.5

Source: *CIDB (1992), Raising Singapore's Construction Productivity, Construction Industry Development Board*

finished floor space.

Using square-metres per manday as the indicator, the productivity levels of the construction sectors of Japan and Finland were compared with that of Singapore's. Japan's construction productivity levels averages 0.44 square-metres per manday whilst Singapore only achieves an average of 0.34 square-metres per manday (refer to Table 1.2). Broadly speaking, Japan's productivity levels are about 29 per cent higher than Singapore's.

The comparison with Finland, a highly industrialized country, had revealed an even more alarming widening gap between the construction productivity levels of Finland and Singapore. Figure 1.1 shows that Finland has a construction productivity level averaging 0.55 square-metres per manday. This is 62 per cent higher than Singapore's productivity level.

Comparisons with Japan and Finland thus give an indication of Singapore's comparatively low construction productivity level. In view of this inferior productivity position, it is therefore imperative for productivity performance in the local construction industry to be raised. The major strategic reasons for this need are set out as follows:

1   Construction must keep pace with other economic sectors which are under even more severe pressure to use fewer workers than construction.

2   The future attraction of the construction industry must be maintained as the industry is still suffering from an image problem due to its large number of foreign workers and its attendant social and safety problems.

4

Table 1.2
Construction productivity of Japan and Singapore

Building category	Productivity (m²/man-day)	
	Singapore	Japan
Commercial	0.29	0.34
Residential	0.27 (Private Sector)	0.46
	0.64 (Public Sector)	
Industrial	0.38	0.53
Institutional	0.24	0.37
Overall	0.34	0.44

Source: *CIDB (1992), Raising Singapore's Construction Productivity, Construction Industry Development Board*

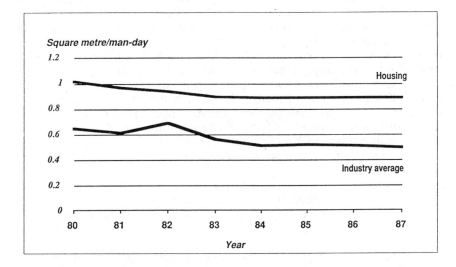

Figure 1.1   Construction productivity in Finland

Source: *CIDB (1992), Raising Singapore's Construction Productivity, Construction Industry Development Board*

3   The engineering prerogative towards excellence and innovation needs to be fulfilled.

4   Singapore's future competitiveness through technological leadership must be enhanced.

Just-In-Time concept for improving construction productivity

Heeding the Singapore government's mission to raise productivity in the local construction industry, Lim and Low (1992) pioneered an exploratory study in 1992 to examine the feasibility of using an established concept from the manufacturing industry to raise productivity in the construction industry (Lim and Low, 1992). This concept is the Japanese "Just-In-Time" (JIT) concept or commonly referred to as the Toyota Production System Concept (Sugimori, et al, 1971). Developed and promoted in Japan by the Toyota Motor Corporation in the early fifties, the JIT concept is a recent but proven and successful philosophy which has helped Japanese automobile manufacturers compete formidably and successfully against American and other European car makers globally. The JIT concept has since then attained a highly respectful credibility as a useful philosophy that have successfully helped the manufacturing industries in Japan and worldwide to overcome the severe problems of low productivity and quality.

The JIT concept is fundamentally a systems approach to developing and operating the manufacturing process. It is basically a philosophy rather than a technique. The term JIT essentially idealizes how the major components of manufacturing - namely, capital, materials, equipment and labour - should be made available only at the right quantity "just-in-time" to complete a specific job. This simply means purchasing or manufacturing only what is needed and delivering only when it is needed. JIT can thus be better described both as a management philosophy which helps to integrate and streamline the manufacturing system into its simplest possible process; and as a continuous process of striving to minimise elements in the manufacturing systems which restrain productivity (Low, 1992).

JIT utilizes simple management tools which are essentially concerned with:

1   Elimination of unnecessary wasteful functions which do not add value to the product such as inspections, rework, inventory, waiting time, etc.

2   Development of simple production systems which encourage early problem identification leading to constant improvement in processes and procedures.

3   Fulfilling the marketing concept by satisfying the customer's need and reducing the customer's cost of purchasing and using a product.

When fully implemented successfully, JIT has proven to bring about the following potential benefits:

1   Decrease in scrap, raw materials and rework rates.

2   Decrease in work-in-process inventory, physical space and factory overheads.

3   Lower production costs.

4   Decrease in manufacturing lead times.

5   Increased teamwork, higher workers' morale and motivation.

6   Improvement of quality.

7   Improvement of customer service levels.

8   Overall improvements in productivity and profitability.

In "Just-In-Time Productivity for Construction", Lim and Low (1992) highlighted that whilst the wide applicability of the JIT concept in construction can only be realized gainfully if appropriate structural modifications are made in the industry, the concept is nonetheless particularly amenable for use in the area of materials management in the construction setting to achieve zero-inventory and higher levels of productivity.

In construction, materials management constitutes an important aspect in the management of construction projects. Inventories or stocks of construction materials are required to be maintained to ensure the smooth flow of construction work. However, holding stocks cost money since capital is required not only for purchasing the stock but also for storing the stock. Too early or too high a level of stock, i.e overstocking, not only ties up a large sum of investment but also subject the stock to the risk of loss due to damage, theft or obsolescence. In addition, overstocking also gives rise to physical problems associated with storage space, handling and utilization. On the other hand, too late or too low a stock, i.e understocking, may result in the risk of shortages and running out of stock, hence delaying construction work. Therefore, construction materials should only be procured just-in-time and at the right quantity in order to minimise total cost and waste (Lim and Low, 1992).

The drive towards prefabrication

The Construction Productivity Taskforce in its 1992 Report had outlined the lack of standardization due to underdevelopment of prefabrication and buildability know-how as one of the major contributory factors towards the currently low level of construction productivity in Singapore. This underdevelopment of prefabrication and buildability know-how was caused by a number of reasons, viz:

1   Cost has often favoured the use of more labour intensive, less productive conventional designs in most construction projects. Too often, designers are not concerned much with standardization and are less familiar with the know-how of more buildable designs which always require additional effort on the part of the designers. While some buildable features can be adopted using common sense, others

7

require considerable expertise and experience.

2   Prefabrication technology, in particular, is not for the amateur. The Housing and Development Board (HDB) started with using foreign design-and-build contractors to transfer the know-how before further developing the systems themselves. Many of these systems have originated from Europe and Japan where extensive research and development (R & D) works were done. Countries like Finland still does R & D to improve their prefabrication systems uptill today. Local problems such as water leakage in joints will require attention and continuous development. Many small local design firms do not have the priviledge of such experience and therefore try to avoid using them altogether. The use of prefabrication is therefore still dependent on the promotional efforts of the prefabricators and the industry's exposure to such projects.

3   Smaller projects are also often disadvantaged in the use of prefabricated components. As an illustration, it does not make sense for a designer to design his own standard components when the number does not justify the costs of producing them. It will be easier to specify such components if these are already available in the market. A greater degree of standardization is therefore required in the industry if small projects are encouraged to use prefabricated components.

The Taskforce was of the view that if Singapore aspires to achieve the Finnish level of productivity, some of the major aspects of the Finnish industrialization model - particularly her prefabrication development experience - must be seriously examined for application in the Singapore context. To this end, some of the main features of Finland's highly industrialized construction industry are worth noting, viz:

1   The extremely cold Finnish weather which sets in six months a year makes it desirable to minimise work on site. The industry has therefore adopted a very high level of prefabrication. Its level of full and partial prefabrication at 60 per cent for all buildings is probably the highest in the world. In contrast, the prefabrication level in Singapore's industry is currently only about five per cent.

2   The development of prefabrication was carried out in a systematic and concerted manner involving the professional, construction and manufacturing bodies. A high level of standardization was therefore achieved. In addition, R & D have enabled advancements to be successfully made in joint technology which is crucial for prefabrication.

3   Finland is extremely stringent on foreign labour. The strategy was therefore to minimise labour usage. Although the resulting wages are very high, the corresponding high productivity levels justify them.

The results of Finland's model of industrialization are impressive. Its absence of foreign workers and concerted industry effort to develop prefabrication has enabled it to achieve high productivity and high wages for its workers, with minimum increase in unit construction cost between 1965 to 1985. With a virtually constant number of workers, the industry was able to increase its output by an average of four per cent per year for 15 years.

In its conclusion, the Taskforce had held that the Finnish level of productivity is certainly a possibility for Singapore. However, Singapore must be prepared for a quantum leap in the level of employment of prefabrication with an accompanying high level and widespread usage of standardization in her construction industry. This strategic direction should be in line with the response to use more labour-saving methods in construction to correspond with the strategic plan to tighten the employment of foreign workers over the next few years. The level of "off-site" prefabrication must increase especially in structural work and "brick and mortar" architectural work which consume the highest amount of unproductive foreign labour.

The focus of this book

In line with the prefabrication drive mooted by the Taskforce as a strategic direction towards improving productivity in the local construction industry, this book will focus on the feasibility of using the JIT concept to raise productivity in the local "off-site" prefabrication sector which manufactures precast concrete components for both civil engineering and building construction projects. As the construction industry spans over a wide spectrum of activities which are complex, diverse and fragmented in nature, it was believed that for a good start, any feasible application of the JIT concept to improve productivity in the entire industry should first be applied to those sectors which exhibit characteristics most amenable for JIT application. In this direction, the JIT concept does appear relevant for the "off-site" prefabrication industry which employs process or repetitive manufacturing processes. The promotion of industrialization in construction to trigger the widespread usage and manufacture of standard prefabricated components mirrors closely the standardized products and repetitive processes found in the manufacturing industry. Also, the "manufacturing factory" nature of "off-site" prefabrication firms offers an ideal environment which is most conducive for the application of the JIT concept.

While Lim and Low (1992) have drawn on a general overview of the applicability of JIT in construction with particular emphasis in the area of materials management, this book will examine how well the JIT concept can be applied to the "off-site" prefabrication industry whose nature is very much identical to that of the manufacturing industry. It is hoped that the conceptual justifications together with the findings presented in this book will provide local prefabricators with a powerful management philosophy to boost their efficiency, effectiveness, profitability and competitiveness.

Because the "off-site" prefabrication industry has been singled out for study in this book, the following hypothesis can now   postulated:

"Although there are fundamental differences between the manufacturing and construction industries, the successful application of the JIT concept in the former can likewise be extended selectively for use in the latter; particularly the 'off-site' prefabrication sector producing precast concrete components for the construction industry."

While it is important at this stage to focus on the application of the JIT concept in the construction industry, it is equally important to be able to measure the effect the concept has within the industry following its implementation. For this purpose, valid accounting procedures which serve to quantify JIT wastes in construction operations are necessary for management control. The accounting procedures which may be used for measuring JIT wastes are explained and tested by means of real-life case studies in this book.

In summary, the objectives of this book are as follows:

1   To study the feasibility of using the JIT concept to improve productivity in the "off-site" precast concrete component prefabrication firms of the local construction industry.

2   To develop and explore the use of valid accounting procedures for measuring JIT wastes which, in turn, will help to facilitate management control.

3   To develop a viable framework for JIT application in the "off-site" precast concrete component prefabrication industry.

2 The Just-In-Time philosophy

Historical background

The JIT system was introduced and promoted in the early 1950s by Mr Taiichi Ohno, former Executive Vice-President of Toyota Motor Corporation (Ansari & Modarress,1990). Although Toyota was not the first firm to use JIT, it is widely recognized as the firm that has done most in promoting and developing the concept, both in Japan and abroad. Indeed, JIT is commonly referred to as the Toyota Production System.

It was argued that this system was developed in response to the special circumstances unique to Japan such as her lack of natural resources, lack of energy resources and limited space. Compared with the United States, for instance, the limited availability of resources and land are major constraints to manufacturing in Japan. It is not easy for Japanese manufacturing plants to expand because of the scarcity of land resources. This had encouraged smaller, more flexible production facilities. The land constraint also means that suppliers in Japan are not as widely distributed geographically as they are in the United States. The lack of natural resources such as petroleum, coal, iron and bauxite means that they have to be imported, which discourages production waste.

When the Japanese advantage in producing high-quality manufactured goods at low costs was first noticed, credit was given to the Japanese culture and its strong work ethics. (Ouchi, 1981). Further study then turned to differences in personnel practices including lifelong employment for about 30 per cent of the employees, training multifunctional workers, collective decision-making, implicit control mechanisms and government policy. (Sepehri, 1986)

It was found later that the real differences between Japanese practices and elsewhere might be attributed to good manufacturing management, operational discipline, consistency and teamwork in the Japanese firms.

Examination and comparison of American and Japanese corporations have indeed shown that productivity and performance are matters of management, not culture or worker's background. The success of JIT is, therefore, not the result of cultural, structural or environmental factors. Rather, it stems from planned management action that any manufacturer can implement (Schmenner, 1990).

The Japanese were in fact using many of the techniques already employed and developed in the Western world. A significant difference, though, was that the Japanese were driven by completely different guiding philosophies and work attitudes.

Most quality control efforts in Japan were originally initiated and instructed by American pioneers. Quality control circles started in Japan in the late 1950s and early 1960s following the advice of quality specialists such as Drs Deming and Juran who visited Japan after the Second World War and lectured extensively on statistical quality control and how this could be applied in the manufacturing industry. (Dale & Plunkett, 1990). Almost all of the JIT principles are stated in Henry Ford's book, *My Life and Work*. This book, published in 1924, explains how the iron ore at the River Rogue plant in Detroit was smelted into iron, re-melted with scrap into steel, and poured into mould for engine blocks. Engine blocks were then cooled, machined, assembled into an engine, tested, transported to the automobile plant to be assembled into a final car and delivered. The manufacturing time from raw ore to a finished and delivered car was an astonishing forty-eight hours in 1924. (Hay, 1988)

Although the JIT philosophy flourished in Japan, United States managers paid little heed to it until about 1980 when Kawasaki in Lincoln, Nebraska, successfully adopted the philosophy. (Schroeder, 1989) Since that time, numerous organizations such as Hewlett-Packard, Sperry, Omark, General Electric (GE), IBM, Harley Davidson, Eaton, and Tennant Co. have utilized JIT techniques successfully to improve their manufacturing operations.

GE was perhaps the first, outside of Japan, to mount a JIT campaign. Two GE plants had JIT projects in 1980; there were ten GE plants in 1981, twenty in 1982, and forty in 1983. GE's JIT efforts are in a variety of manufacturing types: locomotives, dishwashers, huge vacuum circuit breakers, jet engines, switches, generators, coffee makers, etc. (Sepehri, 1986)

JIT projects are now being launched in most of the better known North American industrial corporations. As of March 1985, as many as 250 of the Fortune 1000 companies reported considering some form of JIT for their operations. The concept of JIT has also been applied in Europe and the United Kingdom. (Voss & Clutterbuck, 1989)

JIT philosophy and concept

JIT marks a substantial shift away from major traditional approaches to manufacturing management. JIT is not likened to typical software packages like optimized production technology (OPT), materials requirements planning (MRP) and manufacturing resource planning (MRP II) systems, and reorder level/ reorder quantities (ROL/ROQ) systems. Instead of feeding collated data into computer packages and using the output as a basis for managerial action, the JIT approach examines thoroughly and gradually evaluates the fundamental problems that are holding the manufacturing organization back

12

in terms of its efficiency, productivity and profitability. JIT is, therefore, best defined as a philosophy that, when implemented correctly, will permeate every department of the organization and change the way in which everyone operates.

JIT is thus a philosophy that relates to the way a manufacturing organization organizes and operates its business. It is more than an inventory and quality control methodology. It is a philosophical way of organizational life that promotes an aggressive search for wasteful, inefficient and ineffective activities (Thomas, 1987).

JIT is basically a disciplined approach to improving overall productivity and eliminating waste. It provides for the cost-effective production and delivery of only the necessary quantity of parts at the right quality, at the right time and place, while using a minimum amount of facilities, equipment, materials and human resources (Voss, 1987). It is an aggressive philosophy which stimulates workers to identify and resolve problems and operational weaknesses which hinder organizational effectiveness and efficiency (Schonberger, 1982; Hall, 1983). A key element of JIT is simplification. JIT is seen as a philosophy of total pride in making the business lean, more simple and effective to operate, and with a higher degree of integration (Mortimer, 1986). JIT is in fact simplicity, efficiency and minimum waste.

As a management philosophy, JIT is mainly concerned with creating the right environment for effective operations. The first environment area is strategic. This covers the major, fundamental issues that govern the operation of the organization. Examples are the choice of products to be manufactured, the control mechanisms for the factory and the cost of production, including set-up time, scrap and other quality costs. The second area is tactical, which is concerned with actions and decisions that have a relatively small impact on the operation of the organization. Examples are deciding job priority for a particular process or determining quantum to be purchased from an external supplier. The JIT approach seeks to focus attention away from the detailed tactical decision-making towards the more strategic areas to bring about greater effectiveness in the manufacturing processes.

The concept of JIT manufacturing systems is described by Schonberger (1982) as follows: produce and deliver finished goods just in time to be sold, sub-assemblies just in time to be assembled into finished goods, fabricated parts just in time to go into sub-assemblies and purchased materials just in time to be transformed into fabricated parts. Like perfect quality, absolute just-in-time performance is never attained but rather is an ideal to be pursued aggressively.

JIT in the narrow sense means having only the necessary part at the necessary place at the necessary time. In the broadest sense, it refers to all activities that combine to make transfer of parts possible - everything from market research to design of product and on through production to final delivery to the customer (Sepehri, 1986). It is a problem-identifying way of looking at everything connected with manufacturing. In other words, in its broader sense, JIT is seen as a total corporate philosophy which must be embraced in all aspects of the firm's behaviour. It stresses not only the need to reduce inventories but also the need to involve all workers and managers in the production process. Improving worker commitment, feelings of responsibility and work satisfaction are all necessary if the demands of JIT are to be fully met.

Principles of JIT

There is no one way of conceptualizing or classifying the principles of JIT. The views of some key authors on Japanese manufacturing systems are presented here in order to distill from these views some general guiding principles of JIT for application.

Professor Robert W. Hall (1983) in his seminal work on "Zero Inventories" states that JIT is not confined to a set of techniques for improving production defined in the narrow sense as material conversion. It is a way to visualize the physical operations of the company from raw material to customer delivery. Hall (1983) suggests the following principles of the Japanese manufacturing system:

1   Produce what the customer desires.

2   Produce products only at the rate the customer wants them.

3   Produce with perfect quality.

4   Produce instantaneously - with zero unnecessary lead time.

5   Produce with no waste of labour, materials or equipment; every move has a purpose so there is zero idle inventory.

6   Produce by methods that allow for the development of people.

Monden (1983), who is more concerned with the technical aspects of JIT, identifies the following as important basic elements of the JIT production system:

1   Smoothing of production - an effort should be made to minimise the fluctuations of production from a workstation to the next workstation. If the subsequent process withdraws materials in a fluctuating manner with regard to quantity and time, then it becomes essential for the preceding workstation to have enough inventory to meet this fluctuating demand.

2   Standardization of jobs.

3   Process designing - the machine layout should be re-arranged to improve on the process and work flows to allow multi-functional workers to perform multi-operations and operate on many machines. In JIT, each worker is familiar with many functions and machine operations and can assist in time of troubles.

Richard J. Schonberger (1982), one of the strongest advocates of JIT, identifies nine simple yet hidden lessons from the Japanese. These lessons are as follows:

1   Management technology is a highly transportable commodity.

2   Just-in-time production exposes problems otherwise hidden by excess inventories and staff.

3   Quality begins with production and requires a company-wide "habit of improvement".

4   Culture is no obstacle; just-in-time techniques can change behaviour.

5   Simplify plant layout, and goods will flow like water.

6   Flexibility in production - line management opens doors.

7   Travel light and make numerous trips in purchasing - like the water beetle.

8   More self-improvement, fewer programs, less specialist intervention in worker development.

9   Simplicity is the natural state.

Lubben (1988) views JIT as a systems approach to developing and operating the manufacturing process. It helps management to achieve a competitive edge through three simple management tools:

1   Integrating and optimizing to reduce the need for unnecessary functions and systems such as inspections, rework loops and inventory.

2   Improving continuously to develop internal systems that enhance constant improvement in processes and procedures.

3   Understanding the customers to meet their need and reducing their overall cost of purchasing and using products.

Edward J. Hay (1988) identifies seven elements of JIT; six internally focused and one externally focused. The first internally focused element is the Just-In-Time philosophy itself. The second is quality at the source. There are three manufacturing engineering elements: uniform plant load, overlapping operation, (machine cells or group technology) and minimum set up time. The sixth internally focused element is the pull control system, Kanban or linking operations. The externally focused element is Just-In-Time purchasing.

Voss and Robinson (1987) describe JIT as a tool box of techniques although with little agreement on what comprises the core elements. Some of these tool box techniques include the Kanban system, JIT purchasing, zero defect philosophy, cellular or team based manufacturing, work team quality control and set-up time reduction.

Wantuck (1989) gives the most elaborate view of the concept of JIT. He suggests that there are seven principles of JIT strategy, seven principles of Quality at the source and ten core elements of JIT. The seven principles of JIT strategy are as follows:

1   Produce to exact customer demand.

2   Eliminate waste.

3   Produce one-at-a-time.

4   Continuous improvement.

5   Respect people.

6   No contingencies.

7   Long-term emphasis.

Quality at the source principles emphasize the control of quality at the source of supply by identifying the defects at that point rather than at the end of the production line after a product has been made. These principles are as follows:

1   Perfect parts every time.

2   Operator's responsibility.

3   New customer definition.

4   The quality at source tool kit.

5   Stop and fix the problem.

6   Visibility management.

7   Machines always ready.

The ten core elements are those that are essential for the implementation of the JIT strategy. These are as follows:

1   People policies and practices.

2   Quality circles.

3   Focused factories.

4   Group technology.

5   Design for automation.

6   Set-up reduction.

7   Uniform scheduling.

8   The "Pull" system.

9   Supplier relations.

10   Transport innovations.

Although there are different views among the authors on the principles of JIT, they all agreed that the key element in JIT is "stockless" production. The JIT system is geared to reducing inventories in both raw materials and work-in-process. Everything is ordered, made and delivered just when needed. Production is objectively "just-in-time".

In achieving the "just-in-time" goal, the JIT system should therefore be equipped with the following eight distinctive features and broad principles:

1   Attacking fundamental problems.

2   Elimination of waste.

3   The "Kanban" or "Pull" system.

4   Uninterrupted work flow.

5   Total quality control concept.

6   Top management commitment and employee involvement.

7   Supplier and client relations.

8   Continuous improvements.

Each of these principles is explained in detail as follows:

Attacking fundamental problems

As already mentioned, the JIT approach thoroughly examines and seeks out fundamental problems impeding the efficiencies of manufacturing processes. To describe this first principle of the JIT philosophy, attacking the fundamental problems, it is useful to illustrate this principle using the analogy of the "river of inventory" (see Figure 2.1).

The level of the river represents inventory and the company operations are visualized as a boat navigating up and down the river. When a business

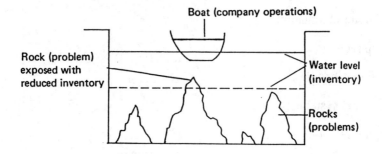

Figure 2.1 River of inventory

Source: *O'Grady, P.J. (1988), Putting the Just-In-Time philosophy into practice: A strategy for production managers, Kogan Page Ltd*

attempts to lower the level of the river (i.e. to cut its inventory levels), it uncovers rocks, that is, problems. In a traditional manufacturing environment, when such problems arose, the typical response was to put increased inventory in place to cover up the problem. A typical example of this kind of problem would be a plant which contained an unreliable machine feeding parts to another, more reliable, machine - and the typical response of traditional management would be to keep a large buffer stock between the machines to ensure that the second machine will not run short of work. By contrast, the JIT philosophy indicates that when problems are uncovered they must be confronted and solved (ie. the rocks must be removed from the river bed.). The inventory level can then be gradually reduced until another problem is uncovered; this problem will then be attacked, and so on. In the case of the unreliable machine, the JIT philosophy would indicate that the problem should be resolved either by a preventive maintenance programme that would improve the machine's reliability, or if all else failed, by the purchase of a more reliable machine. This difference between traditional and JIT approaches is illustrated in Figure 2.2. Some of the other problems (rocks) and JIT solutions are shown in Table 2.1.

Where there is a machine or process that is a bottleneck, one of the traditional approaches has been to aim for better and more complex scheduling (using, for example, MRP II) to ensure that it never runs short of work, so reducing the effect of the bottleneck. However, the results of such policies have frequently been disappointing with low stockturn figures. The JIT approach to the presence of a bottleneck machine or process would involve reducing set-up time to produce greater capacity, finding alternative machines or processes, purchasing extra capacity or even subcontracting excess work. The JIT approach recognizes that neither increased buffer stock nor more complex scheduling will solve the fundamental problem; all they do is to temporarily cover over the rocks.

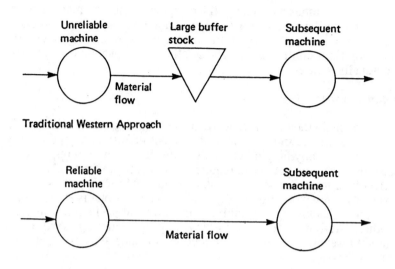

Traditional Western Approach

JIT Approach

Figure 2.2 Approaches to unreliable machines

Source: *O'Grady, P.J. (1988), Putting the Just-In-Time philosophy into practice: A strategy for production managers, Kogan Page Ltd*

Table 2.1
Problems and JIT solutions

PROBLEM (ROCKS)	JIT SOLUTION
Unreliable machine	Improve reliability
Bottleneck areas	Increase capacity
Large lot sizes	Reduce set up time
Long manufacturing lead times	Reduce queuing, etc. by using a pull system
Poor quality	Improve processes and/or supplier

Source: *O'Grady, P.J. (1988), Putting the Just-In-Time philosophy into practice: A strategy for production managers, Kogan Page Ltd*

As regards the issue of long lead times, the JIT approach seeks to identify the fundamental problems that cause them. JIT would not simply try to expedite certain orders through the factory, but will seek to discover why the manufacturing lead times are so long. JIT recognizes that long manufacturing lead times can be the result of a number of factors, including bottleneck machines or processes, poor reliability of machines, poor quality control, and poor shop floor control. By attacking all of these problems, lead times can be gradually reduced.

Elimination of waste

This forms the main theme associated with JIT - the crusade to eliminate all forms of waste for the improvement of product quality and productivity. Waste is defined as anything other than the absolute minimum resources of materials, machines and personnel required to add value to the product (Hay, 1988). An operation consists of motion and work. Motion alone is a waste that adds costs. Only work produces the added value customers are willing to pay for. Hence, machining, assembling, finishing and packaging add value to a product. Activities such as moving, storing, counting, sorting and scheduling, however, add cost to a product but no value. Cost without value is considered waste. Waste incurred in the production processes also includes over-production and defective units.

As a good illustration, the Toyota Production System described by Shigeo Shingo (1982) identified seven prominent causes of waste, viz:

Waste from over-production Over-production is one of the worst wastes commonly found in factories.This is typically created by getting ahead of the work in order to prevent shortages. However, more raw materials would have to be consumed and wages paid for unneeded work, thereby creating unnecessary inventory. This in turn requires additional handling of materials, additional space to hold inventories, and additional cost for carrying the inventories. The unfortunate result is that it often obscures fundamental problems, since operators seem busy and machines are occupied unnecessarily, and additional equipment may be purchased on the mistaken assumption that it is needed.

Waste of waiting time The waste of waiting time is usually easily identified and corrective action should be taken to remove it.

Transportation waste This refers to waste caused by an item being moved a distance unnecessarily, being stored temporarily or being re-arranged. For, instance, parts may be transferred from a large storage pallet to a smaller one and then placed temporarily on a machine several times before they are finally processed. Another instance of waste occurs when parts are moved from a warehouse to the factory, from the factory to the machines and from the machines to the hands of workers. In order to eliminate this waste, improvement in layout, coordination of processes, methods of transportation, housekeeping and workplace organisation need to be considered.

Processing waste The processing method itself may be a source of problems, resulting in unnecessary waste. This often occurs when the

20

equipment or fixtures used for production are not well maintained or prepared and operators may have to use extra effort in processing the materials. Sometimes, certain fixtures may be added or modified to facilitate operation such as the use of a gravity-fed chute which makes automatic loading possible without operator involvement.

Inventory waste As mentioned earlier, excessive inventory adds cost to production. It requires extra handling, extra space, extra interest charges and so on. Because of the problems associated with unnecessary inventory, attempts should be made to reduce inventory levels as follows:

1   Dispose of obsolete materials through proper housekeeping / workplace organisation.

2   Not to produce items not required by the subsequent process.

3   Not to purchase or bring in items in large lot sizes as savings achieved through volume discounts may be more than offset by inventory waste.

4   Manufacture products in small lots which will reduce set-up time and changeovers.

Waste of motion Any motion that does not add value to the product is considered waste and should be eliminated. Pick and place is an example of movement that can be reduced by keeping parts or tools closer to where they can be used. Walking is another kind of wasteful movement, especially when one person is responsible for operating several machines.

Waste from product defects When defects in products are found, re-work may be required or the defective products are scrapped. If a defect has occurred in the assembly operation, operators at subsequent work stations will be kept waiting, adding to production lead time while labour is required to disassemble the defective product. To eliminate these problems, a system must be developed to identify the defects or the conditions that produce defects so that anyone present can take immediate corrective action. For example, statistical quality control is a good technique that can be used to arrest wasteful product defects. Its essential features can be illustrated using the JIT approach to tolerances as shown in Figure 2.3 where it is compared with the traditional approach to inspection and quality control. The traditional approach has been to set upper and lower bounds (i.e. tolerances) and if the measurements fall outside either the upper or lower bound, then the product item is scrapped or reworked. By contrast, the JIT approach is to reduce the deviation from the ideal nominal; any deviation from the nominal not being tolerated. Furthermore, JIT places the responsibility for detecting and correcting deviations for the nominal on the operators of the processes. They are expected to make it right the first time and to prevent any items from deviating too far from nominal.

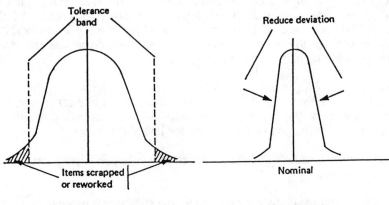

Traditional Western Approach   **JIT Approach**

Figure 2.3   Approaches to tolerances

Source: *O'Grady, P.J. (1988), Putting the Just-In-Time philosophy into practice: A strategy for production managers, Kogan Page Ltd*

In summary, waste is anything other than the minimum amount of equipment, materials, workers and time that are absolutely essential to production. Inventory or buffer stocks are regarded as evidence of waste. The goal in JIT is therefore to achieve zero-inventory levels, or stockless production. Inventory is regarded as masking unseen problems which are only exposed as stock levels are reduced.

Too often, organisations cover their weaknesses and problems by having extra workers, extra inventory, and backup equipment. This only hides problems and does not allow one to address the crucial areas of concern. The JIT concept is therefore concerned with having only the right part in the right place at the right time. Having even an extra part is a waste because it is not needed at that place or at that time.

The "Kanban" or "Pull" system

Production can basically be organised in two ways, namely, produce on demand (pull system) or produce to forecasts of demand or make to stock (push system).

Most manufacturing organisations operate in the traditional push environment. They use master schedules and material requirement planning (MRP) outputs to drive their production schedules and the movement of materials in the factory. MRP (and also optimised production technology, OPT) are push systems in the sense that they plan what is to be produced which is then pushed through the factory. Bottlenecks and other problems are supposedly detected beforehand and complex monitoring systems are installed to feedback factory floor changes so that corrective action can be taken. By contrast, the JIT approach using the pull system eliminates the complex set of data flows since it is essentially, in its original form, a manual system. It uses "bottom-up" demand, which is driven by the actual consumption rates of parts in individual processes to pull materials through the entire manufacturing process.

Pull systems Pull systems pull work through the factory to meet customer demands. The basic concept on the application of a pull system is shown in Figure 2.4. In Figure 2.4, the items pass through the flow line from operation 1 to 2 to 3 and then to the final operation, 4. When there is a demand for an item, it is produced by operation 4 and then taken away. This demand can come from a subsequent process or from a customer. When operation 4 runs short of components as a result of finished products being removed, a signal is sent to the preceding operation (operation 3). Operation 3 then produces components for operation 4. When the component supply for operation 3 is running low, it sends a signal to operation 2. The process is repeated all the way backwards through the manufacturing system. In this manner, work is pulled through the factory. If no work is taken from the end operation, no signals are sent to the preceding operations and hence no work is done. This is a major departure from previous approaches to material control. Some points about pull systems should be noted:

1   Machines / operations do not produce any item unless required to by a subsequent machine / operation.

2   Control information flows backwards through the manufacturing system whilst the material flows in the opposite direction.

3   Pull systems help identify problems.

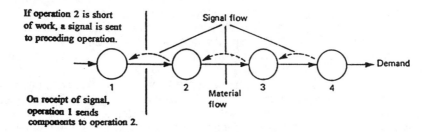

Figure 2.4   The operation of a "pull" system

Source: *O'Grady, P.J. (1988), Putting the Just-In-Time philosophy into practice: A strategy for production managers, Kogan Page Ltd*

23

The first point (that machines / operations do not produce any item unless it is required by a later machine / operation) is considered to be especially important. There is little point in operations producing items unless they are needed; the items would lie around as work-in-progress on the factory floor. With reduced demand, personnel and machines do not produce any items. JIT proponents suggest that they do other tasks such as cleaning the machine, adjustments, checking for any required maintenance, etc. With more traditional approaches, most managers are less keen to have personnel and machines remaining idle. Work would be scheduled even if it was not required in the near future. The manufacturing control then has been to run each machine / operation at full speed even if the subsequent machines / operations cannot handle the output. In effect, the traditional approach attached the highest priorities to keeping machines and personnel producing, even at the cost of manufacturing items that only contribute to an already swollen inventory and a high scrap rate. The result has often been large amounts of work remaining at subsequent machines / operations, increasing manufacturing lead times and work-in-progress levels as well as exacerbating clutter and confusion on the factory floor.

The second point (that control information flows back through the system whilst material flows forward) becomes a factor to be considered when long lead times (usually from suppliers) mean that the system is slow in responding to changes in demand. This is the main disadvantage of the pull system. The pull system has no built-in safety factors. It therefore places great demands on those responsible for its maintenance. Machines must be in good working order at all times when demand is expected. Relationships with the workforce must be such that stoppages are virtually non-existent, motivation levels are high and skill levels are adequate to perform the task in hand (Hutchins, 1988).

The third point about pull-type systems is that they help identify problems. One of the major features of the JIT philosophy is to set up systems that help identify problems. To illustrate with a simple example, suppose operation 3 in the flow line shown in Figure 2.4 is a temporary bottleneck. Operation 3 therefore cannot process as much as operations 1 and 2, so they remain idle for much of the time. This is immediately visible to the supervisor of the flow line and remedial action on operation 3 can be taken. Bottlenecks are frequently dynamic and transitory in nature. The pull systems help to identify and remedy them quickly.

The JIT approach, based on the use of pull type systems, hence ensures that production does not exceed immediate needs, thereby reducing work in progress and inventory levels as well as cutting manufacturing lead times. The otherwise idle time can be productively spent removing the source of future problems by a preventive maintenance programme.

Kanban systems Kanban, literally translated, means visible record or visible plate. The Kanban system is an information system that controls the production of the necessary products in the quantity that is required at the right time in every process of a manufacturing company (Henderson, 1986).

More generally however, Kanban is taken to mean card. The Toyota Kanban system employs a card to signal the need to deliver more parts and an identical or similar card to signal the need to produce more parts. A Kanban system therefore consists of a set of cards that travel between preceding and subsequent processes, communicating what parts are needed in the subsequent processes.

The Toyota Kanban system differs from the generic pull system described earlier by using two types of signal (equating to two types of card or Kanban). This dual card system uses both withdrawal or conveyance Kanbans and production Kanbans. The withdrawal or conveyance Kanban is used when parts are to be moved between the output and input buffer stocks whilst the production Kanban is used when production is to take place.

The main reason for using a dual card system is that Toyota uses both an input and output buffer store, especially where processes are physically separated, for example, in different plants. This is shown in Figure 2.5.

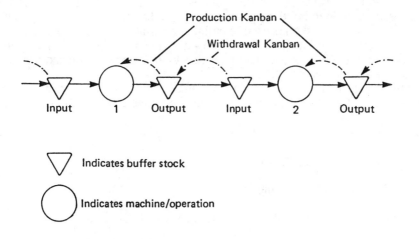

Figure 2.5   Toyota dual card kanban system

Source: *O'Grady, P.J. (1988), Putting the Just-In-Time philosophy into practice: A strategy for production managers, Kogan Page Ltd*

As machine operation 2 uses up its input buffer stock, a withdrawal or conveyance Kanban is sent to the preceding output buffer stock and parts are taken from there and delivered to machine / operation 2 input buffer stock. As machine / operation 1 output buffer stock is reduced, a production Kanban is sent to machine / operation 1 which then begins manufacturing, using parts in the machine / operation 1 input buffer stock. The process is repeated backwards along the production line.

The main advantage claimed for the dual card system is the extra control it gives. However, the extra complexity of the system as compared with the single card approach has led to relatively few companies using it; even though Toyota has persuaded most of its suppliers to adopt a dual card system.

In western industries, the single card system is used much more frequently. Another variation is a system based on the use of cards (or other signals) that replenish queues in front of machines (process Kanbans) and those that replenish products (product Kanbans).

Whichever pull / Kanban-type system is used, they can provide a very simple and clear mechanism for shop floor control, "clear" in that they are readily understood and the factory floor worker is furnished with a simple and visible feedback signal (cards).

Figure 2.6 shows the flow of a pull / Kanban System for a typical manufacturing process. The system uses the master schedule and MRP output to forecast the parts needed from suppliers and to establish the production rate schedules in the factory. Then, starting at the last process work center before the finished goods inventory, the system pulls the material required to build the products listed in the forecast. According to the figure, a Kanban system is used to pull the materials from the supplier center and from the stock location. The figure shows the pull process with a reverse arrow pointing up from the factory process to the stock location and from the stock location to the suppliers.

Finally, there are a number of proven major benefits to be gained from the use of the JIT Kanban / pull type systems. These include the following:

1   Reduced work in progress levels.

2   Reduced inventory levels.

3   Reduced manufacturing lead times.

4   Gradual reduction of work in progress levels.

5   Identifying bottleneck areas.

6   Identifying quality problems.

7   Simple management.

From the above, it can thus be seen how pull / Kanban systems bring out production problems. Under JIT, any system which brings out problems is considered beneficial and any which masks problems, detrimental. Pull / Kanban systems identify problems and are thus beneficial. Previous approaches have tended to obscure fundamental problems and thus delay or prevent their solution.

The systems set up for implementing JIT should be designed so that they immediately trigger some warning whenever a problem arises. Once again, the Toyota production line can be referred to as an illustrative example. On this line, each worker is allocated parts on a one-to-one basis; that is, if each car requires one centre stoplight then the worker is only allocated enough stoplights to cover the number of cars produced. If there is a fault with one

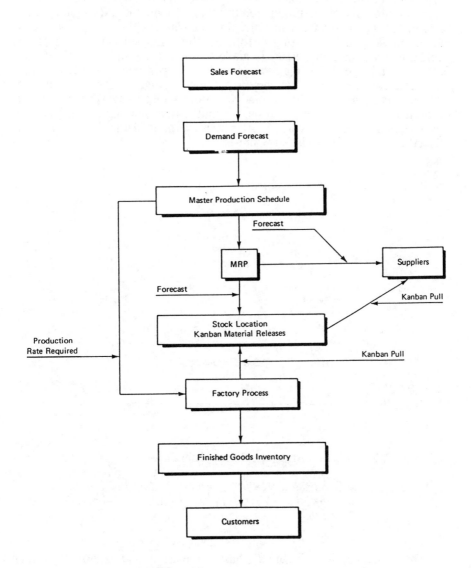

Figure 2.6 Build schedule and materials flow in a pull / kanban system

Source: *Hernandez, A. (1989), Just-In-Time manufacturing - A practical approach, Prentice-Hall, N.J.*

of the stoplights, then the worker is forced to draw attention to it. He does this by pulling on a rope that is dangling above his workstation and when the rope is pulled, the entire production line stops - something, it can readily be imagined, that guarantees that the problem is brought to the manager's attention! This dramatic step is followed by a hurried conference of all concerned where every effort is made to solve the problem. This whole process can be described diagrammatically as shown in Figure 2.7. The line is operating at a certain efficiency, a problem occurs, the line stops and the problem is identified, some remedial action is taken and later the line is restarted. Since a problem has been confronted and wholly or partially solved the restarted line is less likely to suffer from that particular problem again and the efficiency of the line is thus increased.

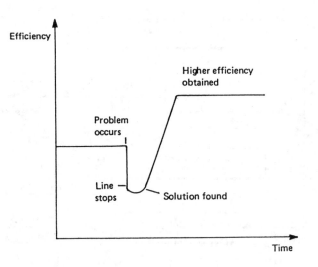

Figure 2.7 Incremental efficiency increase

Source: *O'Grady, P.J. (1988), Putting the Just-In-Time philosophy into practice: A strategy for production managers, Kogan Page Ltd*

The vertical scale in Figure 2.7 has been exaggerated to show the effect but it can easily be seen that the approach works by the gradual accumulation of a series of small increases in efficiency. When enough of these small increases are combined, the result is major increase in efficiency. This has been the experience of the Toyota production line.

In designing a JIT system, the aim is therefore not only to lower work in progress levels and manufacturing lead times but also to identify problems as soon as they occurred so that immediate remedial action could be taken. However, in order to identify a problem properly, a manufacturing process

28

should be prepared to pay the price in terms of some short-term setbacks. In the hypothetical example given earlier, the entire Toyota line was stopped because of a fault in a single centre stoplight; this is something many traditional approaches which take a short-term view would consider unthinkable. In the long term, however, it is often only by ensuring that even a small problem has a major impact that attention will be concentrated upon it. The serious implementation of JIT would thus require two things:

1   To set up "pull" / "kanban" mechanisms so that problems can be easily identified.

2   To be prepared for a short-term drop in efficiency to gain a long-term advantage.

Uninterrupted work flow

In JIT, the master schedule (or final assembly schedule) is planned for one to three months into the future to allow work centres and vendors to plan their respective work schedules. Within the current month, the master schedule is levelled on a daily basis. In other words, the same quantity of each product is produced each day for the entire month. Furthermore, small lots (preferably lot size equal 1) are scheduled in the master schedule to provide a uniform load on the plant and vendors during each day.

JIT uses the Kanban to pull parts from one work centre to the next. The final assembly schedule pulls parts from one work centre to the next just in time to support production needs.

In order to achieve just-in-time production, it is imperative that the various work flows of the manufacturing process be uninterrupted as absolutely as possible. To accomplish uninterrupted work flows, JIT calls for the following four improvements:

1   Usage of "focused factory" and "group technology" (GT) techniques.

2   Design for simplification and automation.

3   Reduction of process set-up times.

4   Implementation of machine / equipment total preventive maintenance (TPM) programme.

Each of these four improvements is examined in details as follows:

Focused factory and group technology techniques Focused factory or group technology (GT) is a management philosophy which identify and exploit the "sameness" of items and processes used in manufacturing industries. Focused factory can be defined as a manufacturing layout dedicated to the production of a single family of parts; whilst GT refers to an equipment layout dedicated to the complete production of a family of similar parts, one at a time, by linking all possible operations in the process. The majority of batch manufacturing plants are organized in what may be termed a process layout; a typical example being that shown in Figure 2.8.

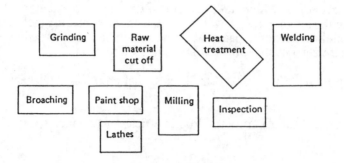

Figure 2.8 A typical process layout

Source: *O'Grady, P.J. (1988), Putting the Just-In-Time philosophy into practice: A strategy for production managers, Kogan Page Ltd*

Most items going through such a factory would follow a tortuous route going from, for example, raw material cut off to lathes then to broaching, welding, grinding, heat treatment, grinding and paint shop. Each process usually involves a considerable amount of waiting added to which is the time taken (amid the general confusion of shop floor activities) to transport items from one process to another. The consequences of this are high work-in-progress levels and long manufacturing lead times. The problems of trying to plan and control such a factory are phenomenal, with typical symptoms being late items rushed through the factory whilst others, no longer being immediately required because of a cancelled order or a change in forecast, are stopped and remain stagnant on the factory floor. These symptoms have very little to do with the effectiveness of management. Any good management system would encounter problems in controlling such a complex shop floor system. It could be argued that these problems would be solved if a computer control system is implemented; but if the factory still remains tremendously complex, then the benefits obtained will probably be marginal.

The JIT philosophy of simplicity examines the complex factory and starts from the view that there is little to be achieved by placing complex control on top of a complex factory. Instead JIT stresses the need to simplify the complex factory and to superimpose a simple system of controls to produce simple material flows. The simple material flows in the factory can be achieved by using focused factory or group technology techniques. GT groups units or components into families of parts which have similar designs or manufacturing sequences and rearrange their processes so that each product family is manufactured on a flow line. Examples of flow line layouts are shown in Figure 2.9.

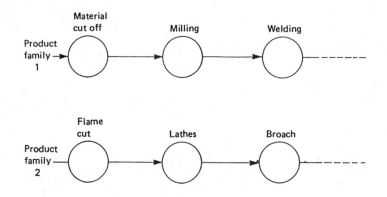

Figure 2.9 Product layout using flow lines

Source: *O'Grady, P.J. (1988), Putting the Just-In-Time philosophy into practice: A strategy for production managers, Kogan Page Ltd*

Items in each product family can now move from process to process more easily as the processes are placed adjacent to one another, hopefully thereby reducing work in progress levels and manufacturing lead times. This reorientation of the processes layout will greatly simplify the management of the factory. Instead of an extremely complex operation based on a process layout where each product follows a lengthy route through the factory, a simple, unidirectional flow with a limited range of products being produced on each flow line is now achieved.

With these small flow lines in place, other advantages follow. For example, management becomes much easier than in the case of a process layout since each flow line is, to a large extent, separate. A sub-manager can be responsible for each flow line. In addition, quality will tend to be improved; since there is less likelihood of panic with fewer rushed orders, more time can be spent addressing the quality problems.

The ideal layout is often the U-shaped flow line dedicated to a particular product family. This layout simplifies control, allowing gradual reduction of inventory and work-in-progress levels. The advantages of the U-shape over a linear flow line are, firstly, that it assists communication, since workers on a particular flow line are physically closer to each other. The operator, for example, of the last machine in the flow line can easily tell the operator of the first machine of a quality problem arising from the first operation and action can be taken quickly. The second reason that U-shaped flow lines are preferable to linear flow lines is that the layout allows the workers access to a number of machines (see Figure 2.10), each worker being physically closer to more machines than in a linear flow line and therefore able to operate several machines.

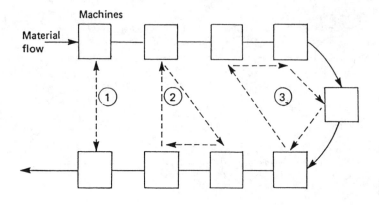

Material flow

Machines

──────── Example route followed by operator

(a) Operator number

Figure 2.10 Example of the flexibility of workers in U-shaped lines

Source:　　*O'Grady, P.J. (1988), Putting the Just-In-Time philosophy into practice: A strategy for production managers, Kogan Page Ltd*

It can be seen from the U-shaped flow line example that a flexible multi-skilled workforce is required for efficient operation of the flow line (i.e. a worker is required to possess skills to spontaneously operate different machines). As part of the switch to product flow lines, many Japanese companies now employ a flexible workforce with each worker having skills in a variety of areas. This is called shojinka. The use of shojinka allows the manning level of each flow line to rise and fall with demand for a product family. When demand is high, each machine has one or more workers to operate it. When low, each worker may have two or more machines to operate. If there is no demand for a particular product family, then all the workers are reallocated to another product flow line. This can, of course, only be effective if the workers are trained to operate several different machines and there is a suitable employee and union environment.

In order to establish suitable flow lines, the first step is to divide the product range into product families. In many cases, this will be relatively easy - each family will be one distinctive part of the product range. In other cases, when there is a finer distinction between products, the division can be more difficult and some sort of group technology analysis may be needed, often using coding and classification systems.

As well as dividing the product range up into families, it is also necessary to reorganise the machines in the process-oriented layout into suitable product flow lines. This again is usually straightforward but there may be complications with large facilities that service several product families.

Examples are paint shops and heat treatment furnaces. Splitting such facilities into small units for individual flow lines is not usually possible; they may have to be shared amongst several flow lines.

To sum up, GT groups interrelated operations together and physically links and overlaps as many operators as possible. Pieces of equipment are placed very close to each other in a cell-like mode. Balance, synchronisation and smooth flow are achieved, while lead times are reduced from days to minutes, which eliminates work-in-process (WIP) inventory. Communication too will be enhanced and the ease of identifying the cause of any problem will increase. Quality feedback is immediate, and high quality products emerge.

Design for simplification and automation An important element of the JIT philosophy is simplification, i.e. striving for simple rather than complex solutions. JIT stresses the desirability of simplicity on the grounds that simple approaches are most likely to lead to more efficient management.

The primary thrust of the drive for simplicity covers two areas:

1   Material flow - group technology is used to design simple approaches to material flow and to eliminate complex route paths by moving towards more direct, if possible unidirectional flow lines.

2   Process control - pull / kanban system is used as a simple information system to control the production of the necessary products only in the quantities that are required just-in-time in every manufacturing process.

Overall, a systematic process of simplifying operations for product design and production engineering should ceaselessly be pursued. Every process should be simplified first before considering automation. The goal is to replace a complex and costly process with one which is simple and less costly.

JIT also stresses the need to improve human operations first before investing in automation. This approach is followed for a number of reasons:

1   The improvement in manual operations will avoid disrupting the operation of the company.

2   The cost of improving human operations is usually low compared with investing in automation.

3   Changes in manual operations can usually be reversed easily if they are not successful, whereas the investment in automation is often wasted if the automation does not work as anticipated.

4   JIT stresses the idea of improving the overall system performance. To do this would initially require improving the overall flow of work through improvement in human operations. Only when the overall flow in the manufacturing system is satisfactory is investment in automation justified. Putting automation investment ahead of investing in human

33

operations is therefore tantamount to putting the cart in front of the horse.

Top priority should therefore be given to gradual improvement in human operations to achieve good overall system performance. This can be aided by an effective total preventive maintenance programme which stresses reliance on the present equipment, with modifications where necessary, rather than a large investment in sophisticated automation. JIT also means emphasizing investment in low cost machines that are flexible in their response to changes in product volume and product type. There is little point in investing heavily in specialized machinery if demand falls for those products that the machinery is designed to produce. JIT implementations are characterized by flexible machines that can be quickly altered from one product to another.

Reduction of process set-up times Set-up time is the time taken to change a machine / equipment so that it can process another type of product. Set-up times can be considerable: it is not unusual to find that it takes eight hours to set-up a machine to run for perhaps one hour. This is a clear instance of the kind of waste which JIT aims to eliminate. Excessive set-up time is harmful for the following reasons:

1   Reducing machine efficiency - due to set-up time being the period when the machine is not producing anything. Human productivity too suffers along with low machine efficiency. An operator usually has to be available to carry out the set-up operation which may also require the services of a skilled set-up technician.

2   Increasing economic order quantity - due to longer set-up times and higher set-up costs. With longer set-up times, it only makes sense to do a set-up operation if there is enough work to justify that time. The consequence of this is pressure to increase the lot (or batch) size. With large batches come the disadvantages of increased queue and lead times. Hence, the set-up time must be reduced in order to minimise the lot size. For instance, the economic order quantity can be decreased by half from 100 units if the set-up time can be reduced to 25 per cent.

3   Increasing WIP inventory and risk of obsolescence - due to increase in the lot size. Increased WIP inventory would occupy more floor space thus disallowing work centres to be moved closer together to form work cells. This in turn increases handling costs and overhead absorptions. Also, the high inventory levels caused by excessive set-up time are not usually used immediately which cause yet another unwanted grave side effect; that of product obsolescence's risk.

4   Increasing quality defects - due to defects not easily and quickly exposed as a result of the large order quantities. The quality of products hence worsens and a high work scrap level is created.

5   Reducing process flexibility - due to the inability to set-up quickly to

manufacture a different product. As the market environment changes, the manufacturer with excessive set-up time and large lot size is increasingly at a disadvantage. The company with short set-up times is much more flexible in its ability to respond to change. With increasing global competition in the manufacturing industries, increased flexibility can mean the future viability of a company.

Implementation of machine / equipment Total Preventive Maintenance (TPM) Programme Cutting set-up time reduces the amount of time that a machine is not running; to reduce the amount of down-time even further, the number of breakdowns must be cut. JIT systems rely on preventive maintenance programmes with the aim of preventing breakdowns rather than repairing them once they occur.

The fact that a successful JIT implementation will reduce inventory and work-in-progress to a minimum means that the manufacturing system becomes more vulnerable to breakdowns. For once a machine does break down there are only small amounts of buffer stocks available and so subsequent machines rapidly become starved of work; whereas without JIT there is more time to repair the machine before the buffer stock is exhausted.

In a conventional manufacturing system, therefore, breakdowns are not particularly important restrictions to the flow of work. There are usually large buffer stocks to help ensure that other machines are not starved of work in the event of a breakdown. In these situations, the only machines that are affected by breakdowns are bottleneck machines. These are the machines that are running at full capacity and a breakdown means that some production will be lost, whereas for non-bottleneck machines breakdown time can often be easily made up.

However, with a JIT system, the buffer stocks have been so reduced that all machines are in some sense bottleneck machines and a breakdown will reduce effective utilization of equipment, and hence lower efficiency as well as increasing shortages and increasing lead times. That is, breakdown will remove some productive time from the machine and thereby lower both its effective utilization and efficiency. Since there is little buffer stock, shortages result and the overall effect is an increase in manufacturing lead times.

Unreliable machines are therefore in direct conflict with JIT and reliability must be improved through the setting up of a TPM programme. Within a TPM programme, one principle guides progress; to decentralize maintenance as far as possible to the operators. More major maintenance tasks can still be undertaken by the maintenance department. Devolving responsibility for the relatively straightforward aspects of maintenance to the machine operators has two major advantages which will increase the effectiveness of the programme. Firstly, the operators are probably the workers who will know most about the operation of their machines and will therefore be the best people to detect unusual noises, wear or vibration. Secondly, the arrangement gives the operators a sense of ownership of their machines and they feel more responsible for ensuring that their machines avoid breakdowns. Such decentralization had proven to result in better maintenance jobs.

Total quality control concept

In a Just-In-Time system, a manufacturer does not carry excess inventory to cover for parts that are defective. This forces the manufacturer to solve quality problems before he can continue building the product.

In the Toyota Kanban system, each time that workers succeeded in correcting the causes of recent irregularity (for instance, machine jamming), the managers remove still more buffer stock. The workers are never allowed to settle into a comfortable pattern; or rather, the pattern becomes one of continually perfecting the production process (Schonberger, 1982).

In order to achieve the progressive reduction of buffer stocks towards zero level, it is essential that errors and defective components are eliminated in each work unit. In other words, in order to have a successful JIT system, it must also incorporate a total quality control system to reduce the risk of frequent line stops.

Under the JIT system, every mistake is an opportunity to understand why the process is not foolproof. By investigating every defect and its cause, one can gradually improve the process so that it does not create defects. To make it easy to identify defects, considerable time, thought and expenses are devoted to developing foolproof devices and automatic defect checks (termed "bakayoke" or "pokayoke" in Japanese) that monitor product and / or process characteristics continuously.

As mentioned, JIT production makes no allowances for contingency. Every piece is expected to be correct when received. Every machine is expected to be available when needed to produce parts. Every delivery commitment is expected to be honoured at the precise time it is scheduled.

In contrast to the traditional western system where quality control is the preserve of specific inspectors from a quality control department, in JIT, quality inspectors are not used to ensure the quality of parts but rather it shifts the responsibility for quality to the makers of the parts. JIT requires that workers, foremen and engineers, or all the firm's employees take primary responsibility for quality.

Very tightly enforced quality control processes help to ensure that the product is exactly specified by the product design or customer requirements. JIT implies a zero defect quality control effort. The elimination of errors, to be cost effective, requires quality at the source, that is, errors should be caught and corrected at the source where the work is performed (Schonberger, 1982). With JIT, each worker involved with the production of a product is personally responsible for a given piece of the process. Before presenting a part to the next station, it must be inspected to ensure it is defect-free. Every individual is responsible personally for the quality of the work that he or she produces. If a quality problem develops, the work is stopped and everybody in the area concentrates on resolving the problem. Work is not started again until the problem is corrected.

The term "autonomation" was used at Toyota to refer to automated inspection or automatic identification of defects in the production process. Basically this requires each workstation to be solely responsible for its own quality control which must, as far as possible, avoid passing on defective parts to subsequent stations. The term "Jidoka" as used at Toyota means "to make the equipment or operation stop whenever an abnormal or defective condition arises" (Sugimori et al, 1986). This is done with the installation of the Andon system. This consists of a set of different coloured lights which are used to summon assistance from the operators of other stations in the event that a particular station is running behind schedule. This prevents the transfer of faulty parts resulting from the pressure of not being able to cope. Typically, there is a red light to turn on to trigger and signal a line stoppage for bad quality, machine trouble, lack of parts etc., and a yellow light to turn on when there is a slowdown but no need to stop the whole production line.

Finally, the total quality control concept in JIT also extends to all the suppliers of the manufacturing organisation because the manufacturer will never be able to produce a first-rate product unless the parts used to build the product are first-rate as well.

Top management commitment and employee involvement

A successful JIT environment can only be achieved with the cooperation and involvement of everyone at all levels in the organisation. The concepts of elimination of waste and continuous improvement that are central to the JIT philosophy can only be achieved through cooperation by people as a team. As stated by Hall (1983), if the inventory is decreased without people being mentally and emotionally ready to overcome the problems that were the cause of inventory, stockless production will not come to anything.

Top management commitment and support for any implemented JIT programme is of the utmost importance. Top management commitment is important for a number of reasons, the primary one being that of authority - top management have the authority to support the changes that JIT requires. Lower management will only be able to authorize investments up to a (often low) set figure. With JIT implementation, this may necessitate a whole series of authorizations to achieve the level of investment required. Each authorization often requires a detailed justification, the preparation of which can frequently divert the JIT team away from the more important work of the implementation itself. If top management is committed, only one justification and authorization is required.

The second aspect of this commitment by top management and its consequent authority is in personnel management. For example, top management can appoint a high-quality employee to the position of JIT project team leader. Other personnel changes may become necessary in the course of the implementation and these may only materialize through top management commitment.

The third aspect is more psychological. If top management is committed to JIT and their commitment is visible, lower management are much more likely to follow. This commitment should be demonstrated and needs to be publicized throughout the company.

The fourth aspect is one where top management can directly contribute to the JIT programme, namely, in dealing with reluctant suppliers. It is likely that some suppliers will be reluctant to accept the idea of short lead times and frequent deliveries of small lots. Top management could contact a supplier's senior management to convince them to accept the new system.

The fundamental idea of employee involvement is both simple and proven: that is, if people are treated with equity and respect, provided with meaningful jobs and the responsibility of problem-solving and decision-making regarding their work, and are given opportunities to learn, then they will satisfy both personal goals as well as organisational goals (Stendel & Desruelle, 1992).

JIT is concerned about workers being given adequate and wide training; be encouraged to actively participate in the JIT programme; and the responsibility for looking after their machines and workplace. With an emphasis on quick changeovers and smaller lots, the multi-function worker is required. Cross-training is needed so that workers can switch from one machine to the next and can perform their own setup and maintenance. This requires a broader range of skills than traditional manufacturing. In fact, JIT requires not only broader skills, but much greater teamwork.

Training workers to perform a variety of jobs will provide the organisation with a great deal of in-house flexibility. Historically, companies have viewed specialisation as the key to increasing efficiency. However, according to Strassman (1985), specialisation creates office work and the resulting relationships amongst specialists determining how much work will be done. Rather than organising a department around specialists with narrow tunnel vision, managers should train employees to perform various jobs. This not only enhances flexibility but promotes wholeness. Employees are in a better position to identify ways to improve operations if they are familiar with the whole organisation rather than a segment of it.

As mentioned before, for a process to continue to produce the required quality, machinery must be maintained in excellent condition. This can best be achieved through a programme of total preventive maintenance. Preventive maintenance starts with daily inspection, lubrication, and clean up. Employees should be concerned to look after their plants and equipment and also the workplace (eg. by good housekeeping practices).

Under JIT, good housekeeping is part of the efforts in visibility management which is concerned with making problems visible by suitable and immediate displays on the shopfloor. The five basic concepts of visibility management in JIT strategy are simplification, organisation, discipline, cleanliness and participation. The aim in visibility management is to provide an environment for continuous enforced improvement by making problems visible and demanding quick response to solve them. Although good housekeeping is a feature of any well-managed operation, under JIT it becomes an obsession. Good housekeeping requires all employees at the shop floor to participate in minimising any impediments to job flow. Poorly maintained equipment, excess dirt or paperwork, extra jobs on the shop floor, additional and complex actions are all disruptive to the smooth flow of job which is critical in JIT. Thus, unnecessary clutter is eliminated and required items are carefully defined and controlled. Less clutter allows the managers of shop floor activities to identify problem areas more easily and to keep better track of jobs as they progress through the factory.

The implementation and maintenance of relations with suppliers and clients are very important to the success of a JIT system in that they broaden the scope of cost reduction and the drive for quality improvement.

The quality of purchased supplies is critical to the quality of a firm's finished product. It is estimated that 50 per cent of a company's quality problems are caused by defective purchased materials. Lascelles & Dale (1990) highlighted that for many companies, the purchase of materials from suppliers and subcontractors accounts for at least 50 per cent of manufacturing costs and in the case of the automotive industry, this figure can be over 70 per cent. This calls for the need to seek improvements in quality and productivity from the suppliers.

In a JIT environment, the role of a supplier is quite different from that in the traditional environment. The JIT principle with regard to purchasing requires organising suppliers to deliver their materials or parts of high quality in small lot sizes and at frequencies required by production, rather than as dictated by economic order quantity purchasing which generates excess inventory and many other unnecessary costs. Suppliers are often asked to make frequent deliveries directly to the production line. Suppliers received Kanban containers, just as plant work centres do, since suppliers are viewed as an extension of the plant.

The major requirements of JIT supplier links are thus:

1   High quality levels.

2   Reduced order quantities.

3   Reduced and reliable lead times.

These help to reduce inventory levels and uncertainty about suppliers' performances. If suppliers will deliver high quality items on time, safety stocks can be reduced, together with the need for in-coming inspection, and there will be no disruption to production through poor quality items or through late delivery.

Supplier development therefore requires a fundamental shift in the customer-supplier relationship. JIT calls for a single or fewer source suppliers delivering high quality products on time and in small quantities based on the customer's consumption rates, while the manufacturing company will make a long-term purchase commitment to suppliers and provide them with accurate forecasts and technical support (Hernandez, 1989). Indeed, JIT continually emphasises the need to have only a single supplier supplying several parts in a "family" thereby increasing the volume per supplier and reducing the number of suppliers. This will encourage the supplier to make the capital investment required to improve his manufacturing processes.

The advantages in having a single or a few sources of supply are:

Consistency and higher quality A single source of supply can be managed more easily giving the buyer more time to work closely with a supplier and involve him in the early stages of design to provide high quality products.

Better communications A single source of supply poses fewer communication problems. Changes in order quantity and delivery time for specific parts can be made quickly.

Operational advantages There will be less production and paperwork time required for fewer suppliers. Easily scheduled deliveries are also possible since orders are placed with one or few suppliers.

Cost reduction A single supplier can constantly contribute to cost-cutting ideas. Overall cost is also lower because of higher volume of items purchased from any one supplier. This cost reduction is eventually passed back to the customer in terms of lower prices.

Certainty Long-term relationships are established which encourage supplier loyalty and reduce the risk of an interrupted supply (Ansari & Modarress, 1990).

Apart from single source of supply, JIT also encourages long-term agreements with a few carefully selected suppliers for the following reasons:

1   More reliable deliveries.

2   Greater opportunities for investment.

3   Better quality products.

4   Lower cost.

A supplier with a long-term agreement is more likely to keep to delivery promises, frequently at the expense of short-term agreements with other companies. The company now becomes a major customer (especially if the company is purchasing a product family from the supplier) and their demands will be met first.

The long-term agreement also gives the supplier a greater sense of security. It is therefore appropriate for the supplier to make some investment to help the production of the product family, investment in machinery, control systems or in training personnel.

Generally, most of the long-term agreements have the advantage of specifying the due date and the quality levels. Before JIT, when contracts were often awarded solely on the basis of price, there was perhaps little incentive for the suppliers to improve the quality of their products. Some gave up even trying to deliver items of an acceptable level of quality. The long-term agreement specifies required quality levels (usually at an increasingly high level), with suppliers left in no doubt as to the importance of maintaining this high quality.

These investments together with the higher production volumes for each supplier lead to cost reduction, part of which benefits the supplier and part of which is passed on to the purchaser.

Lastly, the close or near proximity of suppliers are often required to integrate suppliers effectively with JIT procedures. Under JIT, the ideal transport system is one which can move parts in small lots from the supplier to the customer's point of use without transit to storage or other intermediate stations. The location of dedicated local supply plants or in-plant stores close to customers help to achieve this. Quite often, the deliveries will be made directly to the point of use rather than to the stores or a quality inspection station.

As with suppliers, clients are also important in JIT implementation because, from the financial point of view, they supply the money and, from the manufacturing management point of view, they drive the whole manufacturing process. Obviously, with no clients demand, there would be no manufacturing.

Firm schedules of orders without erratic variations given by clients will definitely ease planning problems of the manufacturer and the clients would be relatively assured that their delivery schedules will be met on time. This reduces costs and disruption both for the manufacturer and for the client.

Continuous improvement

JIT is a never ending process of continual improvement. JIT does not seek one-off improvements that will only produce results in the short-term, but rather looks to the long-term by setting in place mechanisms that will result in continual improvements. This is illustrated with respect to stock turn in Figure 2.11.

With JIT, performance ratings such as stock turn, productivity and quality would improve year by year after implementation. At the end of the implementation stage, the trend of the performance ratings would be evaluated. Any deviations in the performance ratings will be examined and measures taken to ensure that the improved trend is maintained. This means that the task of the JIT project team is not finished upon completion of the JIT system implementation. Rather, JIT progress is continually monitored after implementation and the JIT project team is maintained in place to ensure the upward trend in performance ratings.

For continual improvements to flourish, JIT embarks on an ongoing educational programme to reinforce the message about JIT at regular intervals over the years after an implementation. JIT, like any other discipline, has a learning curve, and the organisation can learn from experience how to do things better the next time round. That is the reason why it is so important to continue the educational program once the original goals have been achieved. The only difference as the programme progresses is that the goals set will be more difficult.

Costs / benefits of implementing JIT

The conventional approaches to manufacturing control such as MRP or OPT

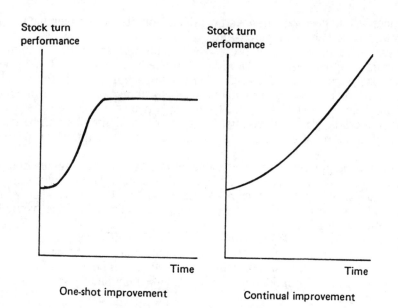

Figure 2.11 One-shot and continual improvement

Source: *O'Grady, P.J. (1988), Putting the Just-In-Time philosophy into practice: A strategy for production managers, Kogan Page Ltd*

require large injections of capital. For example, implementing MRP II is estimated to cost each company an average of over US$1 million (Wallace, 1985). Much of this cost is in computer hardware and software. Typically, an implementation of MRP or OPT involves an eighteen-month implementation sequence to solve the data flows; the system is then tried out in parallel with the existing system, initial troubles are remedied and finally the company is switched over to the new approach.

By contrast, JIT involves little capital expenditure. What is required is a reorientation of people toward their tasks. With JIT implementation, any costs involved are mainly costs of education. The personnel within a company have to be aware of the philosophy behind JIT and how that philosophy impinges on their own particular function.

But while the cost of a JIT implementation is lower than that of a typical MRP II implementation, the benefits brought about by JIT are potentially much greater. The benefits associated with JIT can be divided into two types, viz: "hard" benefits which are tangible and quantifiable; and "soft" benefits which are more difficult to quantify. "Hard" benefits include inventory reduction, WIP reduction, increased productivity, reduced obsolescence, reduced premium freight, etc. while increases in sales, customer service, workers morale and quality make up "soft" benefits.

Past evidences have justified and demonstrated that JIT can be a low cost /

high return policy. A successful JIT implementation can thus achieve rewarding benefits for an organisation at relatively low costs, the one proviso being that the implementation is well-planned through expert advice and carefully executed by intelligent management (O'Grady, 1988).

3 Traditional manufacturing management systems

Introduction

This chapter gives an overview of the various traditional approaches to manufacturing management prior to the emerging global era of JIT application in manufacturing organisations. Three traditional manufacturing approaches, viz: inventory control system; materials requirements planning (MRP) system; and manufacturing resource planning (MRP II) system are briefly discussed, highlighting their various operational methodologies as well as their inherent drawbacks. A short description of how these traditional approaches utilise the "push" type of materials movement system in their manufacturing processes is also given at the end of the chapter.

The term manufacturing industry covers a broad spectrum of activities, ranging from the control of chemical processes to precision engineering, from making satellites to making bicycles (Vollman, et. al., 1984). Overall, the manufacturing process can be divided into three major categories:

1   Flow (or mass) manufacture.

2   Jobbing (or customized) manufacture.

3   Batch manufacture.

Flow manufacture consists of high-volume manufacture of a small range of products such as, for example, consumer goods like television sets or vacuum cleaners. Flow manufacture has certain very obvious characteristics: because it is concerned with achieving high outputs of a limited product range, it often makes sense to invest in specialized machinery, and since there is a significant degree of repetition involved, a high proportion of the labour force can consist of unskilled or semi-skilled workers.

The management problems in flow manufacture are therefore mainly concerned with ensuring a continuity in material and component supply as well as a high overall system efficiency. However, in spite of the high output achieved by many flow manufacturers, poor quality has often been a continuing and intractable problem.

Jobbing manufacture is concerned with manufacturing non-standard items in a one-off mode; that is, the manufacturer cannot assume that repeat orders for products will again be received. Jobbing manufacture is therefore characterized by a large range of products, each product being low volume, and the requirements in terms of the machinery used and the skill levels of the workforce are thus quite different from those found in flow manufacture. General rather than special-purpose machinery is needed and workers in this non-repetitive environment must be highly skilled. Again, major management problems are concerned with ensuring that the high system efficiency is commensurate with high quality levels.

The final category of manufacturing, batch manufacture, is concerned with medium-volume products where repeat orders are expected. In such batch environments, a product is manufactured in a batch, or lot, at intervals which vary according to demand and other factors. A batch may be repeated every day, week, month, year or every few years. This kind of manufacturing poses considerable problems for management since high overall system efficiency must be maintained in the face of constantly changing demand patterns.

Nevertheless, whichever category the manufacturing activity is in, there is one feature that characterises nearly all manufacturing enterprises - complexity. Manufacturing systems are inherently complex and a huge range of factors determines the interrelationships between jobs, machines and personnel. The management of most manufacturing operations therefore poses tremendously complex problems. Nowhere is this more true than in batch manufacturing. At any one time, a typical batch manufacturer may have several hundred batches flowing through dozens of work centres. Coordinating personnel and machines to get the right product to the right customer at the right time in the right quantity while also achieving acceptable standards of manufacture at reasonable cost is a mammoth task.

Over the years, a variety of approaches have been adopted in the hope of resolving, or at least simplifying, their problems. The earliest attempts were based on simply monitoring the inventories of the finished products: when the inventory level of a particular product became too low, a new batch was ordered.

Such approaches were (and still are) very simple to operate; but they can only provide a partial solution. In the 1970s, when both offshore competition and interest rates increased, organisations came under even greater pressure to reduce inventories. As a result, attention began to be focussed on materials requirements planning (MRP) and manufacturing resource planning (MRP II) type systems (Orlicky, 1975). These MRP systems produce a detailed plan for material and component requirements.

Inventory control system

The earliest mechanisms used to manage manufacturing did not involve any analysis of the manufacturing aspect at all, but instead concentrated on monitoring the inventories of finished products. When these inventories fell below certain levels (usually called reorder levels or reorder points) a replenishment was ordered and this order passed through the factory and then into the inventory, hopefully before the inventory was exhausted. (Vollman, et. al., 1984) A manufacturer producing several hundred different lines could therefore make all the management decisions on the basis of information about the finished product inventory levels (see Figure 3.1).

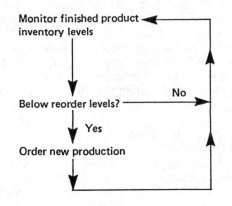

Figure 3.1 Inventory monitoring and reordering

Source: *O'Grady, P.J. (1988), Putting the Just-In-Time philosophy into practice: A strategy for production managers, Kogan Page Ltd*

The inventory control approach to manufacturing management pays little or no regard to how production is going to be addressed; it also frequently results in significant fluctuations in production requirements. If, as often happens, inventory levels of a large number of products simultaneously fall below the critical level, then large amounts of production are ordered, creating production bottleneck problems. Under these circumstances, manufacturing lead times may vary widely, depending on capacity bottlenecks and other factors. These wide variations in lead times make it extremely difficult to organise production efficiently and to replenish inventories promptly.

When long lead times are involved, a host of other related problems are reactively compounded. For example, it then becomes necessary to forecast client demands over a longer time span which may result in an uncertain, inaccurate and risky demand forecast. This in turn, can lead to a decline in the effectiveness of management. If the forecasts of future demand turn out to be inaccurate (as is usually the case), the orderly flow of work through the factory is disrupted. Products which are no longer needed because the forecast over-estimated demand, are put to one side to await an upturn in demand. These stockpiles of partially completed goods disrupt the flow of work through the factory by occupying more factory space thereby creating unnecessary physical obstructions to material movements. Furthermore, the build-up of unwanted inventory levels also severely locks up valuable financial capital which can instead be put to better use to raise productivity. Conversely, part finished products for which the forecast has underestimated now become in demand and have to be pushed through the factory as a matter of urgency. Such sudden changes in priority tend to create confusion and are likely to lead, firstly, to quality problems and, secondly, to inefficient use of resources when partly processed items are taken off a machine and replaced by those that are currently required. The entire plant becomes pervaded by an atmosphere of crisis and factory managers often become totally pre-occupied with the need to resolve short-term problems.

The only two advantages which the inventory control approach have are its simplicity and that it readily lends itself to a manual operation. In practice, the responsibility for reordering is often simply left with warehouse personnel who are ideally placed to monitor changes in inventory levels and react to them. Indeed, the simple and yet manual nature of the inventory control approach had made it the only manufacturing control approach used by manufacturing industries prior to the advent of widespread computer usage in MRP type systems.

The disadvantages of the inventory control approach are however severe. The main ones can be summarized under three headings:

Higher inventory holding costs

Individual inventories of all components are kept with much of this inventory not being used for some time. The inventory that is being held is costly in two major respects; it consumes capital that could be used elsewhere to increase productivity, and it occupies more expensive factory space.

Lack of responsiveness

In any dynamic market, there are likely to be dramatic changes in demand. Where the market demand suddenly increases, then it is likely that there will not be enough inventory to cover any increase and the customer service level therefore falls.

Risk of inventory becoming obsolete

When there is a downturn in demand, a manufacturer may well be left with large quantities of surplus stock. In many cases, this stock will become obsolete and may be kept in inventory for many years (still tying up more money and space) before being written off and disposed of.

Both of the latter two disadvantages arise because the inventory control approach is essentially reactive. It responds to changes as and when they occur without anticipating or looking to the future. By the increasingly competitive atmosphere of the 1970s, when large inventories became very expensive to maintain, it subsequently became clear that there was a need to move towards a more proactive approach. This approach would enable changes to be anticipated and the manufacturing process to be managed in order to ensure that the response was fast and accurate. The proactive systems which were most commonly adopted in the 1970s were MRP and its extension, MRP II (Orlicky, 1975).

Materials Requirements Planning (MRP) systems

As mentioned, the most significant drawbacks of inventory control approaches are their high cost and poor response to dynamic market changes. Under these circumstances many companies looked for approaches which could increase their responsiveness and decrease their inventory levels. As a result, the American Production and Inventory Control Society (APICS) started promoting Materials Requirements Planning; software was written and many manufacturing organisations began to use MRP systems.

The rationale of MRP systems is that they enable factory managers to look to the future and to increase inventory only so far as is necessary to provide for requirements which can be clearly foreseen. The mechanisms of basic MRP are as follows:

1   Forecast future demand and determine, taking the available capacity and on hand inventory into account, how much to produce to meet this demand. This process generates what is usually called a master production scheduling (MPS) that gives the production quantities of products up to a specified time period into the future.

2   After having determined the quantum to be produced, there remains the problem of ordering the material and components necessary to make the products. This is done in the second stage with the help of the Materials Requirements Planning system. This takes the MPS and breaks it down into specific raw materials and component requirements, determining the quantities of each that should be ordered, and when.

3   The output from the MRP system is thus a detailed list of the materials or components to be manufactured or ordered, together with the dates to start manufacture or to place orders. The activities required are to either order the components from the external vendors or to arrange manufacture. In the latter case, the task includes detailed scheduling of jobs on machines in order to ensure delivery on time. Achieving this is a tremendous problem for most manufacturing organisations.

Manufacturing Resource Planning (MRP II) systems

The first MRP implementations were mainly confined to production and inventory control functions within a manufacturing organisation. As experience was later gained, it became evident that the implementation would benefit the organisation further if other departments were included so that the MRP implementation would cover all aspects of the organisation's activities, including sales, purchasing and finance. The basic MRP system was therefore eventually expanded to encompass activities across a broader spectrum of the organisation's activities. This enlarged MRP system was termed manufacturing resource planning or MRP II.

The earlier MRP systems essentially had three levels:

1   Master production scheduling.

2   Materials requirements planning.

3   Ordering.

To incorporate the changes for MRP II, three further layers were added so that the system now has six levels:

1   Business planning.

2   Production planning.

3   Master production scheduling.

4   Materials requirements planning.

5   Capacity requirements planning.

6   Ordering.

The addition of Business Planning and Production Planning broadened the range of functions covered by the MRP II process; while capacity requirements planning gave the detailed capacity analysis of each work centre and provided the basis for priority planning.

In order to carry out the detailed capacity analysis, accurate factory floor data are required. This increased requirement for data, in comparison with the earlier MRP systems, has caused problems in many MRP II implementations with some improvements being less than expected.

MRP and "push" system

This section describes how the MRP system is integrated within the traditional "push" type of operational flowchart in a typical manufacturing organisation. (The term MRP is used to refer to both MRP and MRP II systems in the following sections).

Before the wide spread applicability of JIT, the majority of manufacturing organisations operate in the traditional "push" type environment. They used master production schedules and MRP outputs to drive their production schedules and push the movement of materials in the factory. Figure 3.2

49

shows the operational flowchart utilising the "push" type system in a typical manufacturing environment. The "push" system is a single-flow process in which build schedules and materials travel in the process in the same direction. (Compare Figure 2.6 for a "pull" / Kanban system where materials and build schedules travel in opposite directions, ie. double flow).

To begin, a demand forecast is proposed by the sales department based on a sales forecast (for a specified future sales period) prepared by sales staff in the field. The demand forecast is then passed to the materials department which converts the forecast into a MPS and inputs this data into the MRP system.

The MRP system, being a top-down computer programme, then explodes the product quantities in the MPS all the way down to the lowest-level parts. It takes into consideration all the inventory locations in the factory and nets the parts required to build the products in the quantities listed on the MPS. The MRP system will report the parts that are on order to cover for the materials that are not at hand but are needed to meet the build schedule. It will also report the parts that must be ordered to fill possible shortages. In addition, it can report the excess parts that are not needed for the build plan and the parts that are obsolete or cannot be used by a higher assembly.

In a "push" system, the MRP system triggers a series of work orders required to build the products in the quantities specified on the MPS. A work order is a release mechanism used by the materials planner to provide manufacturing with the materials needed to build a certain number of products. The planner will open a work order on the computer authorizing the stockroom to release the parts to manufacturing. This process is called "kit pulling". The stockroom uses a kit pick list from the computer to pull all the parts required to build the number of units specified by the work order. When the parts are together, the stockroom releases the kit and the work order paperwork to the manufacturing floor.

The MRP system normally has a feedback loop that receives information about the factory work-in-progress (WIP) status at the time it is planning the material requirements. However, the inherent problem is that the response time of the system is too slow. When the schedule corrections reach the manufacturing floor, the excess inventory and product completions are already at hand. This lack of immediate feedback on the status of the materials previously released causes the shop floor to have too much inventory on hand in different states of completion. It also causes waste, since labour and overhead are used in tracking the work orders and the schedules.

Before MRP problems are discussed in the next section, it is also interesting to note here that the traditional "push" type of manufacturing practices are often referred to by proponents of JIT as the "Just-In-Case" (JIC) system (Lim and Low, 1992). In the JIC system, materials and parts are pushed from one process to the next regardless of whether they are needed or will be worked on by the next process. The emphasis of these traditional manufacturing organisations is high volume production of standardised commodities in order to reap the benefits of economies of scale and division of labour. High volume was sought as a means to lower unit costs and long production runs of components are considered necessary in

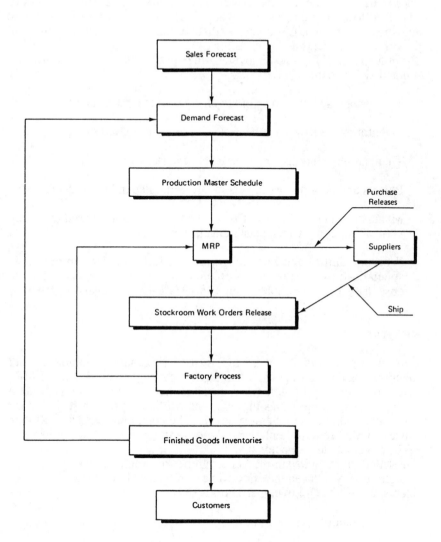

Figure 3.2 Build schedule and materials flow in a push system

Source: *Hernandez, A. (1989), Just-In-Time manufacturing - A practical approach, Prentice-Hall*

51

order to minimise the down-time of machinery. However, such a practice requires a build-up of inventories as "buffer stocks" in case of machine breakdowns, a strike or defective components. To ensure a smooth production flow, ample reserves are kept "just in case". This approach also extends itself to human resources, so that surplus labour is usually hired to cope with contingencies and uncertainties.

Proponents of JIT point to several other problems associated with the traditional JIC system:

1   The system is slow to respond to changes in market demand.

2   Inventories are expensive because of interest rate charges.

3   There are high storage and maintenance costs.

4   Rejects and poor quality in general are concealed in buffer stocks.

5   Management coordination of such a complex system is based on a deep vertical hierarchy which usually leads to rigidity.

6   Workers' ability and knowledge are not fully utilised, and extreme specialisation leads to problems of motivation, satisfaction, absenteeism, etc. (Schonberger, 1982; Hall, 1983; Aggarwal, 1985).

MRP problems

The usual implementation of a MRP system is to have a manual master production scheduling stage with a computer package to carry out the MRP breakdown into requirements for components and raw materials This computer package requires as inputs to the MPS, the product structure (or bill of materials) and the inventory levels. The computer package will then produce detailed requirements with the ordering dates and, in the case of MRP II, more detailed capacity analysis.

The MRP logic looks simple but a number of problems have arisen that have significantly reduced the effectiveness of many MRP operations. These problems fall into the following categories:

1   Poor inventory level accuracy.

2   Inaccurate lead times.

3   Inaccurate bill of material.

4   Poor master production schedule.

5   Out of date data.

6   Poor methodology.

52

The inventory level accuracy is crucial if accurate output is to be obtained from the MRP system. The computer software may be good in itself with very few bugs, but its performance can only be as good as the data fed into it. Most successful MRP systems probably achieve 95 per cent inventory records accuracy. If a MRP type system is implemented in an organisation where inventory accuracy is lower, say only 75 or 80 per cent, then this will probably result in a large number of problems, with final products being overdue and inventory levels being kept higher than necessary (O'Grady, 1988).

In the majority of practical manufacturing systems, lead times vary dramatically even at the best of times. Reasons often quoted for these variations include machine breakdown, quality problems, other products taking priority, component and raw material shortages or tooling problems. This large degree of variation in the lead times would often caused the MRP calculations (which may be based on an estimate of the mean lead times) to become erroneous.

The bill of materials is another item of data that needs to be accurate. Inaccuracies can occur for a number of reasons: when the bill of materials file is built up in the MRP implementation, for example, or when it is altered in updating the product. It is generally recognized by those with experience of MRP implementations that the bill of materials should be 95 per cent accurate (O'Grady, 1988). The goal of 95 per cent accuracy of bill of materials using this definition is probably the minimum standard permissible if the performance of the MRP system is to be satisfactory. If accuracy falls below this level, a significant number of incorrect parts are likely to be ordered or manufactured as a result and this is often only discovered when assembly of these components begins, resulting in a rush to complete the correct component.

The fourth factor leading to poor MRP performance is associated with inaccuracy in the MPS. The MPS acts as the driver of the MRP system. If there are significant inaccuracies in the MPS, these are passed straight through the MRP system leading to errors in the MRP output. Most experts in MRP implementation would suggest that, again, 95 per cent accuracy in the MPS is essential to the MRP operation (O'Grady, 1988). This accuracy is based on 95 per cent of the MPS being correct - in *number of items*, not in money. Reasons for an inaccurate MPS include inaccurate forecasts of demand and inaccurate capacity data. As already indicated, both these elements tend to be inaccurate in practice since, firstly, it is difficult to accurately forecast the demand for most items into the future and, secondly, capacity usage is dynamic, changing rapidly from one time period to another. Under these circumstances, it is extremely difficult to judge levels of capacity availability in the future.

The other difficulty for MRP systems arises from out-of-date data and the time it takes for data to be entered into the system and become accessible. This time delay can be due to the low frequency of computer runs and the time delay between some transactions taking place and the record of these transactions being entered into the computer.

The last problem area associated with MRP implementation concerns poor methodology which clearly points out that the entire MRP methodology is flawed, especially when used for shop floor control. A re-examination of the major features of the MRP system would quickly indicate that each of the features (forecasting demand, MPS determination, inputing MPS into MRP) does actually involve some error being placed into the calculation at each stage. What should end up as a highly accurate requirement for raw materials and components together with a highly accurate schedule of deadlines often contains considerable errors.

In conclusion, this chapter has given an overview of some major well-established traditional approaches to manufacturing management. But it should be borne in mind that they have not always succeeded in significantly improving manufacturing efficiency (Anderson, et. al., 1982). Indeed, the available data indicate that western countries using these traditional approaches still lag behind the countries in Asia (which apply the JIT philosophy) in such performance measures as stockturn, customer service and quality levels. A proper understanding of these "traditional" approaches is, however, necessary in order to fully appreciate the JIT approach, if only because it enables the identification of some of the pitfalls that must be avoided in the course of a JIT implementation.

4 Comparison between construction and manufacturing

Introduction

Unlike the manufacturing sector, the construction industry is a more complex and fragmented industry. Construction activities are generally complex due to the vast number of tradesmen, materials, machineries and construction methods used in any one construction project. The industry is also highly fragmented with different transient professionals (project consultants), builders and suppliers entwined in different procurement and contractual arrangements.

As the JIT concept has its principal origin in the manufacturing industry, it is only appropriate therefore to make some structural modifications in the construction industry for the concept to be applied gainfully to the latter. Before such structural modifications are made, it is imperative that the fundamental differences between the manufacturing and construction industries be explored and closely examined. As a subset of the construction industry, the prefabrication sector should gain from this comparison of the construction and manufacturing industries and derive a framework within which JIT may be applied for precast concrete production.

Differences between construction and manufacturing

The fundamental differences between the construction and manufacturing industries should not negate nor inhibit the applicability of the JIT concept in the former. Rather, these differences should instead strengthen the need for applying the concept more rigorously to construction. A good example of this is the quality assurance concept which originated in the manufacturing industry. This concept has been applied rigorously and successfully in recent years in construction. Some of the major fundamental differences between construction and manufacturing are discussed below. It should, however, be noted that some of the points raised below may create more controversy than agreement. Nevertheless, this should help to place the prefabrication sector within its proper context within the construction industry and provide an appreciation of how JIT may be applied in the latter and, by extension, into the former.

Vagaries of inclement weather

Almost an outdoor activity, traditional construction is commonly subjected and severely affected by the vagaries of inclement weather. Adverse climatic conditions often interrupt the smooth flow of construction works and disrupt its productivity. This adversity may be alleviated to a certain extent by covering the exposed site temporarily with some make-shift shelter (for example, tarpaulin roof). However, this may be feasible only on small localised sites but will be constrained by the vagaries encountered on large or extremely exposed sites (such as large scale civil engineering projects having an extensive geographical area coverage).

Manufacturing, on the other hand, is normally carried out almost exclusively indoors under the shelter of factory premises and is thus provided with ample protection from the disruptive effects of inclement weather.

In view of the inherent disadvantage construction has, the JIT concept should therefore be vigorously applied to the construction setting to raise productivity, thereby leading to a shortening of the completion time for construction projects. Achieving this can greatly help constructors to complete their projects just in time or before inclement weather sets in.

Unique "one-off" nature of construction operations

The final product of construction is usually of unique design and often differs from one project to another. Where design is concerned, no two buildings (not even buildings of the Housing and Development Board) or civil engineering structures are exactly alike in the construction industry. Factors like owner's tastes, locational factors, statutory compliances, subsoil conditions, etc. often greatly influence the design criteria of the construction product.

Different or "one-off" designs are therefore a norm in the construction industry unless standard components are prefabricated for on-site assembly. This peculiar trait of the construction industry means that each new project needs to be designed separately even though their functional attributes may be similar. This implies that the beneficial influence of the learning curve cannot to a large extent be exploited to its full advantage as the design experience or lessons learnt from one project could not be repeated elsewhere in other projects.

In manufacturing, the situation is conversely different. In this case, standard designs and repetitive processes are strictly adhered to so as not to make any disruptions and unnecessary modifications to the sound production rhythm. Standard designs and repetitive production runs are usually adopted for a specific period of time until the next change in design arises in, say, a few years' time to accommodate changes in marketing strategies.

Ease of automation and robotisation

Construction often involves large-scale complex assemblies of components for "one-off" type of site operations. These non-standardized operations which are almost non-repetitive in nature for different projects are also both difficult to handle and fasten manually in place. These factors together with the unpredictable nature of construction (uncertainties like vagaries of inclement weather, difficult subsoil conditions, coordination between different trades, etc.) has make the latter less amenable to automation and robotisation.

The manufacturing scenario, on the other hand, is different. Typical manufacturing processes are characterized by components of products being pre-programmed to move along fixed mechanised production lines which are then worked on by workers at specific stages until the final products are formed. Such repetitive and standardized assemblies of products render the manufacturing industry more readily to utilisation of automation and robotisation. The use of robots in the production lines of Japanese car manufacturers is a good indicator of how automation has been exploited fully in the manufacturing industry.

Certainty and problem identification

As construction operations are often carried out in sequential orders, planning for the commencement of different work activities and the deployment of different skilled trades on site is critical. Unless the planned schedules are expedited timely and effectively, delays and cost overruns are almost inevitable. The wide array of uncertainties like inclement weather, subsoil conditions, site constraints, etc. often disrupt the planned schedules for most construction projects. This is particularly so for large civil engineering and chemical processing projects such as highways, underground tunnels, gas pipelines, etc. which run across vast areas of virgin land. Frequently, unforeseen problems like bad subsoil conditions, undulating land contours, site mishaps, etc. disrupt the smooth progress of the construction works. Thus, as products of construction move along their pre-determined routes, abrupt engineering decisions and solutions would have to be made at various stages in order to solve the unforeseen problems. The construction process is therefore a subtle activity in which likely problems are not readily identifiable.

In the manufacturing environment, the above scenario is however reversed. The various production processes in manufacturing are almost invariably carried out in a factory under conditions of certainty. The production processes can be pre-planned, is repetitive and hence problems may be anticipated and corrective actions taken before they occur. Even if problems do occur, the preventive lessons learnt from overcoming them are useful for future production runs as the processes are standard and usually repetitive in manufacturing. Problems are therefore more readily identifiable in the manufacturing process.

Designer-Producer homogeneity

The project developmental process of design and construction is generally a long and arduous one which is too often made complicated by the large number of designers and builders involved in a typical project. In the traditional form of project procurement, the professional designers (i.e. architects, engineers, quantity surveyors) and builders are each engaged separately by the client who is the initiator of the project. As the designers and builders are independent parties, there is a critical need for efficient coordination and effective communication between the various parties for the successful execution of the project. More often than not, this delineation between the design and building teams has gave rise to problems caused by frequent lack of coordination and poor communication between the various parties.

Unlike construction, the designer-producer homogeneity is achievable in manufacturing where the establishment who designs the product will frequently be the same establishment who produces it. In this case, both the design and production teams are part of the larger manufacturing establishment which manufactures the product. Coordination between the designer and the production operator is therefore more profound and effective than in the case of construction. This advantage enables problems to be ironed out before they occur.

Immediate appraisal and possession

A major difference between construction and manufacturing is the principal inability of owners gaining immediate appraisal and possession of their desired products in construction. This is mainly due to the frequently long gestation period between the project inception and commissioning stages in the construction industry. While manufactured products may be purchased off the shelves, or be readily inspected in showrooms, the final construction product does not materialise until it has surpassed the design, construction and commissioning stages. Hence, although a client may be desirous of a building, immediate possession may not often be possible.

Influence of economic performance

At the macro level, whilst adverse economic conditions can severely affect both the construction and manufacturing industry, the latter is not so dependent on the performance of other economic sectors as compared to the former. This is mainly due to manufacturing making up a large part of the national economics of most developing countries, contributing some 20 to 30 per cent of the Gross Domestic Product (GDP) in some cases (Lim and Low, 1992). As a result, most developing countries have also tended to adopt the manufacturing industry as the vehicle for growth, employment stimulation, job creation and import substitution.

The construction industry, on the other hand, frequently make up less than 10 per cent of GDP. This figure has however tended to be higher in the developing than developed countries where government planners have given the construction industry paramount importance for supporting economic development. The relationships between the construction sector and all other sectors of the national economy were also found to be strong, particularly between manufacturing and construction (Lim and Low, 1992). The construction sector is therefore seriously affected by the performance of other economic sectors when the demand for construction infrastructure and supporting facilities falls. Construction is therefore a "buffer" industry used frequently for regulating the national economy. Compared with manufacturing, the performance of the construction industry is often cyclical in nature.

Construction financing

New construction works often involve an initial outlay of capital due to the sizeable mobilisation of resources to start off the project. This capital outlay may be massive for some large scale construction projects. Because of this capital upfront, pre-payment is therefore an important feature to finance construction works. For instance, it is a normal contractual obligation for buyers of new buildings to pay for their purchases either in full or by progress payments as the buildings are being constructed. In contrast, buyers of finished manufactured products only pay for their goods at the time of purchase.

Owner's involvement

In the construction industry, it is a norm that the building owner is often deeply involved in the construction process from the inception to commissioning stages. Building owners are frequently seen to instruct changes by way of amendments, additions or omissions to the original scope of construction works. The building owner therefore appears to be in a position to greatly influence the construction process. Such deep involvements by building owners have often caused marked variations to the original costs and completion time of projects.

In manufacturing, the scenario is different with potential buyers not having the rights to access manufacturing facilities to inspect and comment on the goods undergoing production. Buyers of manufactured products can only exhibit their influence after they have used the products and have channelled their comments through market research feedbacks.

Safety provision

The nature of construction operations is often "messy" with a host of different trade activities and hundreds of material items all being entwined within a congested and often restricted work site. This is particularly so if the housekeeping activity within the work site is badly carried out. It is therefore difficult and hazardous to gain access into a work site (especially a building site) undergoing construction. The provision of safety measures on a permanent basis is thus quite impossible due to the constantly changing scenarios of the various construction phases.

In manufacturing, safety precautions on the other hand can be embarked upon more readily because of the permanency of production facilities and the controlled process environment of which manufacturing is subjected to.

Organisational structure

Compared to manufacturing, the durations of most construction projects or their individual work phases are relatively short. Consequently, the organisational structure for a construction project is also based on a short-term or ad hoc nature. The management team and workforce must thus be assembled quickly, and once assembled, it is often advisable not to restructure the project team before the project is completed. In addition, planning and tooling up equipment for the various phases of operations are also ad hoc in nature and carried out only once. This contrasts sharply with most long-term manufacturing processes which are standardized and repetitive in nature.

Mobility

In construction, specialised construction crews or tradesmen are often required to move from one location to another within the work site after a given operation is completed. This high mobility is inevitable because on-site work stations are not permanent. In contrast, manufacturing activities only require operations to be assigned to and carried out in one place.

Marketing management

Marketing for construction products is quite different from that of manufactured products. Construction products are often intangible in nature because the clients do not actually get to see or appreciate the final constructed products until the latter have been built. Although life-size models, mock-ups and samples of building materials, etc. may provide some indication to the clients concerning the final constructed product, there is a limit as to how far this experience can be translated into reality. In some very rare cases, the final constructed product may differ significantly from what has been marketed and shown in sales brochures and mock-up models during the initial marketing stage.

The buyers of manufactured products, on the other hand, have the opportunity to see, feel and inspect the products before the purchase. As manufactured products are already in their final forms just before their purchase by the buyers, marketing can be carried out much more readily and with greater certainty by the seller because of the element of tangibility.

In summary, construction therefore appears to be a more complex and fragmented industry involving transient players and where the building owner is involved in the design and construction process right from the very beginning. Nevertheless, the fundamental differences between construction and manufacturing do not mean that productivity improvement techniques adopted by the latter are not applicable in the former. Rather, efforts should be made to modify productivity practices in the manufacturing industry for application in the construction industry (Oglesby, Parker and Howell, 1989).

5 Just-in-Time operations in prefabrication

Introduction

To test the hypothesis targeted selectively at the "off-site" prefabrication sector of the local construction industry, an industry-wide survey was carried out in late-1993 to explore the feasibility of applying the JIT concept to raise productivity in the prefabrication industry. The survey covered twenty local precast concrete component manufacturers in Singapore whose products are used in both building and civil engineering works in Singapore and overseas. A total of fourteen prefabrication firms who responded to the survey have contributed invaluable information relating to their business operations which are pertinent for this study.

The following sections highlight the research methodology used, profile of the respondents and a detailed examination of the findings pertaining to the prefabrication industry and how the JIT concept may be appropriately applied to some of its operations.

Research methodology

The opinion research methodology was used for the field study. This methodology is most suitable because the study seeks to obtain factual information about factory operations and views, judgements and opinions of other people with respect to the research problem. The small population of twenty firms targeted for the survey also made the following data collection techniques most appropriate for the study. The two main data collection techniques used for the study were:

1   Questionnaire survey, and

2   Personal interviews.

After pilot-testing, a set of questionnaire survey form was first sent to all the targeted twenty prefabrication firms. This was then followed up a week later with personal interviews with the relevant personnel of those prefabrication firms who responded to the study.

Appendix 1 shows the questionnaire survey form used for the study. The questionnaire has been designed to seek pertinent information on a variety of subjects under three main aspects of the prefabrication business - namely, production processes analysis; efficiency of manufacturing control system; and relationships with suppliers and customers. In addition, the questionnaire also seeks to determine the current state of awareness of the JIT concept amongst the respondents; wide ranging problems facing the prefabrication industry; and total productivity output data.

The subsequent personal interviews were mainly conducted with the factory or production managers and engineers of the responding prefabrication firms.

Profile of respondents

The profile of the fourteen prefabrication firms who responded to the survey is shown in Table 5.1. A majority of the respondents (ie. eleven firms or 79 per cent) manufacture a diverse range of precast concrete products for both the building and civil engineering markets. Only three responding firms or 21 per cent manufacture precast concrete products solely for the civil engineering sector.

Almost all the precast concrete products for the building industry like staircases, refuse chutes, facades, lightweight partitions, etc. manufactured by 79 per cent of the responding firms are catered for the needs of the local Singapore market; the largest client being the Housing and Development Board (HDB) with her massive public housing programme. The demand for civil engineering prefabrication products were mostly from construction projects tendered out by major government bodies like the Public Works Department (PWD), Ministry of the Environment (ENV), and Jurong Town Corporation (JTC).

It is also worthwhile to note that at least three firms or 21 per cent export their precast products to overseas construction markets in Malaysia, Indonesia, Brunei, Guam and Japan. A majority of these overseas clients are contracting organisations undertaking large private sector commercial building projects.

Survey findings

This section highlights the overall findings of the survey for the fourteen prefabrication firms who responded to the study. These findings were compiled through the combined results of both the questionnaire survey and interviews conducted with the responding firms. Wherever possible, explanations are also given to lend support to the findings reported. For ease of analysis and discussion, the survey findings will be reported as per the format order laid out in the questionnaire survey form as follows:

Table 5.1
Profile of responding precast concrete component manufacturers

Manufacturer	Products														
	Staircase	Refuse chutes	Gable end walls	Facades/ curtain walls	Hollow core slabs/ planks	Beams	Columns	Parapels	Fibrecon panels	Fascia/ sun breakers	Lightweight partitions	Balcony	Roof slabs	Water tank	P.C. components for civil engineering *
A											X				X
B	X														X
C	X	X	X	X				X	X	X	X	X	X		
D	X		X	X	X	X	X				X	X			
E			X	X	X							X		X	X
F	X	X	X	X		X	X	X		X	X	X	X	X	
G	X	X	X	X	X			X			X	X			
H				X							X				
I															
J		X						X		X	X				X
K															X
L	X	X	X	X		X	X	X				X		X	
M	X	X	X	X	X	X		X			X	X		X	
N	X	X	X	X	X			X		X	X	X			X

Legend: X - products offered by manufacturer

(*Components for civil engineering include drain channels, concrete pipes, beams for bridges, slabs for footpaths, box culverts, road kerbs, drain sumps, garden benches, etc.)

Just-In-Time (JIT) awareness

Awareness of JIT philosophy It is surprising to note that only three firms (21 per cent) out of the fourteen responding prefabrication firms have actually heard of the JIT philosophy as applied in the field of manufacturing management. These three prefabricators were amongst the bigger organisations within the survey sample who export their precast concrete products to overseas construction markets. The three firms have came to know of the JIT philosophy through reading and their industrial contacts.

It can thus be generally inferred that the bigger prefabrication firms with their possibly better management structures do carry out a higher level of self-improvement reading than their smaller counterparts in the industry. This is probably their efforts towards striving for excellence and competitiveness amongst the bigger prefabrication firms.

Current practical applications of JIT Although only 21 per cent of the survey respondents are aware of the JIT philosophy, it is interesting to note that all the responding firms do practise some form of JIT system in their manufacturing operations. After briefing the JIT philosophy to the respondents, all of them revealed that the so-called JIT system has in fact been unknowingly adopted and is still being used in the area of materials management in some of their manufacturing operations. In this aspect, examples cited for such JIT applications prevalent in the local prefabrication industry are the supplies of ready-mixed concrete, steel reinforcement bars, as well as fabricated steel formwork systems.

It thus appears that whilst the local prefabrication industry does practise some minor forms of the JIT system in their manufacturing operations, the current level of JIT awareness within the industry is still very low as indicated only by the three firms who have heard of the JIT philosophy. This lack of widespread industry awareness may be due largely to a lack of a formal JIT concept promotion campaign within the local prefabrication industry. This is evident from the fact that before the recent exploratory and promotion works were pioneered by Lim and Low (1992) to use the JIT concept in the Singapore construction industry, there was no formal promotion works to encourage the use of the JIT system in the prefabrication industry.

Analysis of the manufacturing process

Manufacturing planning systems Results on the type of manufacturing planning system(s) the local prefabrication industry is currently adopting are mixed. Four firms (29 per cent) have indicated the adoption of only the traditional inventory control system for their manufacturing operations. Seven or half (50 per cent) of the firms surveyed used a combination of both inventory control system and materials requirements planning system(MRP); whilst only two firms (14 per cent) employed the more advanced manufacturing resource planning system (MRP II). Surprisingly, there is one firm (7 per cent) who has not adopted any of the three listed manufacturing planning systems.

The background of the four firms who used only inventory control system shows that they are manufacturers of largely standardised precast concrete products like road kerbs, drain channels, carpark slabs, etc. Regular demand due to the high level of standardisation already achieved for these precast concrete components in the local civil engineering industry have helped sustained the operations of the four firms based on the inventory control approach. The seven firms who adopted a combination of inventory control system and MRP are manufacturers of a diverse range of precast concrete components for both the building and civil engineering industries. Their range of products include the above-mentioned highly standardized precast components as well as customized "one-off" precast components like bridge beams, balconies, external wall facades, gable end walls, etc. It was learnt that these firms have tended to use the inventory control system for the more regular demand stock of highly standardised components which were being used extensively on a large scale by the construction industry. On the contrary, the MRP system was mainly used by the firms to plan the production of non-standardized, customized "one-off" components. The two firms who employed the more advanced MRP II system are amongst the larger firms in the survey sample who supplied the export markets. The "systemless" firm is the smallest one amongst the fourteen firms surveyed and whose production is only catered to customized orders for one type of precast concrete product - bridge beams for civil engineering projects.

As regards the operational performances of the MRP systems (to reiterate, the term MRP is used here to refer to both MRP and MRP II systems), almost 67 per cent (six firms) of the respondents employing MRP systems have lamented on the problem of common inaccuracies in their system outputs. The major problem areas normally encountered which have hindered the efficiency and effectiveness of their MRP systems are as follows:

Poor inventory level accuracy Incorrect inventory level counts have most often resulted in erroneous MRP system outputs. In most cases, the major cause of incorrect inventory level counts had been due to "double-counting" by production staff. This "double-counting" had came about when sales staff disposed off portions of undelivered inventory stockpile meant for a specific client to other valued customers on an urgent basis. In a majority of cases, delays in the site works of some clients had led to the untimely delivery of the finished goods from the prefabricators. This situation had often tempted the sales staff to sell the undelivered inventory stockpile to other customers who could offer timely acceptance. Provided that the internal communication links within the factory is sound, the confusion that followed from this practice of disposing off undelivered goods had inevitably led production personnel to "double-count" inventory levels.

Inaccurate lead times Maintaining accurate lead times for all different product lines had proved to be an arduous if not impossible task for most prefabricators. Given the fixed manufacturing capacities and different number of product lines, lead times for the various products still varied significantly. The reasons frequently quoted by the respondents for these variations include the following:

1   Machinery / plant breakdowns: this is critical especially for high frequent usage types like overhead gantry crane and concrete batching plant.

2   Quality problems: mostly resulting in reworks and delays when production volume is high.

3   Raw material shortages: most severe in steel reinforcement bars during times of high production volume. The main factor contributing to this was the tendency for workers to misuse steel reinforcement bars allocated for a particular product type for another product line. The results of such malpractices were often confusion, material shortages and eventual delays.

4   Constructibility problems: most prevalent for new precast products introduced into the construction industry for the first time. Examples of common constructibility problems were difficulties in placing steel reinforcement bars due to massive congestion and awkward curtailment, clashing of steel reinforcement bars with other components like prestressing ducts, difficulties in formwork assembly and demoulding operations, etc.

5   Absence of "factory-like" environment: the "open-site" nature of most prefabrication firms visited generally put the majority of their manufacturing processes at the mercy of inclement weather.

Poor "Master Production Scheduling" (MPS) No matter how well prepared the MPS was, most respondents employing MRP systems agreed that a highly accurate MPS was quite impossible to attain. The continuum of accuracy as reported by the respondents ranged from 85 per cent to 93 per cent only. The main reason cited for this impossible task was the difficulty in ascertaining accurate manufacturing capacity data. This is largely due to the dynamic nature of manufacturing capacity usage which often tends to change rapidly from one time period to another. Forecasting capacity usage usually becomes worse when certain product lines abruptly took priority for production due to top management's frequent commitment to meet sudden overseas market demands.

Usage of obsolete data Non adjustment for obsolete data, particularly data on "cancelled orders" in the prepared MRP structures, had in the majority of cases rendered the MRP outputs invalid and inaccurate.

Manufacturing flow-line movements and physical factory layout

Results on how well the existing flow-line movements of the respondents' various manufacturing processes performed were contradictory and inconclusive. Whilst ten firms (71 per cent) and four firms (29 per cent) rated "satisfactory" and "good" performances respectively for their flow-line movements, all of the respondents have readily cited that there would be significant increases in output productivity if their physical factory layouts could be re-arranged; particularly if sequential processes for a particular product type are re-located in a cell group using group technology principles. In fact, it is interesting to note that all of the respondents have in some manner exhibited keen interests in group technology techniques to enhance their productivity drive. It may thus be highly probable that the rated flow-line performances given by the respondents do not truly reflect the actual state of events and that the rated data obtained were ironically given only for "window-dressing" purposes to mask over embarrassing productivity performances.

Nonetheless, a careful examination of the survey findings have enabled the physical factory layouts of the responding prefabrication firms to be illustrated generally using two representative types of layout depending on the product backgrounds of the firms. The first physical factory layout type relates to and typically represents those firms who mainly manufacture precast prestressed concrete bridge beams for civil engineering contracts. There are four (29 per cent) firms amongst the respondents who carry out such works. The reason for singling out the factory layouts of the bridge beam precasters as a separate entity is largely due to the unique product characteristics possessed by such precast prestressed concrete products. Bridge beams are generally huge and long structures with prestressing designs incorporated into them in almost the majority of cases. As a result, they occupied more physical spaces in the factory than precast products for building works like staircases, balconies, lightweight partitions, etc. Furthermore, the requirement for prestressing works has rendered the production beds for bridge beams immobile as compared to the flexible mobility of production beds for some precast building products. Bridge beams must generally be cast in the prestressing beds after the entire assemblies of steel reinforcement bars and formwork systems are completed together with all prestressing tendons stressed to the specified design requirements. In contrast, precast building products can be cast anywhere within the factory provided there are no material handling problems. Figure 5.1 shows the typical physical factory layout for the prefabricators of bridge beams.

The second type of physical factory layout which is shown in Figure 5.2 typically represents the majority of the responding firms who manufacture precast concrete components mainly for the building industry. For these building products, it is interesting to note the major advantage of the multi-usable production beds situated between any two overhead gantry cranes for the production of not only one but many types of different precast products. This advantage promotes manufacturing flexibility by enabling the production of many different product lines to be carried out to serve varying periodic market demands.

The following lists some of the more pressing factory layout related problems identified from visiting the responding prefabrication firms. These problems can be seen to impinge adversely on the productivity performance of these firms.

68

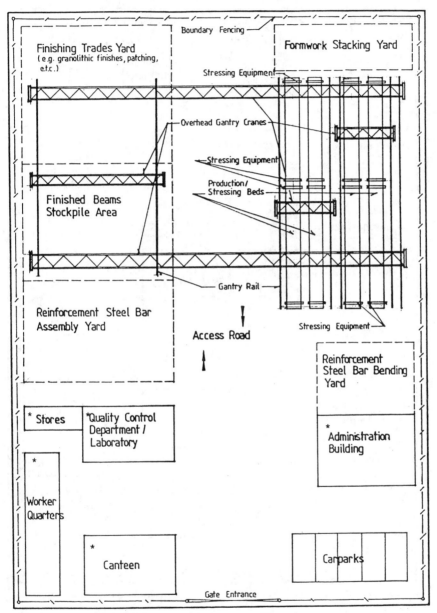

(* Covered premises. All other areas shown are uncovered.)

Figure 5.1 **Typical physical factory layout for bridge beam prefabrication**

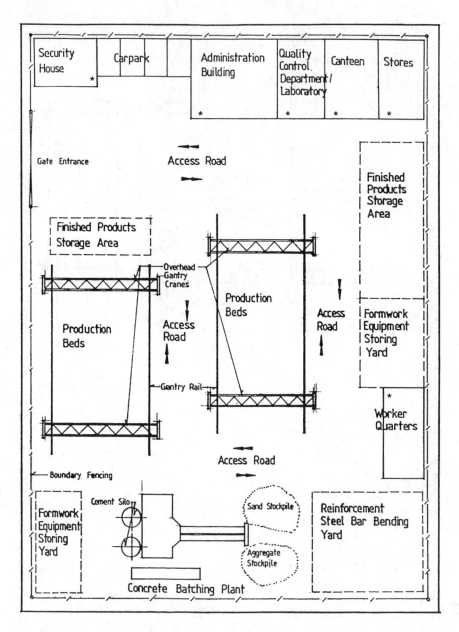

(* Covered premises. All other areas shown are uncovered.)

Figure 5.2   Typical physical factory layout for building components prefabrication

70

Finished goods stockpile The factory visits have revealed an alarmingly massive build-ups of finished good stockpiles waiting to be delivered to their respective clients' worksites. This wasteful situation was found in thirteen of the fourteen firms surveyed. Admittedly, these huge masses of finished goods inventories have gave rise to a growing problem in almost all the prefabrication firms in that they have readily deprived the factories of much valuable physical spaces which could otherwise be used for other productive activities. It was a common sight to see finished precast components being stacked up as high as 12 metres. At a few precasting yards with high volume production, the finished goods were even lined along the sides of the various access routes within the factories, albeit the already narrow access routes. This scenario had inevitably created significant physical obstructions to the smooth flow of transportation and material handling operations within the factories. One precaster of bridge beams had remarked that at times of high job volume, it frequently took them almost four hours to load a finished beam onto the transportation trailer due to the massive physical space congestion which blocks vehicular manoeuvreability.

Exposed (uncovered) production beds Although the prefabrication industry is supposedly a purely manufacturing-based business housed within factory-like environments, it was observed that nine prefabrication firms (64 per cent) undertook their manufacturing operations on exposed or uncovered production beds. This unfavourable practice had put most of the affected prefabrication firms at a great productivity disadvantage in the sense that the uncovered production beds were at all times subjected to the vagaries of inclement weather. The latter had caused significant disruptions to work processes and subsequent delays to production schedules especially during the year end monsoon rain season. According to the affected firms, the reasons for operating on exposed production beds include the following:

1   Most of the "open" factory layouts were inherited from previous owners of the factories and management had been reluctant to invest in erecting covered premises over the exposed production yards.

2   The large number of supporting structural columns of any covered premises would most likely hinder the material handling operations for large prefabrication components: for example, the internal transferring and trailer loading-up operations of bridge beams.

Unfavourable manufacturing processes layout An analysis of Figures 5.1 and 5.2 would show the reason why all the responding prefabrication firms readily agreed to possible productivity increases based simply on a re-arrangement of their existing physical factory layouts for their manufacturing processes. This agreement indicates that the physical layouts of the respondents' manufacturing processes are to some extent unfavourably placed to maximise productivity outputs.

The major problem which hinders productivity of the respondent firms is the tortuous process work-flows that linked sequential manufacturing processes together. These tortuous process work-flows were observed in the following sub-processes:

1   Reinforcement steel bar trade. This normally comprises of the cutting, bending and fixing operations of reinforcement steel bars. Figures 5.1 and 5.2 typically show that the reinforcement steel bar bending and assembly (for bridge beams) yards are generally not located closely adjacent to the production beds. These isolated layout arrangements of the bar bending and assembly yards gave rise to the need for transporting the bent curtailed steel bars either directly to the production beds or firstly to the assembly yard as in the case of bridge beam production. In the latter case, the manufacturing process is even made more difficult as it involves an additional transfer of the fully assembled steel bars from the assembly yard to the production beds. The need for this wasteful handling of massive quantities of steel bars has thus created an unnecessary fleet of fork-lifts, mobile cranes, lorry-cranes, etc. to transport the steel bars between various workstations. The operation of these machineries has most often added to the general confusion amidst the factory production floor.

2   Concrete casting trade. Except for one of the ten building component prebricators, the internal concrete batching plants of all the latter are also isolated and positioned away from the production beds as typically shown in Figure 5.2. Like the case of steel bars, the need to transport ready-mixed concrete to the production lines has forced the prefabricators to invest in machineries like tower and mobile cranes for the high volume of concrete transfers. In addition to increasing fixed capital cost to the manufacturer, the operation of such machineries also seemed to congest the valuable physical space on the factory floor. Although the four prefabricators of bridge beams do not possess any internal concrete batching plant and have to utilise ready-mixed concrete from external suppliers, they too have not been spared from using mobile cranes to carry out their concrete casting operations. A common problem reported by these bridge beam precasters was that at times of high job volume, the physical placements of the mobile cranes would often blocked the operations of other activities like transporting of steel bars, loading-up of finished beams on trailers, general access flow, etc.

3   Finishing trades. These trades involve mainly tiling works such as the installation of granite slabs to precast facade walls, ceramic tiles to precast staircases, etc. for building products; and granolithic finishing works to bridge beams for civil engineering products. In addition, these trades also cover the common face-lift surface treatment works like patching and making good formwork lines, honeycombed concrete, rough concrete surfaces, etc. Once again, Figure 5.1 shows that for bridge beam prefabrication, the finishing trade yard is separated physically from the production beds and is located at one corner of the factory. This again poses the unnecessary need to transfer any constructed beams from across the production beds to the finishing trade yard. For bridge beams, these placement transfers between

locations are often mammoth tasks involving heavy tonnage, high capacity mobile cranes if haulage facilities are not already available through built-in overhead gantry cranes. Needless to say, the problems of clashing work activities and physical space congestion would inevitably follow. In the case of precast building components, it was observed that seven of the ten prefabricators used their production beds dually for the finishing trades as well. Instead of transferring the newly casted precast components to a downstream area (usually designated the finishing trades yard) for the necessary execution of finishing trades, this dual usage of the production beds both for the casting and finishing trades is expected to delay the subsequent batch castings of the precast products. The time and productivity lost due to these delays in production beds turnover may be significantly substantial for large production volume firms.

Set-up times of manufacturing processes

The results relating to attempts made by the responding firms to research into innovative and better ways to reduce the various set-up times for their different product lines were disappointing. Only two firms (14 per cent) have reported on their initiative in attempting to reduce the manufacturing set-up times for their various precast product lines. The average reduction in set-up times that were achieved by these two firms for their families of precast products ranged from 20 per cent to 30 per cent. However, these two respondents were unable to release any detailed information on their innovative techniques employed to reduce manufacturing set-up times because of the confidentiality of classified corporate information. With the remaining nine firms (64 per cent) and three firms (22 per cent) answering "No" and "Never thought about it before" respectively when asked about innovative attempts to reduce processes set-up times, the rest of the respondents seemed to have negated the important need to seek improvements in their manufacturing processes set-up times. Hence, the survey findings clearly show that there is presently a very low embracement of the "continuous improvements" concept being applied to the local prefabrication industry.

Through interviews, the respondents have highlighted the following type of problems currently faced by them and which have caused delays in their manufacturing processes set-up times:

Constructability problems These were found to be the most common type of problems amongst the survey respondents. They include problems like common reinforcement steel bar congestion, clashing of steel bar positions with prestressing design profile (for beams), awkward shapes of precast components requiring unique "one-off" extensive formwork systems, etc.

Repetitive mistakes These problems occurred mostly in the reinforcement steel bar and formwork assembly trades. The affected firms have attributed the severe and constant changing of their labour workforce at the sub-contractor level as the main reason for such wasteful and repetitive human mistakes. Newly employed workers do not often possess the necessary skills to do their jobs right the first time.

Formwork demoulding problems   The unique formwork systems used for casting precast components which have awkward shapes often presented insurmountable demoulding problems after the first batch casting. These extensive formwork systems have thus often lent themselves to be re-designed again for better effective demoulding operations. Even then, the re-designed formwork systems still required extensive time to complete the demoulding process.

Nonetheless, despite the absence of diligent efforts on the part of the local prefabrication industry to research into ways of reducing their manufacturing processes set-up times, a majority (twelve firms or 86 per cent) of the respondents agreed that if their processes set-up times could be reduced substantially, they can ultimately do away with keeping buffer (safety) stocks for all their product lines. Given this positive finding on the relationship between process set-up time and buffer stocks, this is indeed a consoling fact which can propel the prefabrication industry to utilise JIT principles to reduce process set-up times and ultimately increase productivity.

Material handling systems and preventive maintenance management

Overall, the local prefabrication industry uses a wide range of machineries as material handling systems in their manufacturing environments. These machineries include the overhead gantry crane, fork-lift, mobile truck-mounted hydraulic crane, lorry-mounted crane, tower crane and dumper. The overhead gantry crane and fork-lift are by far the most common machineries used in the prefabrication industry and are found in all the fourteen firms surveyed.

The responding firms have highlighted two major types of obstructions which often hampered the peak preformance of the material handling systems. These are:

Machine system breakdown   All the respondents readily agreed that this is the most common type of obstruction that had frequently impeded the smooth performance of their material handling systems, bringing about disrupted production schedules. Not surprisingly, this breakdown is to be expected given that the majority of the responding firms do not implement any preventive maintenance management programmes to adequately and properly maintain all their fleets of machineries which make up the material handling systems. Except for three firms, the rest of the eleven firms (76 per cent) have indicated that they do not practise implementing any formal preventive maintenance management programmes for their material handling systems. Machineries were often used until the worn-out / breakdown stage before repairs were made. Amongst all the machineries used as material handling systems, the overhead gantry crane was cited by all respondents as the most prone to system breakdown. This is probably due to its extensive usage. In fact, during one of the factory visits, the production manager was already complaining about his disrupted schedule due to a shut down of his two overhead gantry cranes. The factory visit coincided with the third day of the gantry cranes' breakdown period.

Congested and insufficient access routes As mentioned earlier, this had been a common sight in some of the prefabrication firms visited. The physical obstructions often created by placing and stockpiling finished goods along the sides of existing access routes have gave rise to congestion problems, interrupting smooth workflow within the factories. At a bridge beam precasting yard, some of the "no through" access routes were even completely closed to vehicular movement due to stockpiling of finished bridge beams which have yet to be delivered to clients' worksites. By closing some of these "no-through" access routes for the purpose of beam stockpilings, the traffic capacity of the overall access route system within the factory was therefore restricted and reduced substantially. This led to insufficient access routes to cater for the firm's intensive material handling needs.

Inspite of the physical obstructions created primarily by stockpiling of finished goods inventories on the access routes, it is also worthwhile to highlight another secondary cause leading to the build-up of physical obstructions on the factory floor. In some of the prefabrication firms visited, it was clearly observed that the practice of poor and inadequate housekeeping had indeed contributed to the build-up of most physical obstructions within the factories. The untidy scene of reinforcement steel bars, formwork equipment, machineries, finished goods inventories, concrete wastes, rubbish, etc. being haphazardly strewn all over the factory floor had caused the material handling systems (particularly machineries like fork-lifts, cranes, etc.) to be operated at less than their maximum efficiency levels. This was principally caused by extremely difficult physical movements involved in using the access routes as a result of the many obstructions created.

Design specifications and buildability

The survey results pertaining to the relationship between engineering design specifications and buildability were contradictory. Whilst eleven respondents (79 per cent) expressed "not at all" when asked whether they find their engineering design specifications complicated, vague and loaded with too much unnecessary information, almost all the respondents (thirteen firms or 93 per cent) stated that there were numerous buildability problems associated with the manufacturing of their precast concrete components. It seems that there is no relationship between engineering design specifications and buildability. However, discussion of this topic is outside the purview of this study and will not be pursued any further here.

The overall buildability problems of the fourteen responding firms can be summarised as follows under three major work process headings:

Manufacturing process The type of buildability problems normally encountered during the manufacturing process include the following:

1   Concrete casting obstructions due to the awkward and unique shapes of precast components. The numerous protruding ends and complex isometric configurations of some precast components often make concrete and vibratory tools difficult to reach these places.

2   Excessive reinforcement steel bar wastage and congestion problems due again to the awkward and unique shapes of some precast components. All the prefabrication firms surveyed have reported a very high reinforcement steel bar wastage level at between 8 per cent to 10 per cent which is about twice the wastage rate for insitu construction works. The main reason for this excessive level of steel bar wastage was attributed to the large number of bar curtailments and non-repetition of bar sizes for the many awkward shapes and sizes of the diverse range of precast components manufactured by the responding firms. Also, the awkward shapes of some precast components often present insurmountable steel bar fixing problems due to frequent congestions at turnings, drops, corner places, etc.

3   Form mould changing (change overs) problems due to the large number of different precast components being manufactured at any one time. These problems were most prevalent in the manufacture of precast building components for private sector projects which have a very low standardisation level in the usage of precast components for construction. The large number of different precast components in production often make form mould changing operations difficult. These always tend to prolong production set-up times.

4   Form demoulding problems due to complex form systems being used for awkward-shaped or non-standard type of precast components. Demoulding problems often arise from complicated form mould systems which normally require the right operational sequencing in closing or opening the many sectional mould faces.

5   The vast number of cast-in items often specified in precast components had prolonged processes set-up times considerably due to the tedious and time consuming installation tasks involved. This scenario was most profound for precast building components like architectural wall panels where the number of cast-in items was not only large but their cast-in positions vary widely as well. Another good example is the many varying strand patterns for precast prestressed concrete planks and hollow core sections.

6   The conventional approach of a long curing time period had significantly led to low production output performance. Unless "steam-curing" or "autoclave curing" methods are specified in the technical specifications, most precasters often resort to the conventional method of "water-spray" curing method for their precast products in an attempt to minimise fixed production costs. The curing times of most precast components using the conventional method usually take about

seven days for the concrete to achieve the required strength before the products can be physically handled. This long curing time often suppresses production and stockturn outputs, increases production costs and therefore lowers productivity performances.

Product handling A major complaint associated with the physical handling of finished precast components was the correct positioning of temporary lifting hooks in the precast members. Three responding firms who are currently supplying precast building components for HDB projects reported that they have had to change the originally specified locations of the lifting hooks for some of their precast wall panels and staircases. The original locations of the lifting hooks for the wall panels were changed as these gave rise to critical structural crackings around the hook positions when the panels were lifted physically. The lifting hook positions of the precast staircases were likewise changed as they obstructed site installation works at the structural joint interfaces.

Product finishing works The usually strict aesthetical requirements associated with the finishes of some precast concrete components like balconies, external wall facades, parapet walls, bridge beams, columns, beams, etc. have inevitably forced precasters to allow for considerable periods of time to satisfactorily make good the finishes to comply with specifications. The period of time allowed for such touch-up works often tend to slow down stockturn output and lower productivity performance in addition to increasing production costs by way of prolonged space utilisation and additional consumption of variable and overhead costs.

Analysis of manufacturing control systems

The following sections discuss an analysis of the manufacturing control systems:

Simple versus complex manufacturing processes

The survey results clearly showed that when compared to the manufacturing sector, the prefabrication industry utilises more simple than complex manufacturing processes incorporating few sub-process or sub-assembly phases. This was concluded from the survey finding which indicated 79 per cent (eleven firms) of the respondents saying that the nature of their manufacturing processes was simple rather than complex or normal. The remaining 21 per cent (four firms) stated as "normal" the nature of their manufacturing processes. No firm however had indicated that their manufacturing processes were complex in nature.

The most likely reason that can explain the largely simple nature of the manufacturing processes in the prefabrication industry could be that the very nature of construction work itself is simply made up of only three major components which give rise to three independent major work processes.

These three major components are simply concrete, reinforcement steel bars and formwork; and the three major work processes are concreting, steel bar bending and assembly, and formwork installation. Of course, there are other sub-work processes (like tile laying, inserting of cast-in items, etc.) involved in the manufacture of some precast components, but these are not so significant compared to the three major work processes. Also, if these sub-work processes are considered significant, they would only constitute the major fourth work process only.

Ease of identification of production problems

Contrary to the normal state of events in the manufacturing sector where production problems are not often easily identified in the many complex work processes, all of the survey respondents have indicated that they could easily and readily identify production problems in their different manufacturing processes. Again, this can be explained by the above-mentioned simple work processes and small number (three or four) of different work processes involved in the prefabrication operations.

Total quality control concept

The survey findings relating to the responding firms gaining certification to the international quality standards SS ISO 9000 for quality assurance practices were comforting. It is reassuring to note that the local prefabrication industry had already shown positive signs of heeding CIDB's call for upgrading the quality level of the industry to improve competitiveness. It is heartening to learn that ten out of the fourteen responding firms (or 71 per cent) had shown concern towards the industry-wide total quality control movement to upgrade the quality levels of their precast products. Table 5.2 tabulates the current status of the fourteen responding firms regarding their decisions to achieve certification under the international quality standards umbrella.

It is clear from Table 5.2 that all of the responding firms who have either undergone or are currently undergoing certification are pursuing SS ISO 9002 and / or SS ISO 9003 in accordance with their roles as producers / manufacturers of precast concrete products. No responding firm has yet to seek certification to SS ISO 9001 which is specifically meant for those manufacturers who are capable of offering a package deal for designing, producing and installing their precast products. It can thus be inferred from the survey findings that none or few prefabrication firms can currently offer design consultancy services for the manufacture of precast products. Table 5.3 shows the contents of the Singapore standards for quality management systems.

In response to the question of whether the respondents have relentlessly pursued continuous improvements in their manufacturing processes through quality control circles in line with the "Zero Defects Construction" campaign mounted by the CIDB in 1991, almost all (twelve firms or 86 per cent) the respondents indicated that it was their corporate philosophy to strive for continuous improvement at all times. Only two firms (14 per cent) who are amongst the smaller firms in the survey sample pointed out that continuous

Table 5.2
Decision status of prefabrication firms towards certification
for quality assurance

Status of certification process	Number of firms	Percentage (%)	Remarks
Certification to SS ISO 9001 to SS ISO 9003	4	29	Mainly certified to SS ISO 9002 and SS ISO 9003
Currently undergoing process of certification	2	13	Undergoing certification to SS ISO 9002 and SS ISO 9003
Intend to undergo certification process soon	4	29	Nil
Never thought about certification before	4	29	Nil
Total	14	100	

Table 5.3
Singapore standards for quality assurance

SS ISO 9000: 1994	Quality management and quality assurance standards - Part 1: Guidelines for selection and use
SS ISO 9001: 1994	Quality systems - Specification for quality assurance in design / development, production, installation and servicing
SS ISO 9002: 1994	Quality systems - Specification for quality assurance in production, installation and servicing
SS ISO 9003: 1994	Quality systems - Specification for quality assurance in final inspection and test
SS ISO 9004-1: 1994	Quality management and quality system elements - Part 1: Guidelines

improvement has never been pursued before. This finding seems to strongly reinforce the fact that the local prefabrication industry is heading along the strategic direction towards producing high quality goods.

Except for the four firms who have already achieved quality certification, all the remaining ten firms have stated "good" performance insofar as the efficiency of their quality inspectors in detecting problems and proposing solutions to production problems are concerned. However, it should be noted that amongst these ten firms, two of them actually do not possess any "in-house" quality inspection team to formally carry out quality management functions. These two bridge beam prefabricators only make use of the project client's (normally governmental bodies like the PWD, etc.) clerks-of-works or engineers to execute the quality inspection tasks. This practice would seem to put the precast products to a higher risk of quality defects. This is because if the client's clerks-of-works or engineers were to miss out on some critical checks, then these defective works would go unnoticed and be cast permanently into the precast structures.

Finally, despite the fact that most of the respondents are already exhibiting concern and priority in getting their firms quality certified, it is interesting to learn that most of them actually do not practise checking the qualities of all their products' sub-components "at source". This is evident by ten of the fourteen firms stating "No" as the answer when asked about checking "qualities at source". Given the nature of the construction process, this practice would seem to have a significant impact on certain sub-trades; particulary the reinforcement steel bar trade. If reinforcement steel bars are not quality checked at the bar bending work station after they are cut and bent to required shapes, any quality defects in terms of wrong bar shapes and sizes discovered later in the concrete casting workstation would certainly result in "double-handling" works and subsequent delays in the overall production schedules. Admittedly, almost all the ten firms mentioned do acknowledge the frequent occurrence of such a scenario particularly at times of high production volume and tight clients' delivery date-lines.

"Pull" (kanban) and "push" systems

The survey findings indicate that the local prefabrication industry presently uses both the "pull" and "push" systems to move production materials or components between workstations in their factories. However, as expected, none of the responding firms has ever heard of the operational mechanism of the pull (Kanban) system. Those respondents who operated using the pull system have merely unconsciously used it without any prior literature knowledge about the system. In fact, all the respondents have shown delightful interests in the pull system when the concept was explained to them during the various factory visits.

Generally, the responding firms have adopted the push and pull systems for their manufacturing processes as follows:

1   The "push" system was commonly used for manufacturing processes producing precast concrete components which are constantly in demand for large scale usage in the local construction industry. These include

those well accepted and established standardised precast products like road kerbs, drain channels, box culverts, pipes, manhole chamber rings, carpark slabs, piles, etc. used extensively in civil engineering works. For building works, the push system was only utilised by precasters to push materials through the manufacturing process in the production of similar products which were specified amongst the precasters' many different contracts for various clients. This situation often arises when the precasters' clients are contracting organisations undertaking HDB projects. The similarity factor had led to standardisation (somewhat to a certain extent) and this in turn had helped to build large production volumes for the precasters. The standardised building component products often involved were hollow core slabs, lightweight partitions, refuse chutes, staircases, water tanks, etc.

2   The "pull" system has only been adopted for manufacturing processes producing "one-off" unique precast concrete components which cannot be universally used in different construction projects. Small demand volumes were often associated with such unique non-standardised products. Examples of some of these products include bridge beams and specialised box culverts for civil engineering works; and balconies, external facade walls and gable end walls for building works.

In summary, it can be inferred from the survey findings that usage of the push system is commonly prevalent for standardised precast products which have high demand usage. The pull system, on the other hand, is only used by the prefabrication industry for unique non-standardised products which have small demand usage.

Another interesting finding also seems to confirm and prove the causal relationship between buffer (safety) stocks and the push system. All the seven precasters who manufacture a mixture of both high volume standardised and low volume non-standardised precast components have indicated that they would only keep buffer stocks for commonly used or standardised products (like road kerbs, precast drains, etc.) and not for "one-off" or non-standardised products (like bridge beams, facade walls, etc.). As the push system is often used in the manufacture of standardised precast components, buffer stocks are therefore an outcome caused by the operation of the push system. On the contrary, buffer stocks were virtually non-existent in the manufacture of non-standardised precast products using the pull system as reported by the seven responding firms.

Labour environment and employee participation

The survey findings relating to the prefabrication industry's labour force strength, skills level, terms of engagement, works training and working environment are summarised as follows:

Labour force strength The labour force strength at the production floor level of the fourteen responding firms are tabulated in Table 5.4. As can be seen from Table 5.4, a majority (93 per cent) of the responding firms have more than 30 workers. Only one firm (7 per cent) which solely manufactures bridge beams and no other precast concrete products have between 15 to 20 workers.

Skills level There is presently no multi-skilled workers being employed by the prefabrication industry at the production floor level. All the fourteen responding firms engaged solely single-skilled workers whereby each category of workers executes only their own specific trade, i.e. a worker who is a concretor does not perform the duties of a form-worker or bar-bender when circumstances demand. This is reportedly due to the absence of skills training in the latter two trades.

Terms of engagement The terms of engagement for the labour force at the production floor level for the fourteen firms surveyed are shown in Table 5.5. From Table 5.5, the local prefabrication industry seems to exhibit a strong preference for both direct employment and sub-contract as terms of engagement for its labour force at the production level. It was learnt that this mixed terms of engagement provides good flexibility, ease of control and effective management for the overall workforce. Otherwise, given the fairly large workforce (more than 30 workers) working amidst the general confusion of the production floor, management of the entire workforce would be a tremendously difficult task if all workers were to be solely engaged by direct employment alone.

Works training Almost all the responding firms have provided their new workers engaged under direct employment terms with proper works training before the assignment of jobs. However, the training of new workers employed through sub-contracts was not provided for by any of the responding firms. According to the firms surveyed, these new workers should first be well trained by their respective sub-contractors before they are assigned to the factories. This misconception did not hold true as most of the prefabrication firms who employ sub-contract labour have complained of high material wastages (particularly in reinforcement steel bars) and repetitive mistakes caused frequently by such workers.

Working environment All the respondents have rated their factory working environments for their workforce as either "good" or "satisfactory" in terms of teamwork spirit and working morale. Despite this harmonious labour environment, some respondents have nevertheless frustratingly highlighted some of their most pressing labour problems currently faced by them. Amongst these were:

1   The presently tight labour market in the construction sector had fuelled high staff turnover at the technical and management level in the local prefabrication industry. Personnel such as the production engineer and line supervisor were the most severely affected. One prefabrication firm had witnessed six and eight turnovers to the posts of production engineer and supervisor respectively over a period of 18 months. The

Table 5.4
Labour force strength for prefabrication firms surveyed

Labour force strength	Number of firms	Percentage (%)
Between 10 to 30	1	7
Between 30 to 50	7	50
More than 50	6	43

Table 5.5
Labour force's terms of engagement for prefabrication firms surveyed

Terms of engagement	Number of firms	Percentage (%)
Direct employment	2	14
Sub-contract	3	21
Direct employment and sub-contract	9	65

reasons given by the responding firms for this exodus of staff include lack of morale due to unattractive renumerations and working incentives, psychological "dullness" due to the homogeneity nature of factory production work, change of career disciplines, etc.

2   As foreign workers (mainly Thailand, Bangladesh and Sri Lanka nationals) make up the bulk of the labour workforce of all prefabrication firms, the maximum working period of stay for most workers is thus limited to only four years under the foreign worker ruling. With these workers having to leave the country after a working stay of four years, whatever work skills which they may have developed and mastered would be lost. This problem is aggravated further by the fact that rugged construction activities at the production level are often shunned by the now much more educated and affluent Singaporeans. Unless automation is introduced on a large scale in the prefabrication industry, this problem cannot be resolved in the long run.

Cost accounting system

Of the fourteen responding firms, seven firms (50 per cent) employed the "work order system" to track labour, inventory and overhead costs in their manufacturing operations for the purpose of cost accounting. Whilst another four firms (28 per cent) employed the "global tracking system" as the cost accounting method, the remaining three firms (22 per cent) have abstained from revealing the type of cost accounting method used by them.

As expected, a majority of the seven firms who employed the "work order system" agreed that they most often faced immense operational problems with the tracking process. Generally, as the number of work orders being opened at any one time is large, workers on the production floor have always tended to move materials (especially reinforcement steel bars and cast-in items) in such a way that they mixed the parts for one work order with the parts for another. Also, due to the often slow feedback response time and inaccuracies from production floor personnel on information pertaining to work-in-progress levels, new work orders frequently have numerous errors contained within them. The tracking process had thus been made time consuming, tedious, complicated and confusing. From a JIT point of view, this is wasteful.

Supplier and client relationships

Some of the more significant issues relating to supplier and client relationships are discussed below:

Supplier relationship

The followings outline the survey findings pertaining to the relationship between the responding prefabrication firms and their suppliers:

Selection of suppliers Generally, the respondents have rated numerous criteria for the selection of their suppliers as follows in decreasing order of importance: Price, On-time deliveries, Quality and Lead time. It can thus be seen that the local prefabrication industry still considers price as the major criteria over and above that of quality for the selection of suppliers.

Problems with suppliers The common type of problems which the responding firms normally encountered with their network of suppliers can be summarised as follows:

1   Quality - Defects in qualities were commonly found in supplies of permanent material items like tiles, cast-in items, prestressing sheaths / tendons, etc. and temporary material items like steel form moulds.

2   Late and untimely deliveries - These affect both local and overseas materials supplies. Amongst local suppliers, prefabricated steel form moulds, cast-in items, reinforcement steel wire mesh and ready-mixed concrete were the materials most affected. Given the presently high construction job volume, the supply of ready-mixed concrete was reported to be the most prone to late deliveries by those respondent firms who are solely bridge beam manufacturers and who do not

possess any internal ("in-house") concrete batching plant. One bridge beam manufacturer complained that at times, it took about two hours for the external supply of ready-mixed concrete to reach his casting yard despite the fact that the supplier's concrete batching plant was located only a 15-minute drive away. For overseas supplies, specialised tiles, aggregates, cement and prestressing tendons were reported to be the materials most frequently affected.

3   Non-compliance to specifications - Cases of non-compliance occurred for both the permanent and temporary material items. Amongst the permanent materials most commonly affected were tiles, prefabricated cast-in items, prestressing tendons, aggregates and wood fibre concrete. Prefabricated steel form moulds made up most of the temporary materials that do not often comply with specifications.

4   Credit payment terms - Some respondents have complained about the strict and short credit payment period imposed upon them by their various suppliers. Instead of a 60-day credit period, some suppliers had pressed for a strict period of 30 days to settle payments. The effect of this has been that some of the big local material suppliers (particularly external ready-mixed concrete and reinforcement steel bar suppliers) have stopped their supplies to some prefabrication firms who do not observe on-time payments.

5   Lead time - A few respondents had also lamented that although they have always observed and allowed sufficient lead times to their suppliers for the supply of materials, such supplies still at times do not meet their specified times for deliveries. The reasons given for this shortcoming were mainly delays in freight documentation (for overseas supplies) and local suppliers intentionally delaying supplies because of late payments by the prefabrication firms.

6   Lack of haulage services - One prefabrication firm has highlighted its frequent encounters with the lack of externally supplied transportation haulage vehicles (like low-bed trailers) needed for its intensive deliveries of finished goods (like external wall facades, balconies) to their clients' worksites. According to this respondent, there is only one transportation haulage contract with one external haulage company. As the owner of the latter company was a close relative of the sole owner of the responding firm, no other external haulage companies were engaged. Due to the currently good business of the engaged haulage company, the responding firm had always experienced the absence or late arrivals of haulage vehicles for delivering finished goods to their clients; much to the chagrin of the latter.

Local and overseas suppliers The survey findings indicate that a majority (nine firms or 64 per cent) of the respondents purchased their supplies of raw components required for their manufacturing processes entirely from local suppliers. The remaining five firms (36 per cent) purchased their raw components from both local and overseas suppliers in the proportions of 80 per cent and 20 per cent respectively.

Supplier delivery systems The prefabrication firms surveyed have generally practised the adoption of a mix supply of bulk and small lots with corresponding few and frequent deliveries respectively for their various purchased supplies of product components. However, bulk lot supplies with few deliveries made up the major proportion of the supplier delivery systems amongst the fourteen prefabrication firms. Only ready-mixed concrete and temporary work materials like steel form moulds were reported to be supplied in small lots with frequent deliveries. Other supplies of materials like reinforcement steel bars / meshes, prefabricated cast-in items, tiles, etc. were normally transacted in bulk lots with few deliveries.

The responding firms have readily agreed that such bulk lots supplies of materials do inevitably tied down their monetary capital in unfinished goods inventories, occupied more physical factory space, caused added physical congestion problems, etc. Nevertheless, all the respondents were confident that their practice of stockpiling huge unfinished goods inventories would not subject the latter to the risk of obsolescence due to product technological innovations. The respondents have strongly argued that such technological innovations in the construction setting were always slow to come by and are not likely to occur in the near foreseeable future to significantly affect their current production processes. Indeed, most of the respondents interviewed seemed to believe that by accommodating bulk lots of production materials, they would be well placed to offer immediate flexibilities to increase production capacities in response to sudden changes in production demands.

Multi and single-sourcing of suppliers All the responding firms have indicated a strong preference for a multi rather than single source of suppliers. The main reasons highlighted to support this strategic preference were as follows:

1   By having numerous suppliers for a particular product component, the prefabricator enjoys the flexibility of a longer credit payment period. Also, if a particular supplier is to stop supplies due to late payments from the prefabricator, the latter can be assured of continuous supplies from other suppliers.

2   The prefabricator would again be assured of a continuous supply of goods in the event that a particular supplier defaults in his contractual obligations to the supply agreement.

3   The prefabricator has the choice of selecting the best supplier whose performance could meet his requirements for quality, timely deliveries and price.

"In-plant" supply stores Except for the four bridge beam manufacturers mentioned above, all the responding firms utilised their own "in-plant" (internal) concrete batching plants to supply ready-mixed concrete for their

production operations. Despite this, a third of those respondents who possessed "in-plant" supplies of concrete do frequently has to source external supplies of ready-mixed concrete for their casting operations at times of high production volume.

As for reinforcement steel bars, all the respondents practised purchasing the raw components and complete the cutting and bending of the steel bars within the factory premises. Welded steel fabric reinforcements (or simply steel wire mesh) which are commonly used for precast drain channels, concrete pipes, etc., were often supplied to the respondents in ready-to-use curtailed bent forms by external suppliers.

"In-plant" supplies of all other major work components like prefabricated steel formwork systems, cast-in items, tiles, prestressing tendons, etc. were virtually not found in any of the fourteen prefabrication firms surveyed. All these components were prefabricated and supplied by external sub-contract fabricators and suppliers respectively.

Duration of "purchase agreement" contract All the respondents have unanimously indicated a short-term duration of less than six months for "Purchase Agreement" contracts entered into between them and their various suppliers. Even though there may be numerous reasons for this short-term agreement, the respondents gave the single reason of "current market practices" for the short-term durations of their purchase agreements.

Client relationships

Generally, the prefabrication firms surveyed have outlined the following as the most difficult problems which they are facing in respect of their relationships with their clients:

Invalid clients' schedules Despite the prefabrication firms' usual good practice and efforts in complying with the seemingly firm and accurate production schedules of their clients, more often than not, most clients would still end up delaying the acceptance of finished goods inventories into their worksites. This is normally due to the construction of in-situ works on the clients' job sites which are not ready yet to accommodate the precast concrete components. This state of events is not surprising given the usual delays often encountered in general construction works which are subject to a whole host of uncertainties. As a result, the clients' production schedules which initially seemed firm and valid would often become invalid eventually.

The above scenario had thus gave rise to the problem of some prefabrication firms being inevitably forced to deliver the finished goods to their clients' sites even though works progress at the latter were not ready yet to receive the precast components. Otherwise, the prefabrication firms would have to end up stockpiling at their factory premises, hugh inventories of undelivered finished goods which would subsequently increase congestion to the factory floor, tie down cost of capital, increase operating costs and hamper productivity performance. This was exactly the scenarios of some of the respondents' factories visited. These prefabrication firms were in fact trying their very best not to tarnish their good long-term relationships with their valued clients by not opting to forcefully deliver the finished goods to their clients' worksites.

As a result, they have to accommodate the stockpile of finished goods at their own factory grounds. Also, some respondents have explained that sometimes they could not even forcefully deliver the finished precast components to their clients' sites especially when the latter were building sites. This was because the frequently restricted site boundaries and site congestion of most building sites would not permit any high stockpiling of finished goods inventories.

Apart from clients not taking stock of finished goods, invalid clients' schedules have also put some prefabricators in difficult situations to effectively and efficiently plan for their production activities. An example to illustrate this scenario was given by a bridge beam manufacturer who undertakes to produce beams for a client who is executing a "design and build" contract for the PWD. For this particular project, although the client has furnished a firm schedule for the beams production at the beginning of the project, the issuance of construction drawings for the beams was somehow delayed by the client's external consultant who is already subjected to a heavy overload of design jobs. As "design and build" contracts are often characterised by construction works following closely behind design works, the prefabricator in this case had found it almost impossible to plan accurately for the beams production due to the uncertain nature of the issuance schedule for construction drawings. Also, the invalid clients' schedules would often disrupt the prefabricator's overall master production schedule as at any one time, the prefabricator is undertaking jobs from not one but many other valued clients as well. Despite this, the prefabricator has still to plan with certainty all his resources to meet the numerous production schedules of his clients'.

Progress payment terms and stock taking of finished goods In a majority of the contracts, finished precast components stockpiled "off-site" at the prefabricator's factory are not normally admitted by the contractor-client under a progress claim as "materials-on-site" in the building contract. The contractor-client will not normally get paid for such materials stockpiled outside his site boundaries. In cases where the contractor-client's in-situ works at the site were also delayed and unable to receive the finished precast components, some of the less co-operative clients would tend to delay taking stock of such finished precast goods as much as possible. As a result, the affected prefabricators would suffer again due to unnecessary build-ups of undelivered finished goods inventories in their yards.

Internal trade "cannibalism" Interestingly, among the survey respondents is a bridge beam manufacturer who belongs to one of the local big groups of companies. One of the core activities of this group is contracting and the company involved often had at hand numerous infrastructural contracts for the local public sector. It was learnt that lately this particular prefabricator has always delayed in producing bridge beams for numerous clients. This was because the prefabricator had been kept busy producing bridge beams for his own group's contracts over and above those of the external clients. As a result, some of these external clients had been annoyed by the cannibalising of priorities caused by the prefabricator's intra company trade activities.

Poor works coordination Although rare and uncommon, at least two prefabrication firms have told of their encounters with poor coordination works on the part of their clients in solving technical problems associated with the precast works. Representatives of clients were accused of being slow to act on the following:

1   Clarification of technical discrepancies in drawings and specifications.

2   Arranging project consultants or clerks-of-works to inspect works on-time.

3   Seeking project consultants' approval for proposal of construction methods.

Such tardiness has contributed to substantial "lost time" and is therefore seen to be wasteful from the JIT point of view.

Overall perspective

An overall perspective of the empirical study is presented below.

Wide ranging problems and issues

The following gives an account of the most pressing problems and wide ranging issues faced by the fourteen prefabrication firms surveyed. In the opinion of the respondent firms, these problems and issues should be brought forward for solution at the industry level.

Invalid client's schedule This formed the most critical problem for all the fourteen prefabrication firms surveyed. All fourteen responding firms had quickly and readily highlighted their grievances caused by frequently invalid clients' schedules. As already mentioned in the last section, the result of such inaccurate and invalid clients' schedules would result in clients refusing or tending to delay taking stock of finished precast concrete components from the prefabrication factories. As explained earlier, this would subsequently set off a chain of problems for the innocent prefabricators like increased inventory build-ups, thereby tying down valuable capital resources; increased occupation of physical factory space thus adding to further congestion and confusion; increased overhead costs due to extra administrative tasks, factory space rental and utilities expenditure; and finally decreased productivity output and profitability.

Labour intensive industry As one prefabricator puts it, the current prefabrication industry is still very much characterised by labour intensive trades. Such trades would include reinforcement steel bar cutting, bending and fixing works; steel forms fabrication and assembly works; concrete casting works; surface finishing works; tiling works; insertion works of cast-in items; etc. Whilst mechanisation can already be seen to operate widely in the material handling systems (like overhead gantry cranes, fork-lifts, etc.) of the prefabrication industry, there is presently a total absence of any signs or forms of automation being used in the industry for substituting the various labour intensive trades.

High workers' inertia for change The prefabrication industry is filled by a large pool of foreign workers executing the various labour intensive sub-trades at production floor levels. Nationalities from Thailand, India, Bangladesh and Sri Lanka made up almost the entire pool of these foreign workers. The different cultural backgrounds, different work attitudes, low educational levels or illiteracies, and language communication barriers which exist amongst this large pool of foreign workers would make it almost impossible for the JIT concept to be applied successfully in the prefabrication industry. Also, the compulsory four-year stay ruling for the employment of foreign workers would pose further difficulties and present periodic hiccups for the smooth realisation of the JIT movement as trained workers would eventually be lost and the re-training of new workers would need to be expedited again. As a few prefabricators had remarked, for the JIT concept to be effectively applied, this inherently high inertia for change must first and foremost be overcome and eliminated.

Buildability A majority of the prefabrication firms have expressed their views that the design of precast concrete components should be made more buildable in the near future in association with the current prefabrication drive in the local construction industry. According to the respondents, the current concern of the local prefabrication industry is the overall low level of standardisation in the entire industry. Insofar as building works are concerned, except for public housing projects undertaken by the HDB, the current level of standardisation achieved for private sector projects is insignificant. The designs of each private sector project are unique and will rarely be used for other projects even if of a similar nature. Even in HDB's projects, the prefabrication designs of each precinct neighbourhood differ markedly from those of others within the same township.

By calling all relevant parties in the construction process to adopt improved buildable designs in precast construction, the respondents hoped that the numerous ills associated with the currently high level of non-standardisation could be minimised if not entirely eliminated. These ills would be: prolonged set-up times, high wastages of raw materials, difficult production control, non-economies of scale, etc. which have always stemmed from the large number of different shapes and sizes of precast concrete components used for different projects.

Other unresolved problems A few of the prefabrication firms had also called for the industry to look into some of the current product manufacturing and installation problems which have yet to be resolved to a satisfactory level. Problems relating to product manufacturing processes like the requirements for long curing times and extensive surface treatment finishing works (like patching and surface smoothening works) would need to be addressed more profoundly for productivity in the industry to be improved further. Prefabrication installation technology, particularly those relating to joint technology, should be researched further to ensure that precast concrete components can be assembled easily on-site and the life-long structural / functional performances of such joints will be free from defects like water seepage, cracks, movements, etc.

"Waste" perception

The survey findings pertaining to the prefabrication industry's perception of "waste" were not conclusive. All the respondents have merely categorized "waste" as being reworks, quality defects, idling time, breakdown of machineries, etc., all of which have been listed down as guiding examples in the questionnaire. Hence, there is no new finding from the survey that would enable further steps to be made in securing a wider understanding of the "waste" subject.

Productivity performance

The survey results obtained for the total productivity performance of the fourteen prefabrication firms were disappointing. Only two of the responding firms (14 per cent) have practised implementing productivity growth plans for their manufacturing operations. The remaining respondents have simply offered the following two main negative reasons when asked why they do not practise setting productivity performance targets for their manufacturing operations:

1   Productivity targets, being intangible, are always difficult in exerting a significant influence in the minds of most senior management staff. This is particularly so for those lowly educated and conservative owners of prefabrication firms who neglect current events and developments that are being achieved in the prefabrication industry. According to this class of owners, the only most important "productivity" indicator to them is the quantum of profit gained from manufacturing operations as shown in their annual "Profit and Loss" financial statement. Furthermore, these owners had argued that they can still manage their prefabrication businesses well today even without having to work with what they termed "ungenuine and misleading" productivity figures.

2   The management staff of some small and medium sized prefabrication firms do not possess the relevant knowledge to compute productivity assessments and set productivity targets.

Despite the above misconception and absence of know-how pertaining to the usefulness and implementation of productivity plans respectively, it should be pointed out at this juncture that the CIDB has in fact launched a productivity assessment scheme to assess the productivity of local prefabrication firms. The productivity outputs of different product categories like precast components for internal and external building works, precast components for civil engineering works, etc. are surveyed by the CIDB on a quarterly basis.

Confidence and willingness to implement JIT concept

It is heartening to note that all the fourteen prefabrication firms surveyed have unanimously shown their strong confidence and willingness to implement the JIT system for improving overall productivity and profitability in their organisations. As pointed out by all the respondents, this would of course only happen if total commitment and support from top management are assured and that the JIT concept is indeed a proven and viable system that could be applied in the local prefabrication industry.

6 Accounting for construction wastes

Introduction

The implementation of the JIT philosophy in the construction industry should be tied to a system of measuring waste. In this context, construction wastes may be divided into material waste, labour waste and machinery waste. The main objective of accounting for wastes is to assist management in improving resource allocation, minimising waste and increasing productivity. Under JIT, apart from material waste control, efforts should also be focused on the elimination of time-based wastes whenever possible in any project or activity it undertakes. Despite the importance of measuring time wastes, no extensive study has so far been undertaken to quantify time wastage. Hence, the purpose of this chapter is to examine and activate an accounting procedure for measuring time wastage in the construction industry. For this purpose, three different building sites which have incorporated the accounting procedure were chosen for measuring time wastage. These three sites include a school, a public housing project and a private condominium project. In the next chapter, these three case studies showed that JIT waste can indeed be measured quantitatively. Using the accounting procedure, time wastage can be identified. Management can then make use of this data to localise bottlenecks and to suggest and implement necessary solutions to reduce the time waste for a particular task. Hence, by applying a quantitative measure for JIT, construction tasks can be performed with better productivity levels.

Accounting for construction wastes

Profit and loss are always of concern to any construction firm. In order to achieve better profit margins, firms will attempt to seek alternative ways of working to raise the productivity of their operatons. However, without a good method to locate bottlenecks in construction processes, it will be difficult to achieve success.

Construction wastes can be divided into three principal components, namely, material, labour and machinery wastes. Traditionally, waste in construction is defined as "the difference between the value of those materials delivered and accepted at site and those properly used as specified and accurately measured in the work, after deducting the cost saving of substituted materials and those transfered elsewhere (Institute of Building, 1979)". The loss is expressed as a percentage of the deliveries. Waste may also be defined as "anything other than the absolute minimum time and resources of materials, machines and personnel required to add value to the product (Lim and Low, 1992)". In the process of developing a site accounting procedure for measuring time wastage in construction, Neo (1995) felt that substantial waste elimination is possible. Furthermore, Neo (1995) felt that the identification of wastage and rectification measures to reduce waste may be performed simultaneously. The following sections will examine the accounting procedures for construction wastes and their validity.

Validity of accounting information

The validity of accounting information is dependent on two factors, namely relevance and reliability. Relevance depends on the decision objectives of the users and therefore may differ between users. Being "relevance in all" means having qualities of predictive and confirmatory value as well as choice for the decision objectives of the users. Relevance also depends on the timeliness of the information as outdated information tends to lose its usefulness. Reliability depends on the errors in information, timeliness of information and source of information. The information must be complete and neutral. In addition to relevance and reliability, the information must be:

1   Understood easily.

2   Well presented.

3   Able to be compared across the board using a common standard.

Accounting for wastes

The main objective of accounting for waste is to assist management in improving resource allocation, minimising waste and increasing productivity. Under JIT, apart from material waste control, efforts should also be focused on the elimination of time-based wastes whenever possible in any project or activity it undertakes. The construction task duration for a product can be expressed as:

Construction Task Duration = Process time + Inspection time + Move time + Wait time

Hence, only process time is considered as a value added activity while the rest are considered as non-value added activities. JIT aims to eliminate these latter activities.

Approaches by Skoyles (1978) and CIOB (1980)

The purpose of developing accounting procedures for material wastes is to exercise waste control and thus help the organisation prevents further losses. The accounting procedure for material waste proposed by the CIOB is shown in Figure 6.1 (CIOB, 1980). Generally, waste can be categorised into direct and indirect waste. Direct material wastage is defined as the loss of those materials which are damaged and cannot be repaired and subsequently used or which are lost during the building process (Skoyles, 1978). It comprises transport and delivery waste, excess materials at the work place, cutting waste, criminal waste, learning waste, management waste and so on. Indirect material waste is distinguished from direct waste as it normally represents only a monetary loss because the materials are not usually lost physically (Skoyles, 1978). These wastes are the result of materials being used for purposes other than those specified or in excess of measured quantities to meet the constraints of production. The Direct Material Waste Calculation Record shown in Figure 6.2 illustrates the total material waste as a percentage of the total material delivered. The percentage derived can be used for comparison purposes with different tasks and across various projects. Through these comparisons, new measures for regulating material wastage can be implemented for future projects.

Neo's (1995) approach to JIT waste calculation

Neo (1995) laments that accounting for material wastage alone is insufficient to account for all wastages in construction. This is because time also plays an important role in the productivity movement. After extensive research and pilot implementatinon on construction projects, an accounting procedure to measure time wastage based on the JIT concept was derived by Neo (1995). In this case, a construction activity consists of work and motion. Motion alone is considered as a type of waste. This is illustrated in Figure 6.3 which shows the task cycle of a typical construction task.

It is to be noted in Figure 6.3 that only process time is considered as value added time whereas inspection time, move time and wait time are considered non-value added time. Wait time is only controllabe in the mobilisation phase and can be eliminated through proper planning and co-ordination. Rectification time, wait time and re-inspection and approval time can be avoided if quality work is ensured.

Move time waste may be avoided as time wastage can be attributed to:

1   Transportation waste - an item being moved temporarily or being rearranged.

2   Waste of motion - materials and tools not kept close to where they are to be used.

3   Inventory waste - excess inventory that adds cost by requiring extra handling.

95

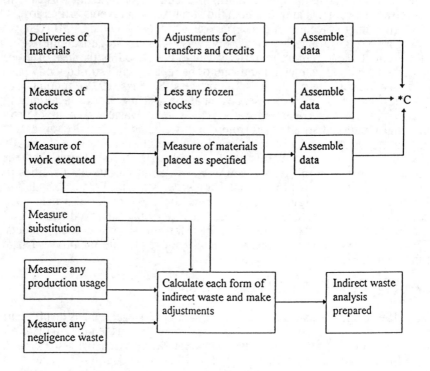

*C = Complete calculations of direct material waste

Figure 6.1   Accounting procedure for waste

Source: *Chartered Institute of Building (1980), Materials control and waste in Building, HMSO*

Although process time is a value added time, it is also vulnerable to wastes. These wastes comprise of:

1   Over-production waste.

2   Construction method waste.

3   Waste from product defects.

4   Poor optimisation in carrying out tasks.

```
┌─────────────────────────────────────────────────────────────┐
│  Site        :                    Date      :                │
│  Material    :                    Location  :                │
│                                                              │
│                                         No./m²/m³            │
│                                                              │
│  A    Total delivered                   ...............      │
│  B    Total transferred from site       ...............      │
│  C    Total available                   ...............      │
│  D    Total measured (as specified)     ...............      │
│  E    Allowances for Indirect Waste                          │
│                              %    No./m²/m³    No./m²/m³      │
│  a)   Substitution         ......  ...........  ...........   │
│  b)   Negligence waste     ......  ...........  ...........   │
│  c)   Production usage     ......  ...........  ...........   │
│       Adjustment for Indirect Waste          ...........     │
│                                              ...........     │
│  F    Total in Stock on Site       ...........  ...........  │
│       Less Frozen Stock            ...........  ...........  │
│       Stock Available for Use                ...........     │
│  G    Materials Accountable for on Site      ...........     │
│  H    = _____ % Waste  (H) = C - G as % of C       │
└─────────────────────────────────────────────────────────────┘
```

Figure 6.2   Direct material waste calculation record

Source: Skoyles, E.R. (1978), Site accounting for materials, Building Research Establishment

To monitor and record the above JIT wastage effectively, an accounting procedure for time wastage was proposed by Neo (1995). This is shown in Figure 6.4. Based on this accounting procedure, Neo (1995) subsequently derived the JIT Waste Calculation Record shown in Figure 6.5. The percentage shown in Figure 6.5 demonstrates JIT waste as a percentage of the whole construction duration. This figure may be used for comparison purposes with different tasks and across different projects. Through these comparisons, new measures for regulating time wastage may be implemented for future projects.

97

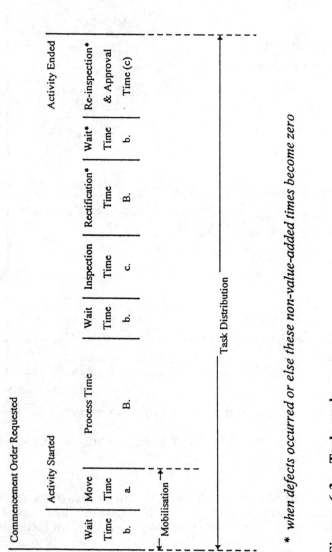

Figure 6.3 Task cycle

Source: *Neo, R.B. (1995), Accounting for waste in construction, In Proceedings of the First International Conference on Construction Project Management, Centre for Advanced Construction Studies, Nanyang Technological University, pp.339-406*

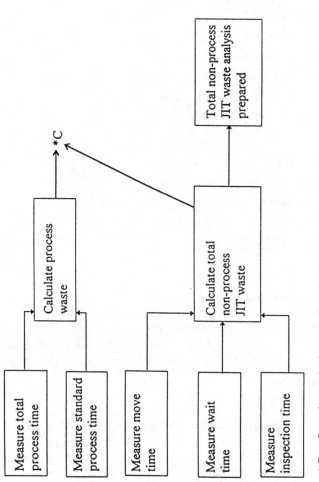

*C = Complete calculations of total JIT waste

Figure 6.4 Accounting procedure for JIT waste

Source: *Neo, R.B. (1995), Accounting for waste in construction, In Proceedings of the First International Conference on Construction Project Management, Centre for Advanced Construction Studies, Nanyang Technological University, pp.339-406*

```
Site          :              Date        :
Material      :              Location    :


                             Week/Day/Hour        %*

A    Total task duration        ...........................   ................

B    Total process time         ...........................   ................

C    Total standard process time   ...........................   ................

D    Total process time waste (B-C)   ...........................   ................

E    Total non-process time waste

     (a + b + c)  This is analysed into   ...........................   ................

                             Week/Day/Hour

a)   Move time            ...........................

b)   Wait time            ...........................

c)   Inspection time      ...........................


F    Total JIT waste (D + E)        ...........................   ................

G    Task Cycle Waste (F/A x 100%)              =  _____ %
```

* percentage of total construction duration

Figure 6.5   JIT waste calculation record

Source: *Neo, R.B. (1995), Accounting for waste in construction, In Proceedings of the First International Conference on Construction Project Management, Centre for Advanced Construction Studies, Nanyang Technological University, pp.339-406*

As demonstrated by Skoyles (1978), CIOB (1980) and Neo (1995) above, the ability to quantify construction wastes is an important one. Their proposals for measuring material wastage as well as time wastage do not contradict one another. On the contrary, they complemented one another. In order to control wastage effectively, both proposals should therefore be used so that total wastage in terms of material and time can be computed. The results of these computations would readily facilitate the comparison of value added work to non-value added work in monetary terms.

Research method for measuring JIT wastage

No extensive work has been undertaken so far to substantiate what Neo (1995) has proposed for quantifying time wastage. Three different building projects in Singapore were therefore chosen to illustrate the practical aspects of Neo's (1995) accounting procedure in terms of its actual inputs and outputs. In this case, Neo's (1995) accounting procedure was incorporated into the three projects chosen for the study. These three case studies include a school, a public housing project and a private condominium.

To ensure a high degree of accuracy and the relevance of data, the study has to be conducted physically on site. The collection of data was carried out at regular intervals, each with an average interval of three days. The raw data collected was processed into information using Neo's (1995) accounting procedure. However, because of the uniqueness of construction sites, Neo's (1995) accounting procedure cannot be applied in its basic form. Hence, slight modifications and customisation were made to suit the situation encountered.

Case study 1: design-and-build school project

The Public Works Department (PWD) school project used the design-and-build method of procurement as well as extensive prefabricated components. The latter, in particular, offered a conducive environment for the application of the JIT concept. The PWD design-and-build school is located at Chua Chu Kang, Singapore. The project has a land area of approximately 30,000 m^2. The development consists of eight main school blocks, one basement level of rifle range cum civil defence shelter, an electrical substation and a bin centre. The duration for the whole project, including design and construction, was 18 months, commencing in January 1994 and ending in July 1995. The contract value of this project was approximately S$18.6 million.

The school incorporates an unprecedented multitude of buildable features such as multi-storey precast columns, precast beams, hollow core slabs and precast shear walls. The extensive use of prefabricated components results in improved productivity and excellent quality. It also gives rise to a significant reduction in manpower requirements on site, yielding in the process, 50 per cent higher productivity compared to other school projects. The precast design also facilitates "fast-track" construction as it reduces dependency on the weather.

The structural construction phase of this school project was selected for illustrating the quantitative measures of JIT deliveries. This phase involved the installation of precast columns, beams, end walls, parapets and hollow core slabs. The installation of precast hollow slabs is the most critical activity in the construction process. It should be noted that the planning and co-ordination for the deliveries of precast materials to site are important. During the scheduling stage, the planner must always bear in mind the following question: "can the columns and beams come just-in-time for the slab installation?" Apart from being a critical activity, the slab has also been chosen as an area of study because people tend to put a value to floor areas more readily. The installation of columns and beams appears to be of lesser value to a client. Hence, columns and beams can only be claimed as materials on site. A good control of time wastage will help the contractor to improve the productivity of the overall project.

In this school project, there is a high degree of standardisation on the precasting of columns, thus achieving JIT delivery. JIT delivery cannot be achieved using the batch concept because having too many different types and sizes of columns would mean long waiting time for fabrication to be completed. This is due to the fact that the normal precast yard's practice is to finish precasting all the Type I components before Type II components can commence and so on. It can be observed from site observations that all precast columns were delivered promptly right after the installation of precast slabs. Subsequently, all beams arrived just-in-time for the slab installation.

Schematic diagrams of the structural construction process for this school project are shown in Figure 6.6.

Case study 2: design-and-build public housing project

This Housing and Development Board (HDB) design-and-build project is also located at Chua Chu Kang, Singapore. The project comprises of seven apartment blocks with a total of 607 housing units. The duration of this project, including design and construction, was 30 months with a contract value of approximately S$71 million. The construction of the flats in this project was carried out using the traditional method of construction, ie. using cast insitu concreting for the structural elements. However, the casting of such elements uses advanced formwork systems. Both the tableform system and metal form system were employed to speed up construction as well as improve safety, thus reducing in the process, construction costs.

The location and site plan of this housing project is shown in Figure 6.7.

Case study 3: private condominium project

This project comprises of the construction of four tower blocks of 16-storey apartments, one block of five-storey multi-storey carpark, one block of half-basement carpark, clubhouse and recreational facilities. The contract value for this project is approximately S$99.4 million and the total duration is 22 months. At the time of this research study in mid-1995, this is still an on-going building project.

The traditional method of using cast insitu concrete for the structural elements was used for the construction of the tower blocks for this private condominium project. However, the casting of such elements are accomplished using the advanced tableform system. This formwork system was employed to speed up building construction and improve safety to achieve reduction in construction costs. Lightweight precision concrete blocks, known as "thermalite" are used to replace bricks in certain areas of the project. Thermalite blocks are autoclaved aerated concrete blocks, with each block equivalent in area to nine standard bricks. However, despite its size, each thermalite block weighs less than half the weight of its equivalent in bricks, thus leading to faster laying. This also results in the structure

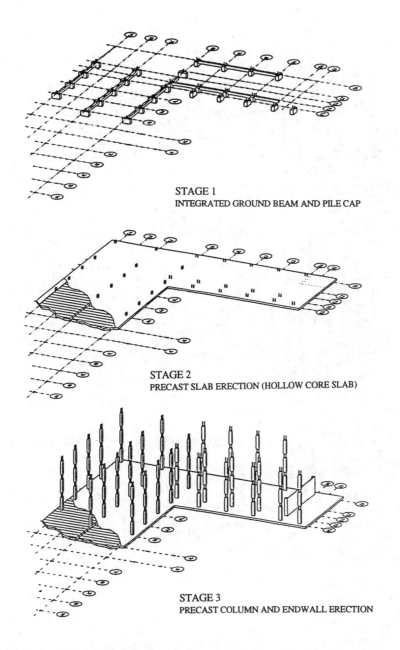

STAGE 1
INTEGRATED GROUND BEAM AND PILE CAP

STAGE 2
PRECAST SLAB ERECTION (HOLLOW CORE SLAB)

STAGE 3
PRECAST COLUMN AND ENDWALL ERECTION

Figure 6.6   Schematic diagrams of the structural construction process

103

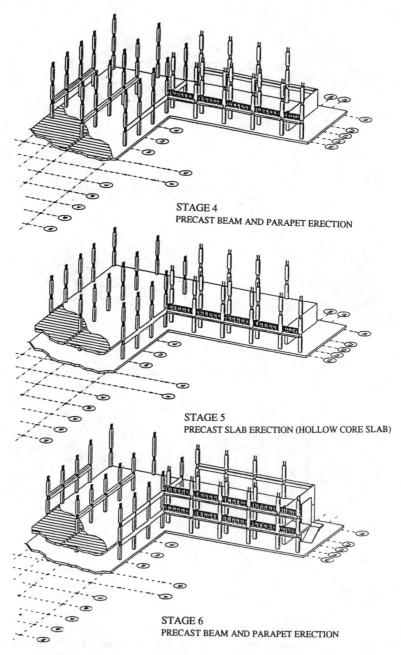

STAGE 4
PRECAST BEAM AND PARAPET ERECTION

STAGE 5
PRECAST SLAB ERECTION (HOLLOW CORE SLAB)

STAGE 6
PRECAST BEAM AND PARAPET ERECTION

Figure 6.6   Schematic diagrams of the structural construction process (cont'd)

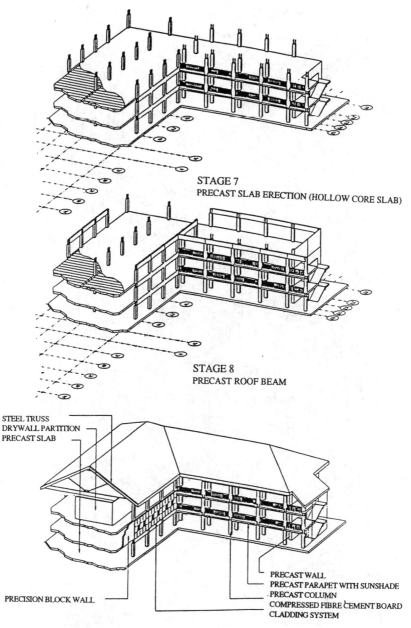

STAGE 7
PRECAST SLAB ERECTION (HOLLOW CORE SLAB)

STAGE 8
PRECAST ROOF BEAM

STEEL TRUSS
DRYWALL PARTITION
PRECAST SLAB

PRECISION BLOCK WALL

PRECAST WALL
PRECAST PARAPET WITH SUNSHADE
PRECAST COLUMN
COMPRESSED FIBRE CEMENT BOARD
CLADDING SYSTEM

ARCHITECTURAL AND STRUCTURAL COMPONENTS

Figure 6.6   Schematic diagrams of the structural construction process (cont'd)

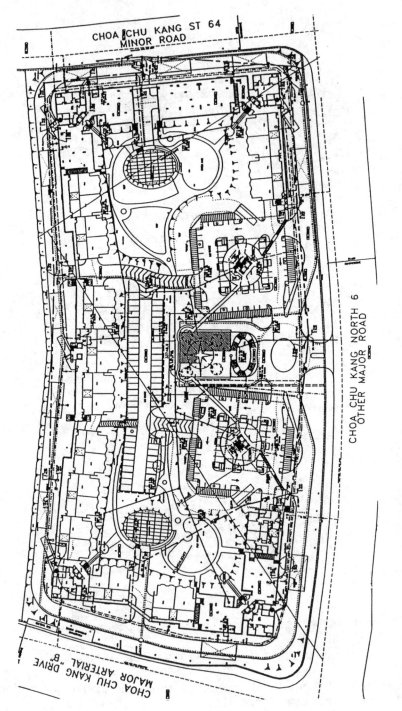

CHOA CHU KANG ST 64
MINOR ROAD

CHOA CHU KANG NORTH 6
OTHER MAJOR ROAD

CHOA CHU KANG DRIVE
MAJOR ARTERIAL "B"

Figure 6.7 Location and site plan

106

weighing 27 per cent less compared with one using conventional brickwall. Furthermore, its higher level of precision facilitates the use of skim coating of 2mm compared with conventional 25mm thick plastering for brickwall. Thermalite blocks therefore help to ensure a good quality finish.

This case study is concerned with two specific trades, namely thermalite laying and bricklaying. Thermalite is essentially used for the construction of internal walls while bricks are generally used for the construction of external walls in this private condominium project.

A typical floor plan of a tower block in this condominium project is shown in Figure 6.8.

Assumptions

Some assumptions need to be made in these three case studies. These are:

1   Since productivity relates to process time, JIT is indirectly affected. However, this study assumes that every worker's productivity is the same.

2   The site operates from 0800 hours to 1800 hours. Out of these ten hours, two hours are put aside for lunch and tea breaks. Hence, the actual working hours per day are restricted to eight hours. Any activities that continued after 1800 hours are considered overtime work.

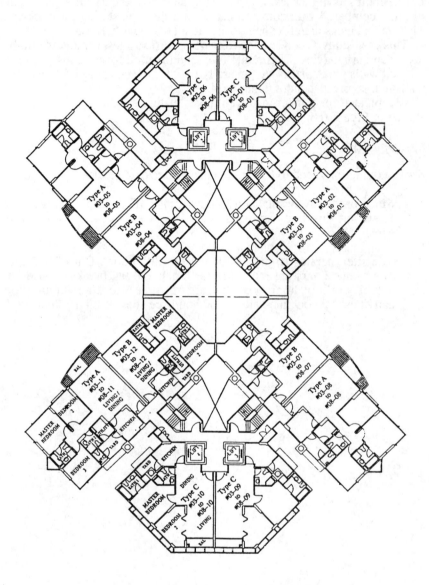

Figure 6.8 Typical floor plan of tower block

7 Measuring Just-In-Time wastes in construction

Introduction

As case studies, three building projects were chosen to illustrate Neo's (1995) accounting procedure in terms of its actual inputs and outputs. These three case studies include a school, a public housing project and a private condominium. The empirical findings of these three building projects are presented below.

Case study 1: design-and-build school project

The entire structural construction process for this project may be divided into eight stages. Stage 1 concerns the integration between the ground beams and pile caps which are both cast insitu. Stage 2 concerns the erection of precast hollow core ground slabs. Stage 3 concerns the precast columns and precast end wall erection. Stage 4 concerns the erection process for the precast beams and precast parapet, after which Stage 2 and Stage 4 will be repeated until the final stage is reached where the precast roof beams are erected.

In this case study, some assumptions are made. These are:

1   Move time and wait time in the mobilisation phase are constant for all activities.

2   The lowest unloading time is the standard process time.

3   Unloading time for precast elements comprises of transportation time from the precast yard to the site and wait time for unloading.

4   Overnight unloading is excluded from the case study.

The raw data collected from site and as shown in Appendix 2 includes:

1   Location of designated precast element installation.

2   Quantity of each delivery.

3   Time in and time out of the trailer transporting the precast elements for installation.

4   Unloading time.

5   Date of delivery.

6   Type of elements delivered.

"Time in" is defined as the time when the trailer leaves the precast yard. "Time out" is defined as the time when the trailer leaves the construction site. For precast columns and precast beams, upon delivery, these will be unloaded and left on the ground at the site. For precast slabs, these will be unloaded and installed at the same time. The unloading time for precast slabs is therefore taken as the process time of slab installation. It is important at this point to note that the data collected for this case study covers the complete set of precast element delivery order for the entire structural construction process. The entire process started in September 1994 and ended in February 1995.

As shown in Appendix 2, the raw data collected is processed into useful information for the purpose of analysis. By grouping data according to the types of elements, time in and time out is used for the computation of unloading time. With reference to Neo's (1995) accounting procedure, this unloading time is considered as the process time (B). In this study, element types are divided into two categories, namely precast slabs and the rest of the precast elements. The minimum unloading time of each category is taken to be the standard process time (C). For each entry, the difference between the actual and standard process time (B-C), known as the total process time waste (D), is taken. This is followed by dividing the total process time waste (D) by the maximum total process time waste (max{D}) and this figure, in percentage format, shows the relative process time wastage (RPT) between entries of the same group. For example, if the figure is 0 per cent, it implies that the particular entry has no process time wastage. On the other hand, a figure of 100 per cent would imply that the particular entry has taken the maximum wastage for the entire project. RPT, being a relative value, can be used to compare against different tasks and different projects.

A sample comprising twelve entries is shown in Table 7.1 to illustrate the detailed calculations for unloading time per slab, process time wastage, RPT and rounded RPT for plotting purposes. Two graphs, Figure 7.1 and Figure 7.2, are plotted to illustrate the trend in process time wastage. The precast slab category consists of 164 entries and the rest of the precast elements category consists of 219 entries. The standard process time (C) for precast slab is 2 minutes 30 seconds and that of the remaining precast elements category is 1 minute 15 seconds. The maximum total process time waste (max{D}) for precast slabs is 57 minutes 30 seconds while that of the precast elements category is 88 minutes 45 seconds. (Important note: the tabulation presented in Table 7.1 is incomplete because of the large number of entries

110

Table 7.1
Sample of processed time computation for design-and-build school project

Location	No of Pcs Delivered	Time In	Time Out	Unloading Time	Date of Delivery	Type of Elements	Unloading Time Per Slab	Process Time Wastage	Relative Process Time (RPT)	Rounded RPT
	a	b	c	d			e	f	g	h
				$(c - b)$			(d/a)	$(e - min(e))$	$(f/max(f)*100\%)$	$(round(g))$
Blk A 1st Storey	6	11:45	13:45	2:00	8/9/94	P.C. SLAB	0:20:00	0:16:00	100%	100%
Blk A 1st Storey	6	12:30	14:20	1:50	8/9/94	P.C. SLAB	0:18:20	0:14:20	90%	90%
Blk A 1st Storey	6	14:55	15:30	0:35	8/9/94	P.C. SLAB	0:05:50	0:01:50	11%	10%
Blk A 1st Storey	7	15:25	16:20	0:55	8/9/94	P.C. SLAB	0:07:51	0:03:51	24%	20%
Blk A 1st Storey	10	10:50	13:00	2:10	9/9/94	P.C. SLAB	0:13:00	0:09:00	56%	60%
Blk A 1st Storey	6	13:20	13:45	0:25	9/9/94	P.C. SLAB	0:04:10	0:00:10	1%	0%
Blk A 1st Storey	7	15:00	15:30	0:30	9/9/94	P.C. SLAB	0:04:17	0:00:17	2%	0%
Blk A 1st Storey	6	16:45	17:10	0:25	9/9/94	P.C. SLAB	0:04:10	0:00:10	1%	0%
Blk A 1st Storey	6	17:35	18:15	0:40	9/9/94	P.C. SLAB	0:06:40	0:02:40	17%	20%
Blk A 1st Storey	5	09:00	09:20	0:20	9/9/94	P.C. SLAB	0:04:00	0:00:00	0%	0%
Blk A 1st Storey	5	10:40	11:05	0:25	9/9/94	P.C. SLAB	0:05:00	0:01:00	6%	10%
Blk A 1st Storey	3	11:30	11:55	0:25	9/9/94	P.C. SLAB	0:08:20	0:04:20	27%	30%

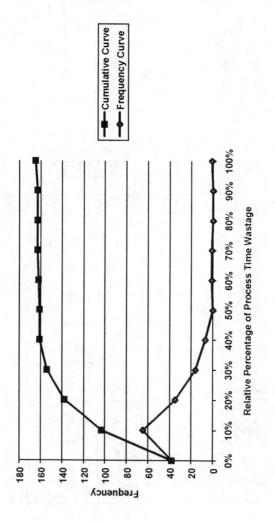

Figure 7.1 Relative process time wastage for precast slabs

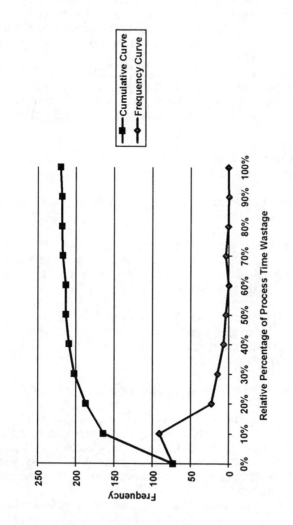

Figure 7.2 Relative process time wastage for other precast elements

involved, ie. 164 and 219 entries for precast slabs and other precast elements respectively. The full data set used to prepare Table 7.1 is shown in Appendix 3. Nevertheless, Figure 7.1 and Figure 7.2 are plotted using the complete data.)

It can be observed from Figure 7.1 that most occurrences of time wastage fall between 0 per cent and 50 per cent, and are particularly high in the range of 10 to 20 per cent. It can be observed further that at the 10 per cent RPT, the time wastage can occur at any time of the day. This trend may be due to the queueing process during slab installation. As for the range between 20 per cent and 30 per cent RPT, 60 per cent of the occurrences happened between 12.00 pm to 1.00 pm and 2.00 pm to 3.00 pm. These may be caused by lunch hours and tea breaks.

Figure 7.2 reveals that most occurrences of time wastage fall between 0 per cent and 40 per cent, and are particularly high at 10 per cent RTP. The high occurrence at 10 per cent RTP may be due to site traffic congestion.

Comparing the RPT for both categories of elements, it may be concluded that:

1   There is less process time wastage in the unloading of other precast elements when compared with the unloading of precast slabs.

2   For other precast elements category, good control over process time wastage has been exercised.

3   Although there is still some process time wastage under the category of "other precast elements", it may be unnecessary to streamline wastage control as there will always be some wastage over time due to external factors such as traffic congestion and unexpected events.

4   It can be seen that there is still room for improvement in the reduction of process time wastage under the precast slab category. A good wastage control system can help to reduce process time wastage.

Case study 2: design-and-build public housing project

The construction of the flats in this project was carried out using the traditional method of construction, ie. using cast insitu concreting for the structural elements. However, the casting of such elements uses advanced formwork systems. Both the tableform system and metal form system were employed to speed up construction as well as improve safety, thus reducing in the process, construction costs.

The entire concreting process for the structural elements was selected for this study. The data collected covers the installation process of reinforcement bar and formwork, inspection time, rectification time, re-inspection time and casting time. The data was collected from all seven apartment blocks (Block 631 to 637) and included the following:

1   Block 631 - 11th and 12th storey slab.

2   Block 632 - 10th and 11th storey slab.

3   Block 633 - 11th and 12th storey slab.

4   Block 634 - 13th and 14th storey slab.

5   Block 635 - 13th and 14th storey slab.

6   Block 636 - 12th and 13th storey slab.

7   Block 637 - 11th and 12th storey slab.

This case study maps the data collected from the site with Neo's (1995) accounting procedure so that both value added time and non-value added time can be evaluated quantitatively.

The formwork systems used by these seven apartment blocks were:

1   Blocks 631 and 637 - tableform system.

2   Blocks 634, 635 and 636 - metal form system.

3   Blocks 632 and 633 - a combination of both tableform and metal form systems.

The standard work cycles for the tableform and metal form system are shown in Figure 7.3 and Figure 7.4 respectively. Each system is made up of a 10-day cycle.

For the tableform system, the work cycle involves slab casting, column steel and formwork, column casting, striking of column formwork, striking of tableform, flying of tableform and reprop tableform, adjustment of gap, beam reinforcement, slab mesh, formation of drop for beam, inspection and slab and beam casting.

For the metal form system, the work cycle involves slab casting, column steel, striking of vertical formwork, kicker casting, hoisting up of column formwork, erection of column formwork, erection of beam formwork, beam reinforcement, slab mesh and formation of drop for beam, drop cleaning and inspection.

Column and slab casting per floor is taken as one single concreting operation. Data in its raw form are then processed. The processed data are then incorporated into Neo's (1995) proposed task cycle. After matching the processed data against each component in the task duration, the following times were idenitifed:

1   Process time 1 - Time taken for formwork and reinforcement bar installation.

2   Process time 2 and 3 - Time spent for concreting.

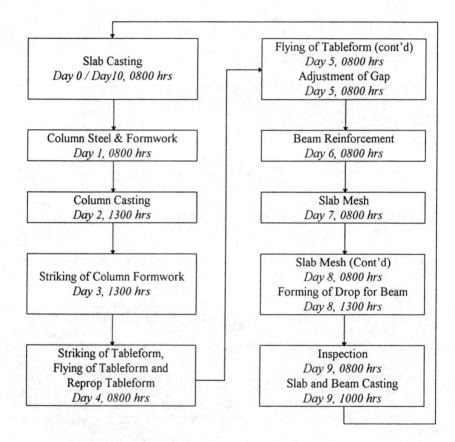

Figure 7.3   Work cycle for tableform system

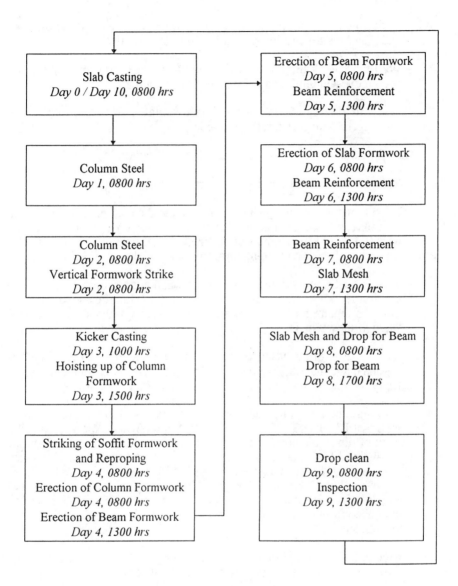

Figure 7.4   Work cycle for metal form system

3   Wait time 1 - Waiting time, calculated from the time inspection had been requested until the time it actually started.

4   Wait time 2 - Waiting time, calculated from the time rectification work ends until the time re-inspection is being requested.

5   Wait time 3 - Waiting time, calculated from the time re-inspection had been requested until the time it actually commenced.

6   Wait time 4 and 5 - Waiting time calculated from the end of the re-inspection until concreting started.

The tabulation of data was undertaken in three stages:

1   Raw data is compiled into a table format.

2   Useful information is obtained by extracting the total process time, total wait time, total inspection time, total rectification time, total rectification wait time and total re-inspection time from the raw data compiled. A summary of the data tabulated for this stage is shown in Table 7.2.

3   To standardise concreting activities between entries, all processed time are divided by the area casted, thus giving a value represented in unit time per square metre. A summary of the data tabulated for this final stage is shown in Table 7.3.

Figure 7.5 is plotted based on the values tabulated in Table 7.3. The observations made therein have been arranged in the order of total duration of the activity. Numerous observations may be made from Figure 7.5:

1   Although the duration of each task increases from left to right, it can be seen that Blocks 631/12, 636/13, 633/11 and 637/11 experienced some form of dip in the process time. This seems to suggest that the ratio of non-value added time to value added time is higher than normal in these cases. (Note: 631/12 means Block 631, 12th storey.)

2   Block 637/12 spent a substantial amount of time in rectification works, thus accounting for the longer period of time for completing the task than expected.

3   Blocks 635/13 and 635/14 performed very well because much of the time duration was used for doing value added activities.

Figure 7.6 illustrates the relative comparison of the total time duration of each entry by expressing the total duration of each task as 100 per cent. Figure 7.6 thus facilitates the component of each task duration between entries to be compared readily. In the process, productivity and wastage can also be identified easily. The following observations may be made from Figure 7.6:

118

Table 7.2
Time computation (Stage II) for concreting activities in absolute terms

(Note: in location, 631/11 means Block 631, 11th storey)

Location	Total Process Time	Total Wait Time	Total Inspection Time	Total Rectification Time	Total Rectification Wait Time	Total Re-Inspection Time
631/11	158:35:00	22:40:00	7:50:00	2:00:00	2:30:00	8:10:00
631/12	89:00:00	19:20:00	10:15:00	5:00:00	3:30:00	4:45:00
632/10	174:20:00	15:50:00	11:35:00	-	-	-
632/11	73:35:00	27:15:00	4:25:00	2:00:00	1:00:00	6:50:00
633/11	209:20:00	35:10:00	19:40:00	3:00:00	2:30:00	1:50:00
633/12	141:50:00	27:00:00	15:45:00	-	-	-
634/13	110:00:00	8:15:00	2:45:00	-	-	-
634/14	100:50:00	2:05:00	12:00:00	-	-	-
635/13	118:30:00	11:30:00	5:30:00	-	-	-
635/14	126:00:00	6:30:00	4:30:00	-	-	-
636/12	148:20:00	7:20:00	5:50:00	-	-	-
636/13	113:02:00	16:15:00	4:05:00	3:00:00	5:30:00	4:20:00
637/11	216:10:00	38:40:00	16:00:00	3:00:00	2:30:00	1:00:00
637/12	75:30:00	10:20:00	11:40:00	11:15:00	1:00:00	1:30:00

Table 7.3
Time computation (Stage III) for concreting activities in relative terms

(Note: in location, 631/11 means Block 631, 11th storey)

Location	Area m²	Total Process Time per m²	Total Wait Time per m²	Total Inspection Time per m²	Total Rectification Time per m²	Total Rectification Wait Time per m²	Total Re-Inspection Time per m²
631/11	590	0:16:08	0:02:18	0:00:48	0:00:12	0:00:15	0:00:50
631/12	590	0:09:03	0:01:58	0:01:03	0:00:31	0:00:21	0:00:29
632/10	949	0:11:01	0:01:00	0:00:44	-	-	-
632/11	949	0:04:39	0:01:43	0:00:17	0:00:08	0:00:04	0:00:26
633/11	949	0:13:14	0:02:13	0:01:15	0:00:11	0:00:09	0:00:07
633/12	949	0:08:58	0:01:42	0:01:00	-	-	-
634/13	286	0:23:05	0:01:44	0:00:35	-	-	-
634/14	286	0:21:09	0:00:26	0:02:31	-	-	-
635/13	590	0:12:03	0:01:10	0:00:34	-	-	-
635/14	590	0:12:49	0:00:40	0:00:27	-	-	-
636/12	585	0:15:13	0:00:45	0:00:36	-	-	-
636/13	585	0:11:36	0:01:40	0:00:25	0:00:18	0:00:34	0:00:27
637/11	590	0:21:59	0:03:56	0:01:38	0:00:18	0:00:15	0:00:06
637/12	590	0:07:41	0:01:03	0:01:11	0:01:09	0:00:06	0:00:09

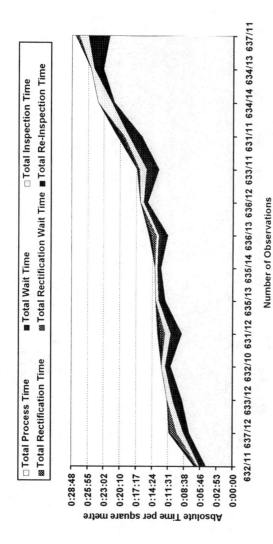

Figure 7.5 Absolute time of task cycle per square metre

(Note: 632/11 along x-axis means Block 632, 11th storey)

121

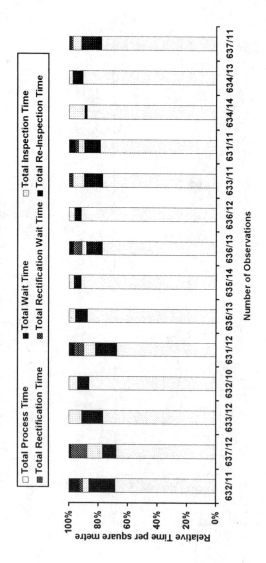

Figure 7.6   Relative time of task cycle per square metre

(Note: 632/11 along x-axis means Block 632, 11th storey)

122

1   Whenever there is re-inspection in the task duration, quite a substantial amount of time would be wasted.

2   Block 637/12 spent more than 15 per cent of the total duration in rectification works, thus resulting in significant time wastage.

3   Productivity levels were high for Blocks 635/13, 635/14 and 634/13 as the value added time chalked up almost 90 per cent of the total time duration. Wastage is minimal in these cases.

4   Productivity level is particularly low in Block 631/12 as the value added time is only about 60 per cent of the total time duration. It can be concluded that there is substantial wastage in this case.

To further illustrate the time wasted for rectification works, a breakdown of relative time wastage for recitification works is shown in Figure 7.7. It can be observed in Figure 7.7 that whenever there are rectification works,

1   An average of 40 per cent of the total rectification time is spent on re-inspection time.

2   An average of 25 per cent of total rectification time is spent on waiting for re-inspection.

The ratio of rectification time to combined time of re-inspection and waiting for re-inspection is very much lower than the ratio of process time to non-value added time in a normal task. Although rectification work is already a form of time wastage, it can be illustrated as a non-value adding activity that wastes more time.

Case study 3: private condominium project

The findings pertaining to this case study are presented below in two sections, namely thermalite laying and brick laying.

Thermalite laying

Raw data are collected from all four blocks (Block A to D). The data collected for thermalite laying covers the following areas:

1   Block A   -   5th Storey Parcel A
             -    5th Storey Parcel C
             -    5th Storey Parcel D
             -    5th Storey Parcel E
             -    5th Storey Parcel F.

2   Block B   -   6th Storey Parcel D
             -    6th Storey Parcel E.

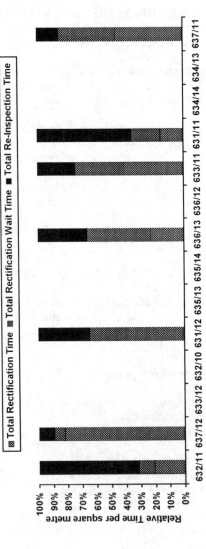

Figure 7.7 Relative time of rectification time, rectification wait time and re-inspection time per square metre

(Note: 632/11 along x-axis means Block 632, 11th storey)

124

3	Block C	-	6th Storey Parcel D
		-	6th Storey Parcel E
		-	6th Storey Parcel F.
4	Block D	-	5th Storey Parcel C
		-	5th Storey Parcel D
		-	5th Storey Parcel E
		-	5th Storey Parcel F.

Data in its raw format are then processed. The processed data are then incorporated into the task cycle proposed by Neo (1995). Following the matching of the processed data against each component in the task duration, the following were identified:

1	Process Time 1	-	Time taken for unloading the thermalite from the container.
2	Process Time 2	-	Time spent to transfer the thermalite to the blocks.
3	Process Time 3	-	Time spent for the crane to hoist the thermalite up to the respective floors.
4	Process Time 4	-	Time spent to lay one parcel of thermalite.
5	Wait Time 1	-	Waiting time, calculated from the arrival of container until the time unloading started.
6	Wait Time 2	-	Waiting time, calculated from the time thermalite is unloaded until the time it is transfered to the respective blocks.
7	Wait Time 3	-	Waiting time, calculated from the end of transfering time until the start of hoisting time.
8	Wait Time 4	-	Waiting time, calculated from the start of hoisting time until the start of laying time.
9	Wait Time 5	-	Waiting time, calculated from the end of laying time until the start of inspection time.
10	Wait Time 6	-	Waiting time, calculated from the end of inspection time until the start of rectification time.
11	Wait Time 7	-	Waiting time, calculated from the end of rectification time until the start of re-inspection time.

The tabulation of data was undertaken in three stages:

1   Raw data is compiled into a table format.

2   Useful information is obtained by extracting the total process time, total wait time, total inspection time, total rectification time, total rectification wait time and total re-inspection time from the raw data compiled. A summary of the data tabulated for this stage is shown in Table 7.4.

3   To standardise thermalite laying activities between entries, all processed time are divided by the area laid, thus giving a value represented in unit time per square metre. A summary of the data tabulated for this final stage is shown in Table 7.5.

The results shown in Table 7.5 are plotted in Figure 7.8 where all observations are arranged in the order of total duration of the activity. The observations which can be made from Figure 7.8 include:

1   Although the duration of each task increases from left to right, it can be seen that all blocks seem to have a relatively constant process time. This is not a good sign as tasks ranging from left to right are wasting more and more time.

2   Wait time seems to be a major problem in thermalite laying.

3   Block A/5/A performs the best among all the observations.

4   Block A/5/E experiences a rise in process time and a slight dip in waiting time.

Figure 7.9 compares the total time duration of each entry relatively by expressing the total duration of each task as 100 per cent. This is useful as one is able to compare the component of each task duration between entries more readily. Productivity and wastage can also be identified readily. The following observations may be made from Figure 7.9:

1   Most operations are quite inefficient as productivity hits a low average of 30 per cent of the total time duration.

2   Block A/5/A performs the best and yet its productivity is only 55 per cent.

3   An average of 55 per cent of the total time duration was spent on waiting time.

4   An average of 10 per cent of the total time duration was spent on rectification works.

Table 7.4
Time computation (Stage II) for thermalite laying activities

(Note: in location, A/5/A means Block A, 5th storey, Parcel A)

Location	Total Process Time	Total Wait Time	Total Inspection Time	Total Rectification Time	Total Rectification Wait Time	Total Re-Inspection Time
A/5/A	48:10:00	25:10:00	1:30:00	2:00:00	6:00:00	1:00:00
A/5/C	35:30:00	40:45:00	1:30:00	11:00:00	5:30:00	0:45:00
A/5/F	44:20:00	42:10:00	2:00:00	9:00:00	7:00:00	0:50:00
A/5/E	45:10:00	34:20:00	1:30:00	10:00:00	6:30:00	0:45:00
A/5/D	48:55:00	48:35:00	1:45:00	10:00:00	6:15:00	1:00:00
B/6/D	48:50:00	161:50:00	2:30:00	10:00:00	5:00:00	1:30:00
B/6/E	41:50:00	158:40:00	2:30:00	9:00:00	6:00:00	1:30:00
C/6/F	42:25:00	191:55:00	2:00:00	10:00:00	5:00:00	2:00:00
C/6/E	40:55:00	190:31:00	2:00:00	10:00:00	5:00:00	2:00:00
C/6/D	53:05:00	160:10:00	2:00:00	10:00:00	5:00:00	2:00:00
D/5/F	42:55:00	71:10:00	2:30:00	10:00:00	4:30:00	2:00:00
D/5/E	33:20:00	80:40:00	2:30:00	10:00:00	4:30:00	2:00:00
D/5/D	35:20:00	81:05:00	2:30:00	9:00:00	5:30:00	2:00:00
D/5/C	39:40:00	75:25:00	2:30:00	9:00:00	5:30:00	2:00:00

Table 7.5
Time computation (Stage III) for thermalite laying activities

(Note: in location, A/5/A means Block A, 5th storey, Parcel A)

Location	Area m²	Total Process Time per m²	Total Wait Time per m²	Total Inspection Time per m²	Total Rectification Time per m²	Total Rectification Wait Time per m²	Total Re-Inspection Time per m²
A/5/A	264	0:10:57	0:05:43	0:00:20	0:00:27	0:01:22	0:00:14
A/5/C	264	0:08:04	0:09:16	0:00:20	0:02:30	0:01:15	0:00:10
A/5/F	264	0:10:05	0:09:35	0:00:27	0:02:03	0:01:35	0:00:11
A/5/E	190	0:14:16	0:10:51	0:00:28	0:03:09	0:02:03	0:00:14
A/5/D	264	0:11:07	0:11:03	0:00:24	0:02:16	0:01:25	0:00:14
B/6/D	264	0:11:06	0:36:47	0:00:34	0:02:16	0:01:08	0:00:20
B/6/E	190	0:13:13	0:50:06	0:00:47	0:02:51	0:01:54	0:00:28
C/6/F	264	0:09:38	0:43:37	0:00:27	0:02:16	0:01:08	0:00:27
C/6/E	190	0:12:55	1:00:10	0:00:38	0:03:09	0:01:35	0:00:38
C/6/D	264	0:12:04	0:36:24	0:00:27	0:02:16	0:01:08	0:00:27
D/5/F	264	0:09:45	0:16:10	0:00:34	0:02:16	0:01:01	0:00:27
D/5/E	190	0:10:32	0:25:28	0:00:47	0:03:09	0:01:25	0:00:38
D/5/D	264	0:08:02	0:18:26	0:00:34	0:02:03	0:01:15	0:00:27
D/5/C	264	0:09:01	0:17:08	0:00:34	0:02:03	0:01:15	0:00:27

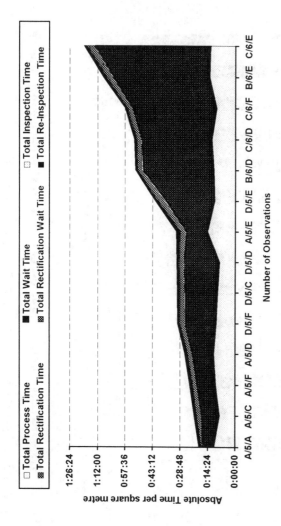

Figure 7.8 **Absolute time of task cycle for thermalite laying per square metre**

(Note: A/5/A along x-axis means Block A, 5th storey, Parcel A)

129

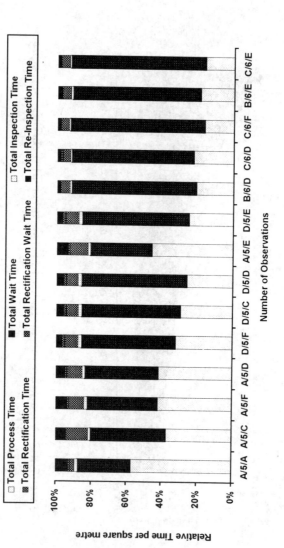

Figure 7.9 **Relative time of task cycle for thermalite laying per square metre**

(Note: A/5/A along x-axis means Block A, 5th storey, Parcel A)

Bricklaying

The raw data collected for bricklaying covers the following areas:

1   Block A   -   5th Storey Parcel A-F.

2   Block B   -   5th Storey Parcel A-F.

3   Block C   -   5th Storey Parcel A-F.

4   Block D   -   5th Storey Parcel A-F.

The data in its raw format was processed and incorporated into Neo's (1995) proposed task cycle. The matching of the processed data against each component of task duration is similar to that for thermalite laying described above. The processed data is then tabulated. Summaries of the bricklaying data as tabulated above are shown in Table 7.6 and Table 7.7 respectively.

Figure 7.10 is then plotted based on the values tabulated in Table 7.7 where the observations are arranged in the order of total duration of the activity. Observations which may be made from Figure 7.10 include:

1   The duration of each task is in decreasing order from left to right.

2   The total rectification wait time is prominent in Block C, but this appears to be an exceptional case.

3   Rectification works take a long time duration.

Figure 7.11 compares the total time duration of each entry relatively by expressing the total duration of each task as 100 per cent. Using Figure 7.11, one is able to compare the component of each task duration between entries easily. Productivity and wastage can in turn be identified readily. Observations from Figure 7.11 include the following:

1   Block C has the best level of productivity despite the long wait for re-inspection.

2   An average of 70 per cent of the total time duration is used in process time, a value added time.

3   The normal wait time seems to be a hindrance to better control of time wastage.

Conclusion

The three construction projects used as case studies have helped to show that Neo's (1995) accounting procedure is workable in practice. Using this accounting procedure, one is able to identify the productivity of each task and

Table 7.6
Time computation (Stage II) for bricklaying activities

(Note: in location, A/5/A-F means Block A, 5th storey, Parcel A-F)

Location	Total Process Time	Total Wait Time	Total Inspection Time	Total Rectification Time	Total Rectification Wait Time	Total Re-Inspection Time
A/5/A-F	73:30:00	24:30:00	1:30:00	7:45:00	1:15:00	1:00:00
B/5/A-F	73:50:00	22:25:00	1:30:00	2:00:00	0:30:00	1:30:00
C/5/A-F	81:35:00	7:00:00	1:15:00	2:00:00	6:15:00	0:45:00
D/5/A-F	63:30:00	8:30:00	2:00:00	7:00:00	0:03:00	1:00:00

the time wastage at various stages. For example, rectification works are very serious forms of time wastage. Hence, to apply the JIT concept to this project, management should request for more quality control measures so as to cut down on rectification works. In addition, management may further streamline operations and optimise schedules so that more wait time could be eliminated, thus leading to higher productivity.

Table 7.7
Time computation (Stage III) for bricklaying activities

(Note: in location, A/5/A-F means Block A, 5th storey, Parcel A-F)

Location	Area m²	Total Process Time per m²	Total Wait Time per m²	Total Inspection Time per m²	Total Rectification Time per m²	Total Rectification Wait Time per m²	Total Re-Inspection Time per m²
A/5/A-F	3049.2	0:01:27	0:00:29	0:00:02	0:00:09	0:00:01	0:00:01
B/5/A-F	3049.2	0:01:27	0:00:26	0:00:02	0:00:02	0:00:01	0:00:02
C/5/A-F	3049.2	0:01:36	0:00:08	0:00:01	0:00:02	0:00:07	0:00:01
D/5/A-F	3049.2	0:01:15	0:00:10	0:00:02	0:00:08	0:00:00	0:00:01

133

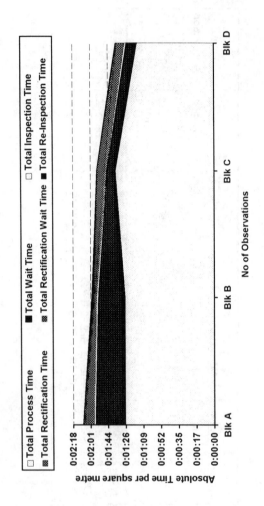

Figure 7.10 Absolute time of task cycle for bricklaying per square metre

134

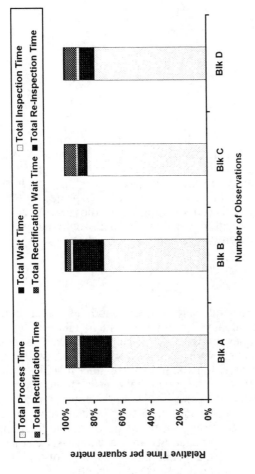

Figure 7.11 Relative time of task cycle for bricklaying per square metre

135

8 Conclusion

Introduction

In the course of explaining how the philosophy of JIT may be applied in the construction industry, two empirical studies were mounted. While the first study relates how JIT can be operationalised within the prefabrication industry, the second study examines the background and methodology for measuring JIT wastes in three different building projects. This chapter concludes the findings of these two empirical studies and suggests relevant concepts and framework within which the JIT philosophy may be adapted to raise the level of productivity in the construction industry.

JIT measurements

With the currently tight and busy project schedules in the construction industry, there is a tendency for practitioners to take process time for granted. Nobody will question whether the same task takes one hour or one day to complete. However, with the advent of JIT, this study shows that some form of time wastage do exist in process time. In addition, this study shows that Neo's (1995) quantitative model can be applied successfully in the construction industry. In using Neo's (1995) approach, one is able to pinpoint the possible time wastage in a task process time, measure and scrutinise the wastage, get to the root of the problem and then apply some corrective actions to achieve productivity improvement. Another advantage is that based on the calculations, a standard process time for each task can be identified and used for planning purposes subsequently.

It is important to acknowledge that daily physical site observations must be made and carefully recorded in order to provide realistic interpretation of the data analysed. This is a difficult task because it is virtually impossible to station the research team on site permanently. As a result, many data sets were collected based on observations recorded voluntarily by many people who are involved in the project. As observed from the data collected, apart from the normal working hours, some construction activities work through the night, especially for trades like thermalite laying. Hence, in order to conduct a reliable study, the research team must be stationed on site at all time to record data. As it is technically impossible for this to be done, the collection of data was dependent on careful co-ordination of the people involved on site. These include the project director, project manager, project engineer, project architect, quantity surveyor, foreman and site clerk. Drawings are also important for obtaining reliable results. Quantities were measured from drawings to, where necessary, obtain floor and wall areas for the entries.

It is obvious from the three case studies presented earlier that JIT waste can be measured successfully using Neo's (1995) quantitative model. The usefulness of JIT waste data arising therefrom will include:

1   Ability to streamline operations.

2   Ability to be more responsive to the environment.

3   Improvement in productivity.

4   Improvement in quality assurance.

5   Improvement in scheduling.

6   More time buffer.

7   Cost savings.

The measurement process will help management to identify time based wastages arising from wait time, inspection time, rectification time and move time. Low and Tan (1996) suggest that the causes leading to time based wastages may include the following:

1   Labour shortage.

2   Shortage of plant and equipment.

3   Inadequate supervision.

4   Poor co-ordination of site deliveries.

5   Inadequate skills training.

6   Traffic congestion on site.

7   Unexpected events, for example, freak weather.

8   Poor workmanship.

9   Insufficient quality control measures.

137

10   Inaccurate programming and scheduling of operations.

It is, however, important to note that the case studies presented earlier were simplified for the purpose of presentation. For more effective results, monetary values can be attached to calculate the actual costs or savings. Adopting the JIT model in construction can help to facilitate planning and co-ordination of deliveries to building sites. Management can make use of the data collected to localise bottlenecks, suggest and implement the necessary solutions to reduce the time waste for a particular task. Hence, by applying a quantitative measure for JIT, the task can be identified and subsequently performed with a better level of productivity.

Application of JIT principles in the prefabrication industry

The study has earlier outlined in details the major survey findings targeted at the local prefabrication industry. The remaining sections in this chapter will attempt to justify the research hypothesis that the JIT concept can be selectively applied in the local "off-site" prefabrication industry to promote productivity. In so doing, the eight major JIT principles described earlier will be used to broadly analyse the survey findings. Wherever possible, the suitability of the JIT principles will be highlighted for their positive and useful applications in suppressing or resolving the major problems and issues faced by the prefabrication industry to bring about further improvements in productivity performance.

Before ending the chapter, a discussion will also be made on the research limitations as applied to this study of operationalising JIT principles in the prefabrication industry. Finally, a list of recommendations for further research work will be given to guide researchers to undertake more broad based studies of the JIT concept for its wider applications to boost productivity across the entire construction industry.

The principles of JIT are first discussed and analysed in detail in this section to ascertain if they could be applied to the local "off-site" prefabrication industry. This is done by primarily considering the major problems currently encountered by the prefabrication industry in the areas of manufacturing planning, process and control; and the relationships between the prefabricators and their suppliers as well as clients.

Attacking fundamental problems

This principle of JIT calls for the eradication of all root causes of fundamental problems. In the context of the survey findings, this principle can be applied in the following aspects to eliminate the fundamental root causes of some of the prefabrication industry's nagging problems:

"Covered" factory concept The underlying problem of "uncovered" factory premises which persist commonly amongst the prefabrication firms can be resolved fundamentally by simply building "covered" industrial premises. By so doing, this would facilitate the smooth running of manufacturing

operations which are unperturbed by the influence of inclement weather. The main resistance would of course be the high fixed capital costs needed for such a metamorphic change. However, these investments should always be weighed against the returns of increased productivity and profitability in the long term.

Constructability problems and promotion of the value engineering concept
More often then not, constructability problems which are commonly encountered in precast concrete component manufacturing are a direct result of the design team overlooking the critical aspect of the construction process. Designers often lack the fundamental foresight to fully understand and appreciate the meticulous operations of the construction team. As a result, constructability problems like congestion of reinforcement steel bars with cast-in items, demoulding problems, wrong positionings of lifting hooks, physical obstructions to concrete casting, etc. are largely prevalent.

With the JIT principle of attacking the fundamental root cause of the problem, constructability problems such as the above-mentioned could well be minimised, if not totally eliminated if a second critical look is made to further evaluate the constructability aspects of the designs completed by the design team. In this direction, the value engineering concept is useful to provide a basis for ensuring second-time checks on completed designs before these are released for construction works on-site. The promotion of a value engineering team is therefore highly recommended for the prefabrication industry if constructability problems are to be arrested. Ideally, the value engineering team should comprise not only design personnel but construction personnel as well who could offer their invaluable expertise and view points on the constructability aspects of precast component designs.

Foreign workers employment policy The compulsory Singapore government ruling to repatriate all foreign workers after a 4-year employment period have gave rise fundamentally to a permanent loss of well-trained workers. Inevitably, this had caused periodic hiccups to the smooth construction work flow for precast concrete components.

In line with the JIT approach to resolve problems at their source, the relevant government authorities and the CIDB should reconsider this problem from the following angles:

1   Extend the current 4-year stay ruling to a longer term. This extended time span will help to ensure that good labour resources are being utilised at their maximum efficiency and also allows for the thorough training of workers in a multitude of trade skills, thereby transforming them into a multi-skilled workforce eventually.

2   Continue to mount a large scale promotional campaign to attract Singaporeans to work in the local construction industry. This direction has long-term gains as citizens will be replacing the currently large pool of foreign workers who will be strategically phased out over the years in line with the existing government's policy.

Elimination of waste

Elimination of waste is the main theme and primary objective of the JIT philosophy. In the JIT environment, waste is anything that does not contribute to the value of the product. Following the Toyota's classification of waste, the identification of waste in the local prefabrication industry based on the survey can be summarised as follows:

Waste from overproduction Except for non-standardised unique precast concrete component products, waste from overproduction has been observed in almost all prefabrication firms manufacturing standardised and commonly used products; particularly those used for civil engineering construction works like road kerbs, drain channels, concrete pipes, carpark slabs, manhole chamber rings, etc.

Waste of waiting time As expected in all types of normal manufacturing operations, the survey has also uncovered a tremendous amount of waste due to waiting time. Lost time due to waiting occurred because of the following:

1   Inaccurate schedule coordination of insitu site works and precast component production works in the factory. This has caused most prefabrication firms to helplessly stockpile within their factory premises, finished goods which are waiting to be delivered to their clients' worksites.

2   Frequent late deliveries of supplies; especially for external supplies of ready-mixed concrete and various overseas supplies.

3   Manufacturing process problems like difficult and time consuming setting-up operations, excessive curing time requirements and extensive surface treatment finishing works (for example, patching works). These problems tend to prolong the manufacturing lead times, thereby subjecting clients to long waiting times.

4   Common problems of reworks because of defective quality and shoddy workmanship and / or mistakes. Reworks were found to occur commonly in the fixing of reinforcement steel bars and cast-in items, and in steel form moulds assembly. The rectification of such reworks demands waiting time.

5   Breakdowns of mechanised material handling systems like gantry cranes, fork-lifts, etc. Production schedules are often kept waiting due to machines downtimes for repair works.

6   An insufficient haulage fleet of vehicles to transport and deliver finished precast components to clients' worksites. Finished goods are again kept waiting in the factory for delivery.

Transportation waste Due to the low level of automation in the local prefabrication industry, transportation waste were almost inevitable in the precast component manufacturing processes. As the survey findings showed, transportation wastes have occurred in the following forms as a result of poor factory layouts and bad housekeeping practices:

1   The many internal transfers of both raw materials and partially finished goods which occur daily within the factory. Examples are partially finished bridge beams being lifted out from their casting beds to another location for subsequent finishing works; and the numerous movements of a large amount of raw materials (for instance, bent steel bars, steel forms, cast-in items, etc.) between various workstations.

2   The numerous unproductive vehicular trips made by machines like dumpers and fork-lifts in disposing of concrete wastes and defective or rejected precast concrete components respectively.

3   The "double handling" motion often required in singling out particular goods amongst huge stockpiles of finished goods inventories for deliveries to clients' worksites.

Processing waste Like all other process operations, processing waste too occurred in precast concrete component manufacturing. The survey findings have identified three major causes of processing waste which resulted in excessive material wastages, particularly in reinforcement steel bars / meshes and concrete. These causes include:

1   The many varied and different designs of precast components being manufactured by a prefabricator at any one time do not permit the efficient utilisation of material resources through repetitive standardisation on a large scale. In the case of reinforcement steel bars / meshes, the unique designs of precast components do not allow the same set of bar sizes and shapes for a particular product to be used for another product design. This, coupled with the further odd and awkward shapes of some product designs, often leads to poor and uneconomical curtailment of reinforcement steel bars / meshes, resulting in excessive wastages. For example, a particular product design may require a bent shape of steel bar length 10 metres. With the raw steel bars being supplied in 12 metres length, a material wastage of 2 metres (or 17 per cent) is incurred for each steel bar curtailed.

2   The inconsiderate "don't care" attitudes of sub-contract labour only workers. Under the common indigenous "kepala" system of sub-contracting in the local construction industry, sub-contractors only provide labour services for construction works to their clients. As materials used for precast component construction are often supplied by the prefabricator clients, sub-contract workers under the "kepala" system have always tended to incur more material wastages than directly employed workers of the prefabrication firms. This tendency is mainly caused by the absence of control and inconsiderate working

attitudes of such sub-contractors.

3   The usage of wrong materials. Although rare in occurrence, this negligent practice does happen in some prefabrication firms. Incidents of such embarrassing and wasteful acts have included the wrong grade of concrete used for casting, wrong sizes of reinforcement steel bars used, wrong types of tiles laid, etc.

Inventory waste The survey findings have shown that waste from inventory build-ups is still one of the dreadful but hidden problem which the local prefabrication industry is currently experiencing unknowingly. Except for customised "construct-to-order" non-standardised precast components, a majority of prefabricators are still seen to adopt the so called "just-in-case" concept in stocking large buffer amounts of both raw components and finished products in order to avoid sudden shortages in supplies. Although the responding prefabrication firms have argued that the extent of standardisation already achieved for such established and commonly used precast components would warrant their safe stocking for long periods in the event of poor demand, there is in actual fact no guarantee that such standardised products are absolutely free from the risk of obsolescence. A good example is the recent design amendment made by the PWD on one of their standardised precast product called "drop-inlet chamber" used for the construction of roads. As a result of this sudden change, a few prefabricators have had to write-off some of their old stocks of drop-inlet chambers as obsolete.

Apart from the risk of obsolescence, inventory waste would undoubtedly also bring along associated concealed problems of higher production costs, extra handling, additional space occupation, added congestion and so on, often at the peril of most ignorant prefabricators.

Waste from product defects From the survey findings, waste from product defects were seen to originate from two main causes, viz:

1   Quality defects in raw product components' supplies. An example would be "rusted" or "bird-caged" quality defects found in prestressing tendons.

2   Quality defects in finished precast components. Such product defects have often forced prefabricators to either reject the products or undertake wasteful reworks which result in prolonged production lead time, increased production costs and decreased productivity.

From the above discussion, it is apparent that the elimination of waste is crucial for the local prefabrication industry if it is to enjoy productivity improvements and their associated benefits. In this direction, the fundamental principles of the JIT approach can well be applied to the industry in overcoming or alleviating its problems to bring about increases in productivity. The principles of the JIT concept can be applied in the following manners to eliminate waste:

1   The JIT approach utilizing the "kanban" / pull concept can be used specifically to overcome wastes from overproduction, inventory build-ups and transportation by way of simply eliminating buffer stocks of both raw product components and finished goods. In applying the "kanban" / pull concept, production runs should only be effected based on exact demand orders from clients and not from forecasted demand some, say, three months into the future. By so doing, buffer stocks of raw product components (like reinforcement steel bars, cast-in items, etc.) would also be eliminated in the process as only the right quantities of raw components would be ordered just-in-time to produce the exact quantities of finished precast products required by clients. Managing the manufacturing process in this way would thus eliminate buffer stocks of both raw product components and finished goods as well as all their associated waste problems. It is strongly recommended that this JIT approach be applied in the production of standardized precast components as the survey findings showed that the problem of buffer stocks often correspond closely to such products.

2   The JIT concept of good long-term working relationship with both suppliers and clients should be emphasized within the prefabrication industry. Existing relationships between prefabricators and their suppliers / clients should be re-examined and reviewed on why suppliers could not deliver defect-free quality goods on time and clients are not able to give accurate work coordination schedules for precast component installation works. The guide to eliminate waste from waiting time due to such drawbacks is to firstly engage reliably proven single supplier sources on a long-term basis; and secondly to educate all clients on the useful workings of the JIT concept so as to gain their commitment and support in making the JIT operation a success.

3   The emphasis which the JIT concept places on total employee involvement should be further strengthened and upheld at all times within the working environment of the production factory. All workers at the production floor level should not only be periodically briefed on the workings of the JIT production system but also be trained to improve and fine-tune their job performances. Achieving this would eventually minimise wastes from waiting time and processing operations as reworks due to workers' mistakes and excessive material shortages due to inconsiderate workers' attitudes would be eliminated.

4   Group technology or focused factory techniques inherent in the JIT concept can be used to re-organize and transform the existing physical factory environments into "group" factory layouts to minimise waste due to the unnecessary and frequent transportation of partially finished goods and raw product components over long distances within the factory premises. Ideally, the workstations for the various production sub-processes like reinforcement steel bar cutting / bending; formwork assembly; concrete casting and finishing trades should be positioned

next to each other in a flow line according to work sequence within a "cell". Re-arranging the factory layouts in these cellular modes would thus facilitate the easy, smooth and efficient handling of both raw product components and partially finished goods as the distances travelled are now minimised due to the close proximities of the various work trade sub-stations.

The "kanban" or pull system

It has been observed from the survey findings that the type of material movement system used by the local prefabrication industry is dependent largely on the type of precast components being manufactured. Surprisingly, the "kanban" or pull system has been "subconsciously" used in the production of non-standardised "one-off" precast components. On the other hand, however, the push system is still widely used by the prefabrication firms in the production of standardised and commonly used precast components.

In order for the "kanban" or pull system of the JIT concept to be applied in the local prefabrication industry, certain structural modifications would need to be introduced first to improve and maximise the operating efficiencies of the various precast production sub-processes. Such modifications would include scheduling a smooth sequence of products at the final assembly line, designing appropriate layouts of machines using group technology or focused factory techniques, large scale standardisation of operations and shortening process set-up times. These modifications would seem rather difficult to accomplish in the overall construction setting at first glance. However, given the likeliness and close resemblance of the prefabrication process with the normal manufacturing production process, such modifications are likely to be achieved successfully with proper guidance, positive commitment and diligent efforts. Indeed, this fact has already been proven by the prefabrication industry using the pull system in the production of non-standardised "one-off" precast products. It is therefore recommended that such modifications be made further to the production processes in the manufacture of standardised and commonly used precast products. Attaining this would eventually transform the entire prefabrication industry into adopting solely the "kanban" or pull material movement system in their production operations.

Having outlined the feasible application of the "kanban" / pull system at the macro level, the system can also be specifically applied at the micro level as follows in the light of the survey findings:

Materials management The pull system is best applied in the context of production materials management. The idea is that the movement of various raw production components between workstations should only be effected based on the actual demands made by the "subsequent" workstation. The "preceding" workstation should then only release the raw production components based on the exact demanded quantities just-in-time to the "subsequent" workstation. No buffer stocks of component materials should be allowed to be introduced into the production flow line. This idea of the pull system should also be extended further to the procurement function of the prefabrication production process. Like material releases within the production flow line, procurement of raw production materials should only be made based on exact computed quantities to be supplied just-in-time to meet production targets for confirmed orders.

It has been highlighted earlier that at times of high production volume, there is a tendency for workers to misuse or misallocate material components meant for a particular product type for another different product. The result of this undesirable shortchange has been confusion and delays because of the misallocated material shortages encountered. Material components like reinforcement steel bars or meshes and cast-in items are the ones most often affected. The adoption of the "kanban" / pull system here would thus be most suitable to address and resolve this problem. Like the Toyota production line, "kanban" cards would be recommended for use to effect material movements between the various work stations. All material components issued or released from the central stockroom or intermediate workstations for a particular product type would then bear on their "kanban" cards the same particular product's name and production serial number. The execution of the material movement system in this way would positively eliminate the problem of misallocation of material components.

Finished goods delivery management The "kanban" / pull system can be further extended to the area of management for finished goods delivery. It has been seen previously that due to the frequently invalid work coordination schedules (insitu site and precast components installation works schedules) of most clients, some prefabricators have resorted to forceful delivery of the finished precast goods to their clients' worksites even though the insitu works at the site were not ready to receive the precast components. A feasible solution to this "conflict" would be to firstly educate and convince the client to embrace the merits of the JIT system of operation; and secondly to jointly implement with the client a goods delivery system founded on the principles of the pull system. The way to implementing this is to have the client place orders for the precast goods at a time period exactly equal to the lead time required in producing the goods. The client should of course always bear in mind that the timings for placing orders for the precast goods should be well coordinated with the actual progress of the insitu site works. In other words, the client should only "pull" the exact and right quantities of precast goods from the prefabricator just-in-time to immediately install the goods into the site works upon delivery to site. By successfully implementing this pull concept in the management of goods delivery, the problem of inventory build-ups of finished goods both for the prefabricator as well as the client would be totally eliminated. The prefabricator also do not have to forcefully deliver finished goods anymore to an "unready" client's worksite, thereby still maintaining the good prefabricator / client relationship.

Finally, it must however be pointed out at this juncture that the current contractual practice of honouring material-on-site claims in the construction industry would pose a major hindrance to the successful implementation of the "pull" system of goods delivery management outlined above. This is because at times when works coordination schedules become invalid (as they often are), clients would then tend to stockpile finished precast goods within their site boundaries and claimed for the goods as materials-on-site. This scenario would always happen especially if a large amount of physical space is available at the client's work site. When this state of events happen, the JIT system of finished goods delivery would be defeated completely.

Integrated "MRP / kanban" system One of the major drawback of the "kanban" / pull system is its lack of visibility for macro or high-level planning. The pull system is unable to translate the sales forecast into materials planning and the subsequent detailed breakdown of component requirements. On the contrary, in a push system, the master production schedule and the MRP system do the planning and the detailed materials requirements breakdown. This software also provides an inventory control system to track production components in inventory locations and all materials transactions in the factory. This part of the push system works well, but the system gets into trouble when the prefabricator cuts purchase orders to suppliers and issue work orders to the factory floor without considering the actual materials needed. Pull systems, conversely, work very well in self-adjusting the process variations once the factory's production rate is determined. The individual workstations do not need to know the complete picture to do a good job in scheduling materials through the production process.

By combining or integrating the best features of both the "kanban" and MRP systems, an effective JIT system is developed that can efficiently plan, forecast and control the materials requirements for production. The survey findings have indicated that the prefabrication industry is currently using the push / inventory control approach system for the production of standardised and commonly used precast products whereas the pull / MRP system is being used in the production of non-standardised "one-off" precast products. In view of these divided approaches used and the demerits of each individual MRP or pull system, it is recommended that the prefabrication industry should adopt the integrated "MRP / kanban" system universally for all types of precast component products in production. This integrated system would be a powerful planning and controlling tool for the future management of production operations just as it has done so for the manufacturing industry.

Figure 8.1 shows the integrated "MRP / kanban" system, highlighting the areas of cooperation between an MRP push system and a Kanban pull system. The master production schedule and the MRP system are used to do the high-level translation of the sales forecast into a production schedule and materials requirements to meet the build schedule. This information is then used to alert the suppliers and the factory of the daily parts requirements. In simple terms, the idea is to use the MRP to plan the materials requirements and to use this information as a forecast to be provided to the different supply centres. Then, using a Kanban system based on actual demand, the pull system moves the materials on the production line or pulls the materials from the suppliers at the time they are actually needed. This last activity must however be carefully coordinated so as to produce a realistic MRP output for suppliers to use this information to plan the output of their production lines. In summary, it can be said that MRP systems will be used to keep global

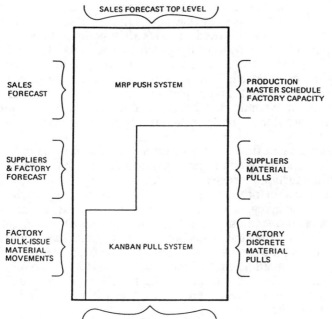

SALES FORECAST TOP LEVEL

SALES FORECAST

MRP PUSH SYSTEM

PRODUCTION
MASTER SCHEDULE
FACTORY CAPACITY

SUPPLIERS
& FACTORY
FORECAST

SUPPLIERS
MATERIAL
PULLS

FACTORY
BULK-ISSUE
MATERIAL
MOVEMENTS

KANBAN PULL SYSTEM

FACTORY
DISCRETE
MATERIAL
PULLS

MANUFACTURING PROCESS LOW LEVEL

Figure 8.1   Integrated "MRP/kanban" system

*Source: Hernandez, A. (1989), Just-In-Time manufacturing - A
practical approach, Prentice-Hall, N.J.*

control of the factory while detailed control will be achieved by JIT
approaches.

Uninterrupted work flow

In order to produce just-in-time, the JIT concept requires the production
process to be made as rationalised, simplified and synchronised as possible.
Achieving these would ensure that the work flows in the production
processes proceed with minimal interruptions. For uninterrupted flows, the
schedule for final assembly must be smoothed out. In the context of the
survey findings, this JIT principle of uninterrupted work flow can be applied
in the following manners:

Focused activities and group technology It has been highlighted in the
previous chapter that all the prefabrication firms surveyed have readily agreed
that there would be significant increases in output productivity if their
physical factory layouts could be re-arranged; particularly if the sequential
processes for a particular product type are relocated in a cell group using

147

group technology principles. The reason for this unanimous consensus was revealed from an analysis of the prefabrication firms' physical factory layouts. It has been observed that generally, process work flows in the respondents' factories followed tortuous flow paths in moving from one workstation to another. Most of the production sub-process activity centres (like steel bars storage yard, cutting and bending yard; concreting yard; finishing trades yard; etc.) are scattered away from one another. These isolated physical layout arrangements of sub-process workstations would require more movement and handling and have often resulted in site congestion problems, undesirable transportation waste, and higher production costs.

It is thus evident from the above discussion that there is indeed a great potential in applying group technology techniques to improve the physical layouts of production processes in the current prefabrication industry to bring about increases in productivity. In using the JIT approach of group technology techniques, factory layouts would need to be re-structured such that interrelated operations are grouped together in cells. This manner of locating together sequential production sub-process activities would minimise costly space and resource (particularly material handling systems) requirements. In addition, balance, synchronisation, communication enhancement, quality improvements and smooth work flow are achieved; whilst production lead times are reduced which subsequently eliminate work-in-process inventory.

Figure 8.2 shows a proposed physical factory layout designed on group technology techniques that can be recommended for implementation by prefabricators of bridge beams. (Compare Figure 5.1 which shows the typical physical factory layout representative of the bridge beams prefabricators surveyed). It can be seen that the various sub-process activity centres (with the exception of only the formwork fabrication trade) like steel bars storage; steel bars cutting and bending; steel bars fixing; modular formwork assembling and concrete casting (both on the stressing beds); finishing treatment works and finished beams storage are all arranged in a straight flow-line in a sequential order. As modular formwork systems are normally used in precast concrete components prefabrication, it is assumed here that the prefabrication of discrete modular formwork units are carried out in a separate building or that they are being supplied by externally engaged sub-contractors. The formwork yards shown in Figure 8.2 thus only serve the purpose of storing these discrete modular formwork units after being dismantled upon completion of concrete casting works. It must be pointed out here that for the proposed physical factory layout to operate efficiently and effectively, the following two facilities must be provided for sufficiently:

1   Overhead gantry cranes of sufficient capacities and operating area coverage to cover the entire physical factory layout. This would ensure total lifting services to be provided for all the production material components within the factory layout.

2   Access ways and roads of adequate sizes and number for use by

148

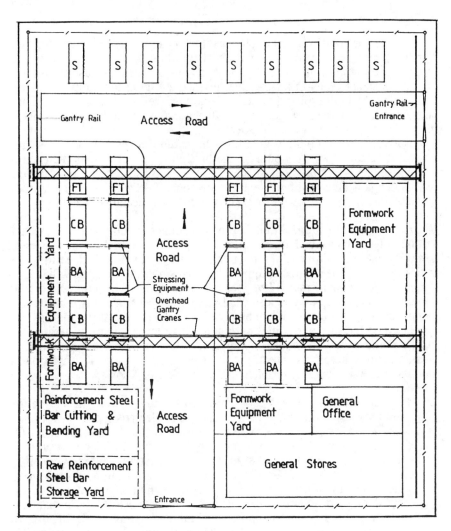

Legend:

BA - Reinforcement steel bar assembly
CB - Casting bed for bridge beam
FT - Finishing trades (eg. granolithic finish, patching works)
S - Storage of completed bridge beam

Note:

1. The entire proposed physical factory layout should be housed within covered premises.
2. Concreting works are assumed to be executed by means of automated overhead mobile gantry system.

**Figure 8.2   Proposed typical JIT based physical factory layout
for bridge beam prefabrication**

149

workmen and vehicular machineries (fork-lifts and lorry-trailers) respectively.

In a similar manner, another physical factory layout can also be proposed for implementation by prefabricators of building components. Again, the point to remember here is to separate out all the various production sub-process activities in a flow-line in a sequential order. In this way, the existing problem of utilising the same factory space for both concrete casting and finishing treatment works (as prevalent amongst current prefabricators of building components) would be solved.

Lastly, it should be highlighted that the main drawback of the proposed physical factory layouts would be the high initial capital costs incurred in setting-up such large factory spaces. Nonetheless, this should be critically weighed against the positive rate of returns in terms of increased productivity and profitability in the long term if such factory layouts are adopted.

Design for simplification Simplification constitutes an important key element of the JIT philosophy. The simplification process seeks to streamline and simplify operations for both product design and production engineering. The rationale behind the simplicity approach is that simple approaches will lead to more efficient management. The goal is to accomplish production operations which are as simple and as less costly as possible. When this is achieved, simple control schemes can then be used to control the simplified system.

Based on the survey findings pertaining to major problems of buildability in the manufacture of precast components, the need for simplification in design cannot therefore be over-emphasized. By using the JIT approach of simplicity, the buildability problem can be tackled as follows:

1   Standardisation - It has been observed that the current prefabrication industry uses too many variety of precast designs which have given rise to problems like excessive material wastages; specific need for unique formwork systems; operational problems such as difficulties in demoulding, obstructions to concrete casting, extensive set-up changeovers; handling problems like improper lifting hooks positions; etc. One way of using the JIT approach of simplicity to suppress these buildability problems is to call on the entire construction industry to adopt some significant degree of standardisation in the design of precast components. As standardisation would however result in design homogeneity and hence dullness in the aesthetical appearance of construction products, an optimum trade-off would therefore need to be struck between standardisation and varying clients' aspirations and tastes. Nonetheless, in the more affected field of building works (as compared to civil engineering works), a recommendation would be to adopt large-scale standardised designs for internally "concealed" structural components like beams, columns, slabs, staircases, partition walls, refuse chutes, water tanks, etc. whereas for the externally "exposed" architecturally aesthetic facade walls, gable end walls, parapet walls, etc., differing precast designs could be used to off-set dull appearances.

2   Production lead time - The survey findings have indicated that the excessive curing time requirements and extensive finishing treatment works are the two major factors which impinge severely on the production lead times of precast components. As one of the major benefits for the precast construction movement in the industry is speed of construction, anything that inhibits or prolongs the production cycle times of precast components are therefore highly undesirable. It is therefore of paramount importance that both the issues of excessive curing time and extensive finishing treatment works be fully addressed without further delays for the industry to achieve full support for the precast construction campaign.

Adopting the JIT approach of simplicity here to resolve the problem of long production lead times would simply mean cutting down the curing time requirements to as short a period as possible; and reducing the finishing treatment works to as little as possible. It is even better if the curing time can be cut short to only hours and the finishing treatment works reduced to zero. In short, the overall main theme to be observed would be to design for the shortest production lead time. In this aspect, it is heartening to note that the prefabrication industry had in fact to a small extent, already embarked on some active measures to cut down on requirements for curing time and finishing treatment works in its bid to shorten production lead times. Through technological advancements, new methods and materials have been used over the last four years in the prefabrication industry for the manufacture of precast components and innovative products that virtually require only hours of curing time and minimal finishing treatment works. Some well-known examples of such innovative products are lightweight blocks or partition walls made from autoclaved aerated concrete (AAC) or wood fibre concrete; and external wall panels made from carbon fibre-reinforced concrete (CFRC). These innovative products have not only better physical properties, durability and ease of workability than conventional concrete but also multiple uses as well such as in fire protection, thermal insulation, sound insulation, load-bearing, etc. The only common disadvantage of using these products is that they are not cost effective as compared to conventional precast concrete components. Generally, these products cost more to produce then conventional products. For instance, CFRC wall panels cost 30 per cent more than conventional precast concrete wall panels.

Although the current production scale of innovative precast products in the local prefabrication industry is small, nonetheless, in view of the ground-breaking effort already made by the construction industry to use such products, it is strongly recommended that the construction industry should on a larger scale further explore more opportunities, carry out extensive research works and develop more of such innovative products for use in the industry. Special efforts should be put in by all those concerned to make such innovative products as cost effective as conventional products, if not more effective. This can be made possible through the better characteristics of such innovative products such as functional performances, durability, workability, ease of installation, cost savings in erection works, etc. A markedly significant reduction in production lead times for precast components can then be achieved for the prefabrication industry.

Finally, in order to encourage the local construction industry to adopt large scale standardisation in the manufacture of precast products and in the use of more innovative products, incentive schemes drawn-up by the government (notably the CIDB) should be fully exploited by all parties in the construction process to reap maximum benefits and returns. Currently, two such incentive schemes are in place in the Singapore construction industry.

The first incentive scheme is the Buildable Appraisal System. This is an assessment system drawn up to assess designs of construction projects for buildability at the design stage. The system assesses project designs based on the degree of technical innovation and buildable features employed which would give rise to cost-effective and aesthetically appealing designs. The resultant Buildable Score will give an indication of the productivity potential on site. This system has since been used in the CIDB Best Buildable Design Award assessments introduced in 1991.

The second incentive scheme is the Product Development Assistance Scheme (PDAS). Presently, this is a financial incentive scheme administered by the Productivity Development Unit of the CIDB to help contractors increase their construction productivity and quality. The scheme provides financial assistance to encourage companies engaged in research and development of a new or substantially improved product, process or technique for use in the construction industry. Appendix 4 gives a summary of the scheme. This scheme should be fully utilised by all design consultants and / or precast components manufacturers for the research and development of more innovative precast products that could shorten production lead times.

Mechanisation and automation It has been observed that the production activities of the local prefabrication industry are generally labour intensive. Mechanical plants or equipments used on the factory floors generally serve only as material handling systems for activities such as transporting, hoisting, placing and positioning. As mentioned before, the degree of automation currently adopted by the prefabrication industry is also very low, and near to insignificant levels. As the use of appropriate machines, plants, equipments and robots would greatly help in expediting speedier and more uniform work flow in factory environments, mechanisation and automation would need to be addressed urgently.

1   Mechanisation - The survey findings have shown that the most hard pressed mechanisation problem currently faced by the prefabrication industry is the lack of good total preventive management (TPM) programmes for the various mechanised material handling systems used. This lack has caused frequent machine breakdowns, resulting in undesirable interruptions to the smooth flow of production works. In

this case, the most obvious JIT solution would be for the prefabrication firms to adopt effective TPM programmes for their fleet of machineries. By so doing, this would help to ensure that such machineries will have longer economic lives, better operating efficiencies and fewer breakdowns. Eventually, this would add up to costs savings in machineries repair works, smoother work flow, speedier production and finally good value for the capital invested.

The way to implement an effective TPM programme is to employ an "in-house" mechanic team on a permanent basis to oversee the fleet of mechanised material handling systems. In-house mechanic teams were found to be lacking amongst a majority of the prefabrication firms surveyed. These firms have merely depended on externally engaged mechanics to repair their machineries in the event of breakdowns. This sort of practice has one very big disadvantage: namely, frequent delays being incurred due to late arrivals (which can be a time lapse of days) of external mechanics thereby further prolonging machines downtimes unnecessarily. As the overhead gantry crane is the most heavily used equipment amongst the fleet of usual material handling systems, the "in-house" mechanic team will help to ensure that immediate repair works will be carried out in the events of breakdowns. Otherwise, costly disrupted production schedules would occur if external mechanics do arrive late for the repair works.

2   Automation - In the context of the prefabrication industry, automation can only take place after all production work flows are simplified to move along uniform and smooth operational lines. As discussed in the previous section, simplification of these work flows can be brought about by adopting large scale standardisation of designs to be used in the production of precast components. In this respect, given its massive public housing programmes, the HDB can play a key role in taking the lead in the construction industry by adopting large scale standardisation in precast components. It is only when a substantial degree of standardisation has been established can production activities move along standardised and smooth work flows. Only then can automation be introduced to speed up production activities and replace the presently large pool of semi-skilled foreign workers who are comparatively less productive. Automation in the JIT environment is therefore one of the last steps to be taken.

Finally, it is envisaged that future automation in the prefabrication industry can be adopted to carry out the following production sub-process activities. These activities include the installation of cast-in items by simple pick-and-place robotic equipment; form mould assembly and demoulding works; precast components casting works (especially for innovative products); and curing of finished precast components by autoclave methods.

Reduction of process set-up time In order to achieve flexibility in the manufacture of precast components, changeovers of production setting-up operations must happen swiftly and quickly. The survey findings have indicated that presently, there is very little attempts made by the local prefabrication industry in researching into ways to reduce production set-up times. Despite this, significant reduction of processes set-up times have been shown to be achievable. (two respondents firms reported 20 per cent and 30 per cent reductions in set-up times). This, together with the general consensus amongst the prefabrication industry that reduction in processes set-up times could ultimately eliminate the problem of keeping buffer stocks, strongly points to the fact that the reduction in processes set-up times is indeed a critical issue which needs to be looked further into if the industry is to reap the benefits of increased productivity.

In accordance with the survey findings pertaining to production set-up times, the JIT solutions that could be used to resolve this problem would be as follows:

1   Constructability problems - Problems like common steel bars congestion, extensive time consuming form mould assembly works (due to unique formwork systems used for non-standardised products), etc. can be resolved by encouraging designers to be more flexible in their designs. Steel bars congestion problems can be overcomed by "value-engineering" over "over-engineered" designs; and extensive formwork systems can be eliminated by using simple standardised precast designs.

2   Repetitive mistakes - Mistakes often made by newly recruited workers in steel bars fixing and formwork assembly works can be overcome by firstly offering proper training to these workers before they commence works on the production floor. Experiences gained through the learning curve would greatly help these workers to handle their tasks with better care and finer precision.

3   Demoulding problems - Where it is not possible to use standardised precast designs (particularly for export) and unique and awkward formwork systems have to be used, demoulding problems can be overcome by incorporating flexible designs in the formwork structural system. For instance, the form mould system can be designed to open up in various planes and directions instead of only a few planes. This will greatly help to ease demoulding problems.

Finally, the JIT approach to small lots production can also be further explored to substantially reduce process set-up times through minimal changeover operations. However, small lots production should be considered critically against economics of production and the varying requirements of clients over time.

Total quality control concept

It is heartening to note from the survey findings that the local prefabrication industry is aware of the total quality control (TQC) concept and has sought to recognise SS ISO 9000 certification as an indispensable and effective means of improving their operational efficiencies. Besides furnishing documented proof of the prefabrication firms' capabilities and efficiencies, the SS ISO 9000 certification scheme can also go a long way towards raising the prefabrication industry's standing in Singapore and abroad. With quality providing the extra edge in today's competitive business environment, the prefabrication firms are confident that SS ISO 9000 certification will adequately equip them for export markets in the newly emerging economies like China, Vietnam, Cambodia, Myanmar, etc.

Despite the above awareness towards certification to international quality standards, the survey findings have nonetheless pointed out some crucial quality-related problems which still persist amongst some of the prefabrication firms; particularly those who are intending to undergo the certification process as well as those who have never thought about the quality certification scheme. These problems include the absence of "in-house" quality inspection teams and quality checkings "at source"; poor workmanship quality; shoddy implementation of quality control circle (QCC) concept; and quality defects in design-related informations. The TQC concept of the JIT system can in these instances be applied to "fine-tune" the understanding and practice of quality assurance in the local prefabrication industry and assist all prefabrication firms to eventually attain SS ISO 9000 certification. The JIT recommendations pertaining to the TQC concept are as follows:

Quality at source The traditional approach of inspecting quality of production sub-components at their points of usage as currently practised by the local prefabrication industry must be eliminated. In its place, the JIT approach to inspecting quality of sub-components at their source of production should be implemented. This "quality at source" concept emphasizes two imperatives, viz: producing right the first time and making "producers" at the sub-components production source responsible for detecting and correcting quality defects. "Producers" are expected to make sub-components right the first time and to prevent their qualities from deviating too far from specified requirements. By so doing, this would eliminate the practice of "downstream" inspections which are to be replaced with better quality control at source. The quality of all sub-components are determined at the instant the items are made, and no amounts of further inspections are needed.

In the manufacture of precast components, manufacturing quality control at source can happen in the following ways: reinforcement steel bars can be quality checked in the bar bending yard before they are transferred to the steel bar assembly yard; extensive trial tests for concrete design mixes can be carried out at the concrete batching plants before mass volume of demand orders begins; steel form moulds can be checked in the fabrication yard (either "in-plant" yard or external sub-contractor's yard) before their assembly works at the casting beds; cast-in items can be quality checked at the suppliers' warehouses before distribution to prefabricators; etc. Of course, all these processes can only take place effectively and efficiently after JIT education has been extended to all the parties concerned and strong support for JIT management demonstrated by them.

Quality control circles (QCC's) The continuous search for quality improvements through participation in QCC's must be further reinforced throughout the prefabrication industry. The precast component manufacturing factory does provide an excellent environment for the implementation of QCC's to improve the quality of production. Likened to the manufacturing sector, precast components manufacturing operations are generally characterised by a reasonably stable and cohesive workforce and long term tasks. These conditions can offer the environment and time frame appropriate for QCC's to make thorough analyses of the quality problems at hand. Through effective workings of QCC's, current problems such as long process set-up times; poor housekeeping practices; excessive material wastages; poor communication systems; etc. can be solved creatively to improve productivity performance.

Total quality management Total quality management (TQM) is that aspect of the overall management function that determines and implements the quality policy across all organisational activities. Rosenfeld, Warszawski and Laufer (1991) have shown that through effective implementation of TQM, substantial improvements in quality can be achieved amongst construction companies in areas such as waiting times, equipment utilisation, materials waste, project duration, workers' safety, work quality, workers' morale and communication. Similarly, the TQM concept can also be applied to the prefabrication industry to improve qualities in workmanship and design-related information. The recommendations pertaining to TQM are as follows:

1   Workmanship quality - The three-pronged approach suggested by the CIDB on quality control can help to alleviate this problem in the prefabrication industry. These three strategies are proper supervision of work, training and retraining of workers, and use of proper construction and checking techniques.

Supervision and quality control - Proper and sufficient supervision of work is most important in producing good quality work. Generally, better quality products can be delivered where close supervision and continuous checking of the works are emphasized. Sufficient supervision and checking can reduce costly errors. Mistakes are also detected and rectified early. In the long run, better quality final products are made. Workmanship is dependent on the capability, aptitude and temperament of an individual. The achievement of consistently good standards from a worker represents one of the major tasks to be attained by site supervisors. Until today, prefabricators still adopt the practice of sub-letting various work activities to sub-contractors. While this has very definite advantages for the prefabricator, many difficulties remain, particularly those of getting the right number of men on site and doing the right job to an acceptable standard. The prefabricator still carries the overall responsibility for the subcontractors' workmanship. Prefabricators should ensure that measures are taken for quality control when subcontractors are employed, and should take positive steps to encourage their staff to be quality conscious in order to attain higher quality in their work.

Training of workers - Employment of tradesmen should be encouraged because they have been through a trade apprenticeship and have specialised in it. Good tradesmen, however, are always in short supply and they tend to move from site to site, especially during a construction boom, to obtain the most favourable employment terms with each move. The importance of training cannot be overlooked. Trained and skilled workers normally produce better quality work. Today, there are more facilities for training than at any time in the history of the construction industry in Singapore. Training can be in the form of formal classroom teaching, informal on-site or on-the-job training. Continuous on-the-job training is of utmost importance in producing good quality work. Prefabricators should take the initiative to ensure that their workers receive proper training (e.g. tradesmen certification courses conducted by the Construction Industry Training Institute) so that quality becomes part and parcel of their job.

Proper construction and checking techniques - Proper construction techniques and equipment are important in producing quality. For example, improper placing and compaction of concrete could result in segregation and, subsequently, honeycombs. Plastering not carried out according to specifications could result in hollow spots. To check for defects, the use of proper equipment is important. For example, the "CONQUAS rod" used by the CIDB can be used to detect hollow tiles in external wall facade of precast components. When struck across the surface of the wall panel, it is able to detect hollowness through variation in the sound produced. It can thus be used to carry out continuous checking soon after a wall panel has been tiled.

In this way, a prefabricator or his subcontractors can initiate at the earliest possible time the necessary rectification work and improve their work as a project progresses. At the same time, they can also investigate the causes of such defects.

2   Quality of design-related information - Design can exert a great influence on the speed and quality of precast component manufacturing. The survey findings have shown that a significant proportion of precast component manufacturing problems are associated with design-related information. Undesirable complications from defective designs have been reported in various ways, viz. contractual claims arising from vague or inadequate specifications and construction detailings in drawings; delays due to inconsistencies in the production of design information and documentation (especially for "design and build" projects); and constructability problems due to a lack of concern for the practical aspects of buildability.

In suppressing the above design-related problems in the JIT environment, the TQM concept embracing quality assurance schemes should be strongly recommended for implementations by all parties (namely, designers, contracting organisations, clients, and precast component manufacturers) to improve the overall quality and productivity performance of the prefabrication industry. Two suggested schemes that can be applied to improve the quality of design-related information are discussed below.

Value engineering scheme - Vagueness or insufficient information in specifications and construction drawings can be significantly reduced by engaging a competent value engineering team to take a second look and review into first-hand design information. In the context of the Singapore construction industry, the professional accredited checker can take on this additional role.

Design-and-build contractual procurement - Constructability problems inherent in "non-buildable" designs can be resolved by adopting more design-and-build procurement methods for precast component manufacturing. This scheme would of course require that developer clients are willing to procure projects through design-and-build packages and that precast component manufacturers possess their own "in-house" design capability and resources. As the constructor (in this case the prefabricator) will be involved in the construction process during the early stages of design works, likely constructability problems arising from unbuildable features can be detected early.

Top management commitment and employee involvement

As a successful JIT environment can only be achieved with the cooperation and involvement of everyone in the organisation, management and workers should view each other as "partners in business" rather than "hierarchical discriminates". Only then can productivity and quality improvements be achieved through the close working relationships between management and workers in the prefabrication industry.

Top management commitment constitutes the most important driving force behind any JIT implementation scheme. As top management forms the major decision-makers and "main pillars" of any prefabrication firms, all JIT implementation schemes would in no time collapsed if proper and firm commitment as well as support from management are not forthcoming.

Wantuck (1989) expressed the view that blue collar workers are the most undeveloped source of potential improvement because they usually represent about 80 per cent of the total personnel of an organisation and they are on the production floor 99 per cent of the time. This observation also appears to be applicable in the prefabrication industry which is largely characterised by labour- intensive operations.

In the light of the survey findings, the JIT principle of top management commitment and employee involvement can be applied to raise productivity performance in the following manners:

Top management commitment The research findings have shown that all the prefabrication firms surveyed would only adopt the JIT system in their manufacturing environments if the system is proven to be viable to improve productivity and profitability. Given this favourable response, for a start, the prefabrication industry should offer themselves an opportunity to try out the implementation of JIT systems in their manufacturing environments. The chances of successful implementation are great if proper, diligent and committed steps are taken. However, it should be pointed out that top management must be willing and committed to accept some fundamental changes in their factory environments using the JIT system. For example, management must get acquainted with changes like stockless production; operational practice of TQM (for those firms who have yet to practise quality assurance); increased delegation of responsibilities to line workers; single suppliers sources; "pull" / kanban material movement systems; etc.

Lastly, to get the implementation of JIT going in the local prefabrication industry, the best way forward is to first obtain the firm commitment from some of the prefabrication firms surveyed to change their "uncovered / exposed" production areas to "covered" ones (to ward off the effects of inclement weather); and to change their existing physical factory layouts for production processes into suggested JIT based ones using group technology principles.

Employee involvement The survey findings have shown that the current labour situation in the local prefabrication industry is characterised by problems such as absence of multi-skilled workers; absence of "before-job" training for new recruits of sub-contractors'; high staff turnover rate at first line supervisory and middle management levels; and the issue of foreign workers. In view of these problems, the application of JIT would require some radical changes to be made in the organisation of the labour force in the prefabrication factory. These radical changes would include:

1   Multi-function workers - In line with changing the physical factory layouts of production processes into cellular arrangements using group technology principles, the JIT concept requires multi-function workers who can operate effectively several different trades within a cellular group of production activities. This calls for a leaner flexible workforce to replace the currently large number of single-function workers. Moving towards this flexible workforce system will thus require changing the way the entire labour force is organised, selected, trained and rewarded. Workers must therefore be firstly trained or retrained to become more flexible in the tasks that they can perform. For instance, a bar bender should be trained not only to do cutting and bending of steel bars but also formwork assembly and concreting works as well. In addition to their principal tasks, workers are also expected to perform other "secondary" duties like quality inspections at source; and plant, equipment and tools maintenance. Overall, this would require a general upgrading of the skill levels of prefabrication operatives.

2   Education and training - The JIT approach calls on all workers (direct employment as well as sub-contractors' workers) to be educated and trained on the basic JIT principles of waste elimination, worker's responsibility for performing work, ensuring zero defect quality and visibility management. In addition to their greater responsibilities for production, workers are also taught to take initiative in improving the production process. Through QCC's, suggestion schemes, and other

159

forms of participation, workers are encouraged to offer suggestions for improvements to the processes of production. The capability of the worker is thus used to a much greater extent in the JIT system than in traditional production approaches.

With the current labour situation in the local prefabrication industry, it would be extremely difficult to undertake a major revamp based on JIT principles for the organising, training and education of the entire workforce. The main drawback would be the large pool of foreign workers. The entire workforce (with the exception of "kepalas", foremen and line supervisors) of the local prefabrication industry is almost made up of foreign workers of various nationalities who are generally illiterate or lowly educated and speak different languages. Even with good JIT education, these workers may not be able to comprehend the full workings and benefits of the JIT system because of the numerous communication barriers. Rather than understand what stockless production and quality assurance mean to the production process, most of these workers are only interested in performing their daily tasks and be rewarded with the right wages. These workers know very well that their employment period here is only temporary and for a maximum period of four years. After this period, they would have to be repatriated to their homelands. Therefore, most of these workers would not be interested or at all concerned with what JIT means.

In view of the above issue of foreign workers, a better JIT strategy in the medium term would be to educate and train all employees only up to first line supervisor or sub-contractors' "kepalas" / foremen levels on the full workings of the JIT system. Since almost all of these personnel are of local or neighbouring Malaysian nationalities (with similar cultural affinities), there exists good communication channels necessary for effective teaching and training to take place. Comprehension and appreciation of the JIT system would be more effective for these groups of employees, thereby bringing about higher chances of productivity improvement through the JIT philosophy.

There is also a need to reward the workforce, which is largely made up of foreign workers at the production line level, with monetary incentives over and above their normal wages for good performance. Because of these workers' general inabilities and difficulties in understanding the JIT system, this strategy would be effective to "push" production operatives to work harder for better productivity output. Good performances may be assessed based on criteria such as punctuality, efficiency, working attitudes, responsibility, intelligence, diligence and initiative. This strategy may increase production costs at first glance but should be offset by gains in higher productivity.

3 Career prospects and flexi-wage system - One solution to the problem of high turnover rate for staff at the supervisory and middle management levels in the prefabrication industry is to offer these categories of employees a working environment with good career prospects. An environment which offers good opportunities for personnel development and advancement should be created. This can

take place constantly through formal teaching, on-the-job training, workshops, seminars, etc. for upgrading their knowledge and skills.

At the same time, to curb rampant "job-hopping", the prefabrication industry should embark on an employee renumeration scheme based on the flexi-wage system. In replacing the current rewarding system which is based on a fixed salary and / or overtime renumeration, prefabricators should perhaps consider offering profit-sharing and other flexible performance bonuses over and above their competitive salaries.

Supplier and client relationships

Supplier relationships The principle of JIT with respect to supplier relations can be interpreted to mean the procurement and utilisation of the right materials, in the quantity as needed by the next activity, just-in-time before it is needed, and at the closest possible place to the point of use. Materials may have to be delivered on the same day or the day before they are used on site. (Lim and Low, 1992)

In the light of the survey findings, the JIT strategy of fostering a long-term, trusted and profitable working relationship between prefabricators and their suppliers would be appropriate to overcome most of the suppliers-associated problems currently faced by the prefabrication industry. This JIT strategy is particularly applicable in materials management. Some recommendations based on this JIT principle are outlined below:

1   Selection criteria - The prefabrication industry should place an important emphasis on "quality" when selecting suppliers. Quality of purchased supplies was given a lower priority than "price" and "on-time deliveries" amongst the criteria used in the selection of suppliers by the prefabrication firms surveyed. Whilst it is comforting to note that the prefabrication industry is currently beefing up its efforts to attain quality certification for its finished precast products, it is surprising to note that the industry had ignored the important quality aspect at the supplier end. As an estimated 50 per cent of a firm's quality problems are caused by defective purchased materials (Lascelles and Dale, 1990), the quality of purchased supplies is therefore critical to the quality of the firm's finished products.

In view of the competitive business environment, the "price" for a particular sub-component would be more or less fixed at a certain level given the competition that exists today in a majority of the maturing trades. Also, "lead time" and "on-time deliveries" (both of which are interrelated) would also be more or less the same given the fact that most purchased supplies for the local prefabrication industry are bought from local suppliers. In the context of the local prefabrication industry, "quality" would be the overriding and governing criterion in the selection exercise for suppliers.

2   Single supplier sourcing - Instead of the current multi-suppliers sourcing scheme practised by most local prefabrication firms, the

prefabrication industry should consider trying out the single supplier sourcing scheme based on the JIT approach for some of its purchases of production raw materials and sub-components. The single supplier sourcing scheme can be applied for the following raw materials and / or sub-components.

Concrete - Due to the presently intense price competition in the local market, prices for the constituents of concrete like cement, sand, aggregates, admixtures, etc. are more or less fixed with minimal price differentials between different suppliers. For those prefabrication firms (mainly bridge beam prefabricators) who do not possess "in-house" concrete batching plants, prices for the supply of ready-mixed concrete from external sources are also very competitive and more or less the same. As such, in any of these cases, single sources of supply are possible if the suppliers can offer good quality and on-time deliveries for their purchases on a long term basis.

Reinforcement steel bars - This item has the greatest potential of being supplied single-sourced. As prices for steel bars are regulated and controlled by the National Iron and Steel Mills (NISM) in the local market, all appointed supplier agents of NISM would charge the same prices for steel bars. The only difference is in the quantum of discounts allotted to any sales transaction. By purchasing single sourced on a long term basis, single suppliers are bound to offer good discounts, efficient services, small lots deliveries, etc. in good faith.

Cast-in items - Cast-in items like architectural tiles, window frames, mounting brackets, prestressing tendons, connecting hooks, etc. also lend themselves to be suitably purchased from single supplier sources (either locally or overseas). This of course only works well if single suppliers are engaged on a long-term basis and can offer the right prices and credit terms; good quality of conformance; timely deliveries; etc. in accordance with the JIT system.

3   Local and "in-plant" supply stores - This JIT approach would need no further emphasis as most of the prefabrication firms are purchasing their supplies from local suppliers. Given Singapore's excellent telecommunication facilities and infrastructural system, there is virtually no major problem with the logistics aspect of local supplies made out to local prefabrication firms.

However, emphasis would need to be further reinforced at the more micro level of "in-plant" supply stores for the entire prefabrication industry. The "in-plant" supply stores concept can be used for the following selective supplies of both tangible material components and intangible services normally required in the manufacture of precast concrete products.

Concrete - All prefabrication firms should be recommended to set-up their own "in-house" concrete batching plants. This is especially so for those firms who use a variety of concrete mix designs (like normal concrete, lightweight concrete, wood fibre concrete, etc.) for their production works. Particularly, this recommendation of "in-house" concrete batching plant should first be applied to the four bridge beam prefabricators who do not presently possess any such plant. In addition to giving greater flexibility to the timing of orders, the ownership of concrete batching plants also offers better quality control at source, long term economies of scale and elimination of wasteful activity like unnecessarily long waiting times.

Form moulds - All prefabrication firms should engage either a team of directly employed workforce or sub-contractor to be stationed "in-factory" for the primary purpose of fabricating all necessary steel form moulds for the various designs of precast component production. The sub-contractor gang should be recommended for those prefabrication firms who have high production volumes for a substantial time period, say one to two years. In the case of the directly employed gang, and in line with the JIT strategy, these workers can be put to other functional uses like bending steel bars, casting concrete, etc. during times of low production volumes.

Transportation haulage facilities - As these facilities are necessary for delivering the finished products to clients, prefabrication firms are therefore recommended to own their fleet of transportation vehicles (comprising prime-movers, low bed trailers, lorry-cranes, etc.) to ensure the timely delivery of goods to clients. This is especially so for the bigger prefabrication firms who manufacture a large variety of precast components for a large clientele base. Ownership of these transportation haulage facilities would be economically justifiable in the long term as the frequent and intensive delivery demands for finished goods inventories can then be efficiently met, thereby eliminating undesirable problems of untimely deliveries, wasteful waiting times, inventories stockpile build-ups, escalating production costs, etc.

4   Delivery mode systems - The JIT recommendation of effecting supplier deliveries in small lots quantities at frequent intervals should be further extended to other production material sub-components like reinforcement steel bars / wire meshes, cast-in items, etc. apart from concrete and steel form moulds. (The latter two items are already reportedly being supplied in small lots quantities at frequent intervals in the local prefabrication industry). This approach would be highly successful if prefabricators and their suppliers fully understand the workings of the JIT system and both parties are firmly committed to work closely in accordance with JIT principles.

In this instance, it should be highlighted that there is tremendous potential in using the JIT principle of "kanban" / pull system to move materials from suppliers to the prefabricators' factories. Prefabricators could use "kanban" cards to pull the needed materials (be it reinforcement steel bars or cast-in items) in the right quantities in small lots just-in-time for their various production requirements. By moving materials from suppliers in small lots at frequent and regulated intervals, the need for stockpiling buffer inventories for such materials would eventually be eliminated totally.

5   Duration of purchase agreement - The "current market practice" of

entering into short-term (less than six months) purchase agreement contracts between prefabricators and their suppliers should be abolished. In its place, prefabricators should encourage their suppliers to enter into longer term (say, two years and above) purchase contracts in order to reap the full benefits of a valuable long term and profitable working relationship. There should be no major hindrances to this JIT orientated arrangement if the supplier networks are all proven and reliable.

Client relationships As clients are both the creator of demand and also the paymaster in all business transactions, good client relationships are therefore by far the most important and precious type of relationships which all prefabricators should strive to attain with their clients. However, in view of the survey findings pertaining to client-associated problems in the prefabrication industry, it is crucial for both prefabricators and clients to play their respective roles well enough for good long-term client relationships to be built upon JIT principles. Some suggested recommendations are as follows:

1   Prefabricators' role - Refering to the earlier case of the bridge beam prefabricator who used to place priority in manufacturing beams for its sister company at the expense of delays to other contracting organisation clients, prefabricators should not indulge in this "priority game" when it comes to accepting prefabrication contracts from a large pool of clients. Delays in finished goods deliveries due to the "cannibalising" of priorities would eventually jeopardise and damage any good working relationships with existing and prospective clients. On the contrary, prefabricators should exercise fairness in their dealings with clients. All clients, regardless of their backgrounds, should be entertained on a "first come - first serve" basis in relation to production works scheduling. Also, prefabricators should be advised to set a limit for the maximum quantum of jobs they can handle at any one time in order not to tarnish their corporate image when finished goods cannot be delivered in the times stipulated.

2   Clients' role - Refering to client-related problems like invalid production schedules, inaccurate site works schedule, reluctance in accepting finished goods, poor works coordination, etc.; there is no doubt that JIT education would also need to be extended to cover clients as well as the prefabrication firms and their suppliers. To resolve these problems, the JIT approach would require clients to play the following roles.

Invalid client's schedules - To minimise the disastrous effects of invalid clients' schedules, the JIT strategy of "pull" system can be used by clients as a kind of ordering system to order the commencement of production works in the prefabricators' factories. Instead of furnishing to the prefabricator a master delivery schedule of precast components for an entire construction project at the time of signing the prefabrication contract, clients should adopt the practice of "phase ordering" for precast components production in line with their insitu works schedule on-site. In other words, clients should only order the right quantities of precast products each time which are required for each phase of the completed construction works on-site. Clients could do this by timing an order based on a time frame equivalent to the lead times required for the precast products production. Of course, it could be argued that it is extremely difficult to take order in line with the production lead times given the complexity and irregular lead times at the prefabricator's factory production floor. Nonetheless, this approach would be feasible if a JIT educated client is to work closely with a JIT based prefabricator who has already successfully streamlined and regulated his production lead times.

Works coordination - Clients should engage a team of competent and efficient works or project coordinators to coordinate on their behalf the various work interfaces between the prefabricator and their project consultants. Matters pertaining to the clarification of technical discrepancies in drawings and of vague and unclear specifications, arranging for inspection checkings, expediting approval for proposed construction methods, etc. would need to be quickly and effectively coordinated to prevent any interruptions to the smooth workflow of precast production operations. In particular, important emphasis should be focused on coordination works for "design and build" projects whereby the timely issuance of approved construction drawings is critical to the timely production of precast components necessary for just-in-time installation works at clients' construction sites.

Stock taking - In situations where the progress of insitu works at clients' construction sites is lagging behind the production schedules of precast components in the factories, clients should be encouraged to take stock of the finished precast products in order to free the prefabricators the costly dilemma of holding such undelivered stocks of finished precast goods. It would be justifiable for clients to initiate such stock-taking actions as they could subsequently recover the costs of such precast goods through progressive "material-on-site" claims which are normally permissible under many forms of standard contracts. By working in-line with the JIT approach of valuing the relationship between prefabricators and clients, prefabricators would not need to forcefully deliver finished precast goods to reluctant clients who wish to delay the acceptance of such goods due to delays in the progress of their insitu works. From the clients' viewpoint, the only drawback that would hinder them from the stock taking action will be the availability of physical site space required to stockpile the finished precast components. It would seem that clients undertaking civil engineering construction projects will be better placed to initiate stock takings of finished precast products than those clients undertaking building construction projects. This is because surplus and free physical spaces are much more available in civil engineering construction sites than in the normally congested building worksites.

As with all good philosophies, the JIT philosophy also stresses the importance of upholding the continuous improvement theme at all times in its working environment. Dubbed the "kaizen" concept by the Japanese, the continuous improvement theme is both a vital catalyst force and "watchdog" control instrument that helps a JIT organisation to scale further new heights in its achievements or to prevent the firm's performance from deteriorating back into a state when JIT was not yet introduced.

Based on the survey findings, the continuous improvement theme of the JIT philosophy can be used to promote productivity in the local prefabrication industry as follows:

Productivity performance assessment The low level of productivity in the local prefabrication industry must be addressed urgently if the industry is to uphold the main theme of continual productivity improvements. Conservative "first generation" owners of prefabrication firms (the majority of whom are typically lowly educated or illiterate) should be guided to understand and accept innovative ways of managing their businesses in today's competitive business world market. In particular, this group of prefabricators should be steered away from their traditional practice of only assessing their "profit and loss" financial statements for profits whilst totally ignoring productivity issues. This is because profitability figures alone would be misleading without considering the productivity factor. For instance, a prefabrication firm can attain the same profitability level as another prefabrication firm over a shorter time frame by manufacturing at twice the productivity rate as the latter firm.

In addressing the low level of productivity and management participation in the prefabrication industry, the following two-pronged approach is recommended:

1   CIDB productivity assessment scheme - The assessment scheme set up by the CIDB to monitor the productivity performance of the local prefabrication industry should be expanded to include other useful indicators of productivity; for example: labour productivity for different work trades. In addition to this, the CIDB will also need to take the lead in transferring the necessary "know-hows" of productivity management to the prefabrication industry. Transfers of such knowledge concerning productivity management can be done through the organisation of compulsory teaching programmes; workshops, seminars; etc. for the participation of the entire prefabrication industry.

2   Government incentives - In addition to launching the above productivity assessment scheme on a larger scale, the government should also come forward to play a major role in helping the local prefabrication industry boost its productivity performance. The government could do this by way of offering incentives to prefabrication firms who excel in their productivity performance. Incentives can be in the forms of reduced corporate tax rates; subsidies

for employees' works training schemes; reduced levies for foreign workers; etc.

Concerted industry effort In order to promote better buildability in the construction industry, the various parties (namely owners, consultants, contractors and suppliers) to the construction process should come forward to set standardisation rules for the wider use of precast components. In this direction, to rationalise construction operations, the two concepts of standardisation and modular coordination should be given further consideration and emphasis for effective utilisation.

However, as standardisation would lead to aesthetical homogeneity of the constructed products, the differing aspirations and tastes of owners would be a major hindering force towards the achievement of the standardisation movement. Nonetheless, individual preferences should be conditioned by the economic benefits that can be reaped through successful standardisation practices.

High value-added prefabrication manufacturing The prefabrication industry should gradually transform its labour intensive production operations into one of high value-added manufacturing activities using automation. This move should be expedited simultaneously with the above call on the prefabrication industry to practise broad based standardisation in the use of precast components for construction works. It is only through this establishment of broad based standardisation in the prefabrication industry that high level automated manufacture of precast products can be made economically justifiable. The two issues of standardisation and automation should therefore be developed hand-in-hand and integrated slowly into the construction process for precast components. The eventual achievement of a higher value-added precast manufacturing environment would certainly be a welcoming solution to the current labour intensive nature of the industry who relies on a large pool of foreign workers.

Addressing unresolved problems The current hordes of unresolved structural performance and manufacturing process related problems pertaining to precast construction should lead to opportunities for more research and development works to be promoted within the prefabrication industry to continually improve and further develop the science of precast construction. Innovative solutions would need to be developed to resolve structural performance problems like precast joint failures and water seepages; and manufacturing process problems like the requirements for long curing times and extensive finishing treatment works. These research and development efforts could be jointly expedited through associations of prefabricators and institutions of higher learnings; periodic workshops; technological seminars; study group exchange programmes; dialogues; etc.

However, it should be noted that the main resistance to promoting innovative changes would be the inherent selfishness concerning "trade secrets" prevalent in the industry. This is evident from the unwillingness of some respondent firms to release technical information on successful process set-up time reductions and also on the fact that no cameras were allowed during all the factory visits made in this research study.

Proposed framework

The foregoing discussions have outlined the feasible applications of the JIT concept in the local prefabrication industry. From this, it can be envisaged that for a good start, the best JIT framework that can be proposed for the promotion of the JIT concept in the local prefabrication industry would undoubtedly be a framework built on the eight fundamental principles of the JIT philosophy. Figure 8.3 shows diagrammatically the proposed JIT framework for pioneering the JIT campaign in the local prefabrication industry.

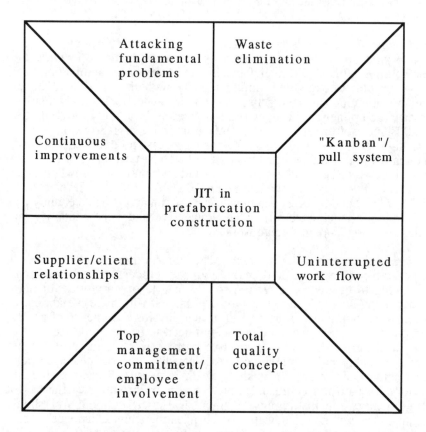

Figure 8.3 Proposed JIT framework for the prefabrication industry

168

Limitations of study

The opinion type of exploratory research employed here for this research study is not without its limitations. Its main limitations are as follows:

Methodological deficiencies

The research work may suffer from methodological deficiencies such as:

1   Biasness inherent in the design of survey instruments. For example in this case, the questionnaire has been designed to "fit into the JIT framework".

2   Systematic bias in the way in which the respondents answered the questions, for instance bias between favourable or unfavourable, or answering questions which the respondents do not quite understand at all.

3   Systematic bias in the administration of the survey instruments such as the role of the interviewer and the spontaneous reactions of the respondents.

Unstable opinions

Opinions of respondents are highly subjective and may be unstable over time. This may affect the development of general inferences or conclusions.

Difficult group dynamics

It is often difficult to capture the opinions of a group of respondents (in cases where the number of interviewees is more than two) or analyse their dynamics in the process.

Recommendations for further research

In view of the limited scope of this study which focuses only on the local "off-site" prefabrication industry, it is pertinent to recommend further JIT-based research studies in other facets of construction works. This is to enable the JIT concept to be promoted widely and strategically applied in the entire construction industry to improve productivity in the near future. The areas of construction works that can be recommended for further JIT-based research studies are as follows:

At the macro level

1   General construction works, i.e. traditional construction management of projects.

2   "On-site" prefabrication works, i.e. manufacturing of precast components in a temporary "in-plant" factory set up within the project site where the precast products are to be installed.

3   Specialist sub-contractor works, for example: structural steel fabrication works, mechanical and electrical engineering works, architectural finishing works, landscaping works, etc.

At the micro level

1   Productivity studies using specific types of indicators. Productivity indicators used can be in the following forms: capital, labour, machinery or total factor.

2   Quantitative productivity studies relating to cost economics based on specific types of indicators.

3   Application of operational research techniques such as queuing theory and transportation modelling to secure a better understanding of how the JIT philosophy may be operationalised in practice.

Conclusion

The survey findings and their subsequent analysis in the light of the eight fundamental JIT principles have strongly indicated that there is indeed vast potential for applying the JIT philosophy to improve productivity in the local "off-site" prefabrication industry. The hypothesis postulated in Chapter 1 can therefore be supported.

As the issue of productivity improvement is of prime national concern to the entire construction industry, favourable consideration should therefore be given to firstly launch a JIT productivity movement in the local "off-site" prefabrication industry as some form of a "kick-off" pilot project. The reason for targetting the "off-site" prefabrication industry for such a pilot project is that if a major and significant productivity improvement is to happen in the construction sector, it has to happen first in the prefabrication industry given its closest resemblance to the manufacturing sector, where the JIT philosophy originates, as compared to other areas of construction works. The highly possible successful outcome of such pilot projects would thus lend substantial weight and support to future productivity improvement projects in other more difficult areas like traditional cast insitu construction works and "on-site" prefabrication works.

However, to achieve a successful and productive outcome for JIT application in the "off-site" prefabrication industry, collaborative and concerted efforts must be exerted by all parties to the construction process in good faith. Clients, consultants, contractors and suppliers alike must learn to understand the JIT system and be willing to adopt and apply JIT principles in every facets of their daily undertakings. Wide ranging issues like the low standardisation of current prefabrication production; the frequently invalid clients' schedule; technical issues concerning joint technology, water seepage problems, long curing times and excessive requirements for finishing treatment works to precast components should be brought forward to be addressed and resolved at the industry level. Only then, can the JIT approach to improving productivity in manufacturing be translated fundamentally into a "Build-In-Time" concept for the construction industry. This will ultimately help all Singapore construction-related companies to boost their "external wings" to export construction services to neighbouring emerging economies in line with the government's "regionalisation drive" strategy.

APPENDIX 1

(Your response to this survey will be held in the strictest confidence. Please mail your completed questionnaire in the pre-paid envelope attached herewith. Thank you for your co-operation.)

A. AWARENESS OF "JUST-IN-TIME" (JIT)

1. Have you ever heard of the existence of the JIT philosophy as applied in the field of manufacturing management?

   [ ] Yes

   [ ] No

2. If yes, do you currently practise any form of the JIT system in your manufacturing operations?

   Please state briefly the form of JIT system practised.

   _____

   _____

   _____

B. MANUFACTURING PROCESS ANALYSIS

1. Please state which of the following manufacturing planning system(s) you are currently adopting:

   [ ] Inventory control system

   [ ] Materials Requirements Planning System (MRP)

   [ ] Manufacturing Resource Planning System (MRP II)

   [ ] Others. Please specify _____

2. If your answer to Questions B(1) above is either MRP or MRP II, please state whether you are encountering any problems with regards to the effectiveness of the MRP systems from the following areas:

   [ ] Poor inventory level accuracy

   [ ] Inaccurate lead times

   [ ] Inaccurate bill of materials

   [ ] Poor "Master Production Scheduling"

   [ ] Usage of obsolete data (for eg. cancelled orders)

172

3. How many different product lines of precast concrete components do your firm currently manufacture?

No. of different product lines: _____

4. How do you rate the existing flow line movements of your various manufacturing processes in your factory?

[ ] Very good

[ ] Good

[ ] Satisfactory

[ ] Poor

5. Do you think there will be an increase in output productivity if the physical factory layouts of your various manufacturing processes are re-arranged, for eg. by locating sequential processes for a particular product in a cell group?

[ ] Yes

[ ] No

6. Please draw a sketch of the physical factory layout for all your manufacturing processes in the space provided in Appendix A attached with this questionnaire.

7. Please tick the type of material handling systems used in your manufacturing operations.

[ ] Overhead gantry crane   [ ] Mobile truck-mounted hydraulic crane

[ ] Lorry-mounted crane   [ ] Dumper

[ ] Fork-lift   [ ] Others. Please specify _____

8. Please state the type of obstructions that often hamper the peak performance of your material handling systems.

[ ] Machine system breakdown

[ ] Movement obstruction caused by congested and insufficient access routes

9. Do you practise keeping a reasonable level of buffer (safety) stock for your various product lines or strictly manufacture exactly to customized orders (ie. no buffer stock)?

[ ] Keeping buffer stocks

[ ] Manufacturing to exact orders

[ ] Mixed practice of buffer stocks and exact orders

10. Is it normally true that buffer stocks would only be kept for commonly used products (like road kerbs, precast drains, etc.) and not for "one-off" products (like bridge beams)?

[ ] True

[ ] No

173

11. Given the relationship between process set-up time and buffer stocks, do you think that if the set-up times for your various product processes can be reduced substantially, you could ultimately do away with keeping buffer stocks for all your product lines?

[　]　Yes

[　]　No

12. Have management ever attempted to research into innovative and better ways to reduce the various set-up times for your different product lines?

[　]　Yes

[　]　No

[　]　Never thought about it before

13. If yes, please indicate the average reduction in set-up times for your various product lines that have been achieved.

Average per cent reduction: _____ per cent

14. For the precasters in the construction industry, preventive maintenance management is achieved by carrying out adequate and proper maintenance to all machineries, equipment and tools that support the various production processes (for eg. maintaining fork-lifts, cranes, steel moulding formwork equipment systems, concrete vibrators, etc.).

Please indicate how well do you practise such preventive maintenance management system in your factory environment.

[　]　Preventive maintenance management system implemented with frequent periodic maintenance programmes.

[　]　No formal preventive maintenance management system implemented. Machineries, equipment and tools are used until worn out / breakdown stage before repairs / replacements are made.

15. How well do you rate the engineering designs of your various precast concrete products in terms of buildability?

[　]　Very buildable

[　]　Satisfactory

[　]　There are buildability problems

16. Please state the types of buildability problems frequently encountered in your various manufacturing processes.

_____

_____

17. Do you generally find the engineering design specifications for your various precast concrete products complicated, vague and loaded with too much unnecessary information?

[　]　At most times

[　]　Sometimes

[　]　Not at all

C. MANUFACTURING CONTROL SYSTEM ANALYSIS

1. Generally, do you feel that your various manufacturing processes are complex or simple in nature?

   [ ]   Complex with many sub-processes / sub-assemblies

   [ ]   Neither complex nor simple but normal

   [ ]   Simple with few sub-processes / sub-assemblies

2. Do the nature of your different manufacturing processes help you to identify production problems easily and readily?

   [ ]   Yes

   [ ]   No

3. Is your firm certified to the international quality standards SS ISO 9000 to 9004 for quality assurance?

   [ ]   Yes. Certification to SS ISO 900 ___ (Please fill in the last number)

   [ ]   Currently undergoing process of certification

   [ ]   No, but intending to undergo certification process soon

   [ ]   Never thought about it before

4. If your firm is not already quality certified, please state how efficient your quality inspectors are in detecting problems and proposing solutions to production problems.

   [ ]   Very good

   [ ]   Good

   [ ]   Satisfactory

   [ ]   Poor

5. Do you agree that once quality problems are identified in any of the sub-process workstations, the entire production line for a product would only be stopped if all the sub-processes are sequentially dependent on one another; otherwise production activities would only be stopped at the faulty sub-process workstation alone?

   [ ]   Yes

   [ ]   No

6. Do you normally practise checking the quality of all the sub-components of a product at their sub-assembly workstation source? (For eg. checking steel reinforcement bars in the bar bending yard before installing them in the casting workstation.)

   [ ]   Yes

   [ ]   No

7. Do you adopt statistical quality control techniques when implementing your quality checks? (ie. checking the quality of a specified number of random samples per production batch.)

    [   ]   Yes

    [   ]   No

    [   ]   Other techniques used. Please specify _____

8. Further to the "Zero Defects Construction Campaign" mounted by the CIDB in 1991, is your firm's quality management system relentlessly pursuing <u>continuous improvements</u> *(kaizen)* in all your manufacturing processes through quality control circles?

    [   ]   Yes, the continuous improvement theme is upheld at all times

    [   ]   The continuous improvement theme is only vaguely upheld sometimes

    [   ]   No, the continuous improvement theme was never pursued

9. Please state your method for releasing the preceding components of a precast product (for eg. steel reinforcement bars) to the next subsequent workstation (ie. casting workstation).

    [   ]   Release only based on actual production rate of subsequent workstation (Pull System)

    [   ]   Release based on a pre-computed daily issuing rate regardless of the production rate of the subsequent workstation (Push System)

10. Is your labour force at the production floor level multi-skilled or single-skilled? (ie. multi-skilled meaning a worker can be a bar bender, concretor or form worker depending on situational demands.)

    [   ]   Multi-skilled

    [   ]   Single-skilled

11. What are the terms of engagement for your labour force at production floor level?

    [   ]   Direct employment

    [   ]   Sub-contract

    [   ]   Direct employment and sub-contract

12. What is the strength of your labour force at production floor level?

    [   ]   Less than 10

    [   ]   Between 10 to 30

    [   ]   Between 31 to 50

    [   ]   More than 50

13. Do you first train your new worker before assigning jobs to them on the production floor?

[   ]   Yes, at all times

[   ]   Sometimes

[   ]   No

14. How would you rate your present labour workforce at the production floor level in terms of teamwork spirit and working morale?

[   ]   Excellent

[   ]   Good

[   ]   Satisfactory

[   ]   Unsatisfactory

15. Please state the method of cost accounting your firm employs to track labour, inventory and overheads costs

[   ]   "Work order system" method where actual consumption costs of labour hours, inventory units and overheads absorption are accounted for in individual product lines.

[   ]   "Global tracking system" method where total consumption costs of labour hours, inventory units and overheads absorption are accounted for across all different product lines.

D. SUPPLIER AND CLIENT RELATIONSHIP

1. Which of the following criteria are important for the selection of your suppliers? (Please tick.)

[   ]   Price

[   ]   On-time delivery

[   ]   Quality

[   ]   Lead time

[   ]   Others. Please specify _____

2. Please state the kind of problems you normally encounter with your suppliers.

_____

_____

3. What are the percentages of all raw components required for your manufacturing processes which are purchased from local and overseas suppliers?

Local suppliers: _____ per cent

Overseas suppliers: _____ per cent

177

4. Please state the kind of supplier delivery system(s) adopted by your firm.

   [ ]   Supply in bulk lots with few deliveries

   [ ]   Supply in small lots with more frequent deliveries

   [ ]   Mixed supply of bulk and small lots depending on product component type

5. Do your firm prefer multi-sourcing or single-sourcing of suppliers? (ie. preference for many rather than a single supplier for a particular product component, for eg. concrete.)

   [ ]   Multi-sourcing

   [ ]   Single-sourcing

   [ ]   Mixed multi-sourcing and single-sourcing depending on product component type

6. Do you utilise your own internal concrete batching plant or external concrete suppliers for the supply of concrete for all precasting operations?

   [ ]   In-plant concrete supply

   [ ]   External concrete supply

   [ ]   Mix of in-plant and external concrete supplies

7. Do you fabricate the steel formwork systems and reinforcement bars required for your precasting operations internally within the factory premises or sub-contract the works to external steel fabricators?

   [ ]   In-plant fabrication

   [ ]   External sub-contract fabricators

   [ ]   Mix of in-plant and external sub-contract fabrications

8. Please state in general the time duration of the "Purchase Agreement" contracts entered into between your firm and your various suppliers (for eg. suppliers of concrete, steel reinforcement bars, prestressing sheaths and tendons, etc.)

   [ ]   Less than 6 months

   [ ]   Between 6 to 12 months

   [ ]   Between 1 to 2 years

   [ ]   More than 2 years

9. Do you usually request monthly rolling schedules from your clients for high volume project-based jobs to facilitate your production planning in order to deliver goods in time?

   [ ]   Yes, in most cases

   [ ]   Only in some cases

   [ ]   No

10. How often do you find that your clients' monthly rolling schedules are invalid due to constant variations in their monthly demands?

[   ]   At most times

[   ]   Sometimes, but within acceptable limits

[   ]   Not at all

11. In your effort to minimise tying capital down in finished inventories, do you normally "forcefully" deliver the finished goods to your clients' sites even though work progress at the latter may not be ready to receive the goods due to delays?

[   ]   Yes, for all cases

[   ]   Only in some cases depending on relationships with clients

[   ]   No

E. OVERALL PERSPECTIVE

1. By taking a macro view across all prefabricators in the local construction industry, please highlight the more pressing problems and issues which you are currently facing. From amongst these problems and issues, which of these would need to be solved at the level of the prefabrication industry.

_____

_____

_____

2. In your opinion, how would you categorise "waste" as seen in the prefabrication industry? (For eg. "waste" can mean reworks, quality defects, idling time, etc.)

_____

_____

3. Please state the total productivity your firm is presently achieving and the likely productivity growth forecast for 1994.

1993 productivity _____ per cent

Productivity growth forecast for 1994 _____ per cent

4. Are you confident of the feasibility of implementing some action plans to improve the overall productivity of your prefabrication business if you are assured of absolute commitment and total support from your firm's top management?

[   ]   Yes

[   ]   No

5. If the JIT philosophy proves to be a viable system for improving productivity and profitability in the prefabrication industry, would your company be willing to implement the JIT system as a comparatively small investment for a high return?

[   ]   Yes

[   ]   No

PHYSICAL FACTORY LAYOUT OF MANUFACTURING PROCESSES

APPENDIX 2

Time computation for precast elements in PWD school project (raw format)

Location	No of Pcs Delivered	Time In	Time Out	Unloading Time	Date of Delivery	Type of Elements
Blk A 1st Storey	6	11:45	13:45	2:00	8/9/94	P.C. SLAB
Blk A 1st Storey	6	12:30	14:20	1:50	8/9/94	P.C. SLAB
Blk A 1st Storey	6	14:55	15:30	0:35	8/9/94	P.C. SLAB
Blk A 1st Storey	7	15:25	16:20	0:55	8/9/94	P.C. SLAB
Blk A 1st Storey	10	10:50	13:00	2:10	9/9/94	P.C. SLAB
Blk A 1st Storey	6	13:20	13:45	0:25	9/9/94	P.C. SLAB
Blk A 1st Storey	7	15:00	15:30	0:30	9/9/94	P.C. SLAB
Blk A 1st Storey	6	16:45	17:10	0:25	9/9/94	P.C. SLAB
Blk A 1st Storey	6	17:35	18:15	0:40	9/9/94	P.C. SLAB
Blk A 1st Storey	5	09:00	09:20	0:20	9/9/94	P.C. SLAB
Blk A 1st Storey	5	10:40	11:05	0:25	9/9/94	P.C. SLAB
Blk A 1st Storey	3	11:30	11:55	0:25	9/9/94	P.C. SLAB
Blk A 1st Storey	5	-	-	0:15	15/10/94	P.C. COLUMN
Blk A 1st Storey	6	-	-	0:30	15/10/94	P.C. COLUMN
Blk A 1st Storey	4	-	-	0:25	19/10/94	P.C. COLUMN
Blk A 1st Storey	3	-	-	0:30	19/10/94	P.C. COLUMN
Blk A 1st Storey	5	-	-	0:30	21/10/94	P.C. COLUMN
Blk A 1st Storey	4	-	-	0:15	22/10/94	P.C. COLUMN
Blk A 1st Storey	4	-	-	0:10	22/10/94	P.C. COLUMN
Blk A 1st Storey	3	-	-	0:20	22/10/94	P.C. COLUMN
Blk A 2nd Storey	2	-	-	0:15	18/10/94	P.C. COLUMN
Blk A 2nd Storey	1	-	-	0:05	18/10/94	P.C. BEAM
Blk A 2nd Storey	5	-	-	0:15	18/10/94	P.C. BEAM
Blk A 2nd Storey	3	-	-	0:20	18/10/94	P.C. BEAM
Blk A 2nd Storey	4	-	-	0:15	20/10/94	P.C. BEAM
Blk A 2nd Storey	3	-	-	0:15	21/10/94	P.C. BEAM
Blk A 2nd Storey	6	-	-	0:25	24/10/94	P.C. BEAM
Blk A 2nd Storey	5	-	-	0:25	24/10/94	P.C. BEAM
Blk A 2nd Storey	6	09:00	09:45	0:45	26/10/94	P.C. SLAB
Blk A 2nd Storey	6	09:45	10:15	0:30	26/10/94	P.C. SLAB
Blk A 2nd Storey	6	13:30	14:30	1:00	26/10/94	P.C. SLAB

Location	No of Pcs Delivered	Time In	Time Out	Unloading Time	Date of Delivery	Type of Elements
Blk A 2nd Storey	6	12:20	12:55	0:35	26/10/94	P.C. SLAB
Blk A 2nd Storey	6	14:50	15:25	0:35	26/10/94	P.C. SLAB
Blk A 2nd Storey	6	15:30	16:05	0:35	26/10/94	P.C. SLAB
Blk A 2nd Storey	4	16:35	17:00	0:25	26/10/94	P.C. SLAB
Blk A 2nd Storey	3	-	-	0:30	28/10/94	P.C. BEAM
Blk A 2nd Storey	6	-	-	0:50	31/10/94	P.C. SLAB
Blk A 2nd Storey	6	-	-	1:10	31/10/94	P.C. SLAB
Blk A 2nd Storey	6	-	-	0:35	31/10/94	P.C. SLAB
Blk A 2nd Storey	6	-	-	0:55	31/10/94	P.C. SLAB
Blk A 2nd Storey	6	-	-	1:05	31/10/94	P.C. SLAB
Blk A 2nd Storey	6	17:00	17:35	0:35	31/10/94	P.C. SLAB
Blk A 2nd Storey	6	17:40	18:20	0:40	31/10/94	P.C. SLAB
Blk A 2nd Storey	8	16:25	19:30	3:05	31/10/94	P.C. SLAB
Blk A 3rd Storey	4	-	-	1:30	27/11/94	P.C. BEAM
Blk A 3rd Storey	6	-	-	1:00	27/11/94	P.C. BEAM
Blk A 3rd Storey	6	-	-	0:30	27/11/94	P.C. BEAM
Blk A 3rd Storey	7	-	-	0:40	27/11/94	P.C. BEAM
Blk A 3rd Storey	6	09:30	11:45	2:15	3/12/94	P.C. SLAB
Blk A 3rd Storey	6	09:05	11:55	2:50	3/12/94	P.C. SLAB
Blk A 3rd Storey	6	10:00	12:00	2:00	3/12/94	P.C. SLAB
Blk A 3rd Storey	6	13:10	14:20	1:10	3/12/94	P.C. SLAB
Blk A 3rd Storey	6	13:30	14:55	1:25	3/12/94	P.C. SLAB
Blk A 3rd Storey	6	13:45	16:20	2:35	3/12/94	P.C. SLAB
Blk A 3rd Storey	4	14:10	16:50	2:40	3/12/94	P.C. SLAB
Blk A 3rd Storey	6	09:25	10:35	1:10	14/12/94	P.C. SLAB
Blk A 3rd Storey	5	10:40	11:05	0:25	14/12/94	P.C. SLAB
Blk A 3rd Storey	5	12:00	12:35	0:35	14/12/94	P.C. SLAB
Blk A 3rd Storey	4	12:40	13:40	1:00	14/12/94	P.C. SLAB
Blk A 3rd Storey	6	10:05	11:45	1:40	16/12/94	P.C. SLAB
Blk A 3rd Storey	6	11:30	13:40	2:10	16/12/94	P.C. SLAB
Blk A 3rd Storey	6	14:05	14:55	0:50	16/12/94	P.C. SLAB

Location	No of Pcs Delivered	Time In	Time Out	Unloading Time	Date of Delivery	Type of Elements
Blk A 3rd Storey	6	14:20	16:45	2:25	16/12/94	P.C. SLAB
Blk A 3rd Storey	6	15:00	17:30	2:30	16/12/94	P.C. SLAB
Blk A Roof	5	-	-	3:15	3/12/94	P.C. ROOF BEAM
Blk A Roof	5	-	-	2:45	3/12/94	P.C. ROOF BEAM
Blk A Roof	6	-	-	1:30	13/12/94	R.C. ROOF BEAM

183

Location	No of Pcs Delivered	Time In	Time Out	Unloading Time	Date of Delivery	Type of Elements
Blk B 1st Storey	6	-	-	0:30	29/9/94	P.C. COLUMN
Blk B 1st Storey	4	-	-	0:35	30/9/94	P.C. COLUMN
Blk B 1st Storey	3	-	-	0:15	30/9/94	P.C. COLUMN
Blk B 1st Storey	1	-	-	0:15	5/10/94	P.C. WALL
Blk B 1st Storey	3	-	-	0:15	6/10/94	P.C. COLUMN
Blk B 1st Storey	6	16:25	16:50	0:25	7/10/94	P.C. SLAB
Blk B 1st Storey	3	-	-	0:30	8/10/94	P.C. COLUMN
Blk B 2nd Storey	3	-	-	0:25	29/9/94	P.C. BEAM
Blk B 2nd Storey	4	-	-	0:15	8/10/94	P.C. COLUMN
Blk B 2nd Storey	2	-	-	0:10	8/10/94	P.C. BEAM
Blk B 2nd Storey	3	-	-	0:20	8/10/94	P.C. BEAM
Blk B 2nd Storey	5	11:15	11:45	0:30	11/10/94	P.C. SLAB
Blk B 2nd Storey	6	09:45	10:25	0:40	11/10/94	P.C. SLAB
Blk B 2nd Storey	5	13:50	14:15	0:25	11/10/94	P.C. SLAB
Blk B 2nd Storey	5	13:15	13:35	0:20	11/10/94	P.C. SLAB
Blk B 2nd Storey	3	14:50	15:15	0:25	11/10/94	P.C. SLAB
Blk B 2nd Storey	6	10:15	11:00	0:45	12/10/94	P.C. SLAB
Blk B 2nd Storey	5	13:20	14:00	0:40	12/10/94	P.C. SLAB
Blk B 2nd Storey	5	14:15	14:45	0:30	12/10/94	P.C. SLAB
Blk B 2nd Storey	5	15:00	15:30	0:30	12/10/94	P.C. SLAB
Blk B 2nd Storey	3	16:25	16:40	0:15	12/10/94	P.C. SLAB
Blk B 2nd Storey	1	16:40	16:45	0:05	12/10/94	P.C. BEAM
Blk B 2nd Storey	4	-	-	0:15	12/10/94	P.C. BEAM
Blk B 2nd Storey	6	14:00	14:45	0:45	13/10/94	P.C. SLAB
Blk B 2nd Storey	5	14:50	15:25	0:35	13/10/94	P.C. SLAB
Blk B 2nd Storey	5	17:10	17:30	0:20	13/10/94	P.C. SLAB
Blk B 2nd Storey	5	16:15	17:05	0:50	13/10/94	P.C. SLAB
Blk B 2nd Storey	6	18:30	18:55	0:25	13/10/94	P.C. SLAB
Blk B 2nd Storey	6	19:10	19:40	0:30	13/10/94	P.C. SLAB
Blk B Roof	4	-	-	1:00	21/11/94	P.C. ROOF BEAM

Location	No of Pcs Delivered	Time In	Time Out	Unloading Time	Date of Delivery	Type of Elements
Blk B Roof	4	-	-	0:30	22/11/94	P.C. ROOF BEAM

Location	No of Pcs Delivered	Time In	Time Out	Unloading Time	Date of Delivery	Type of Elements
Blk C 1st Storey	9	-	-	0:15	15/9/94	P.C. COLUMN
Blk C 1st Storey	8	-	-	0:20	20/9/94	P.C. COLUMN
Blk C 1st Storey	1	-	-	0:25	26/9/94	P.C. WALL
Blk C 1st Storey	1	-	-	1:10	26/9/94	P.C. WALL
Blk C 1st Storey	1	-	-	0:05	27/9/94	P.C. COLUMN
Blk C 1st Storey	1	-	-	0:10	27/9/94	P.C. WALL
Blk C 1st Storey	1	-	-	0:10	28/9/94	P.C. WALL
Blk C 1st Storey	5	-	-	0:10	28/9/94	P.C. COLUMN
Blk C 2nd Storey	6	-	-	0:20	21/9/94	P.C. BEAM
Blk C 2nd Storey	2	-	-	1:25	28/9/94	P.C. BEAM
Blk C 2nd Storey	3	-	-	0:30	28/9/94	P.C. BEAM
Blk C 2nd Storey	4	-	-	0:20	28/9/94	P.C. BEAM
Blk C 2nd Storey	8	09:15	10:00	0:45	3/10/94	P.C. SLAB
Blk C 2nd Storey	8	10:10	10:50	0:40	3/10/94	P.C. SLAB
Blk C 2nd Storey	8	11:05	11:45	0:40	3/10/94	P.C. SLAB
Blk C 2nd Storey	6	13:15	13:40	0:25	3/10/94	P.C. SLAB
Blk C 2nd Storey	5	-	-	0:20	6/10/94	P.C. COLUMN
Blk C 2nd Storey	8	10:30	11:25	0:55	7/10/94	P.C. SLAB
Blk C 2nd Storey	8	13:05	13:45	0:40	7/10/94	P.C. SLAB
Blk C 2nd Storey	8	15:30	16:15	0:45	7/10/94	P.C. SLAB
Blk C 2nd Storey	1	-	-	0:15	2/11/94	P.C. WALL
Blk C 2nd Storey	1	-	-	0:10	3/11/94	P.C. WALL
Blk C 2nd Storey	1	-	-	5:00	22/11/94	P.C. WALL
Blk C Roof	6	-	-	0:15	2/11/94	P.C. ROOF BEAM
Blk C Roof	3	-	-	0:20	21/11/94	P.C. ROOF BEAM
Blk C Roof	6	-	-	0:30	22/11/94	P.C. ROOF BEAM

Location	No of Pcs Delivered	Time In	Time Out	Unloading Time	Date of Delivery	Type of Elements
Blk D 1st Storey	4	08:00	09:30	1:30	13/9/94	P.C. SLAB
Blk D 1st Storey	4	09:25	10:00	0:35	13/9/94	P.C. SLAB
Blk D 1st Storey	4	10:10	10:45	0:35	13/9/94	P.C. SLAB
Blk D 1st Storey	4	14:10	15:00	0:50	13/9/94	P.C. SLAB
Blk D 1st Storey	4	15:00	15:25	0:25	13/9/94	P.C. SLAB
Blk D 1st Storey	3	15:00	15:45	0:45	13/9/94	P.C. SLAB
Blk D 1st Storey	4	-	-	0:10	29/10/94	P.C. COLUMN
Blk D 1st Storey	4	-	-	0:20	29/10/94	P.C. COLUMN
Blk D 1st Storey	5	-	-	0:45	29/10/94	P.C. COLUMN
Blk D 1st Storey	1	-	-	0:10	1/11/94	P.C. COLUMN
Blk D 1st Storey	1	-	-	0:15	1/11/94	P.C. WALL
Blk D 1st Storey	1	-	-	0:15	1/11/94	P.C. WALL
Blk D 2nd Storey	6	-	-	0:35	1/11/94	P.C. BEAM
Blk D 2nd Storey	4	-	-	0:35	4/11/94	P.C. BEAM
Blk D 2nd Storey	3	-	-	0:15	4/11/94	P.C. BEAM
Blk D 2nd Storey	2	-	-	0:15	4/11/94	P.C. BEAM
Blk D 2nd Storey	4	10:45	11:40	0:55	9/11/94	P.C. SLAB
Blk D 2nd Storey	3	12:15	12:55	0:40	9/11/94	P.C. SLAB
Blk D 2nd Storey	3	13:00	13:30	0:30	9/11/94	P.C. SLAB
Blk D 2nd Storey	3	13:35	14:05	0:30	9/11/94	P.C. SLAB
Blk D 2nd Storey	3	14:05	14:50	0:45	9/11/94	P.C. SLAB
Blk D 2nd Storey	3	15:35	16:10	0:35	9/11/94	P.C. SLAB
Blk D 2nd Storey	3	17:00	17:40	0:40	9/11/94	P.C. SLAB
Blk D 2nd Storey	3	17:35	18:40	1:05	9/11/94	P.C. SLAB
Blk D 2nd Storey	1	18:15	18:25	0:10	9/11/94	P.C. BEAM
Blk D 2nd Storey	12	18:25	18:50	0:25	9/11/94	P.C. PLANK
Blk D 2nd Storey	1	-	-	0:15	15/12/94	P.C. WALL
Blk D 2nd Storey	1	-	-	1:00	15/12/94	P.C. WALL
Blk D 3rd Storey	5	-	-	0:35	14/12/94	P.C. BEAM
Blk D 3rd Storey	5	-	-	0:20	15/12/94	P.C. BEAM
Blk D 3rd Storey	5	-	-	0:20	15/12/94	P.C. BEAM

Location	No of Pcs Delivered	Time In	Time Out	Unloading Time	Date of Delivery	Type of Elements
Blk D 3rd Storey	1	17:50	17:55	0:05	16/12/94	R.C. ROOF BEAM
Blk D 3rd Storey	3	09:55	11:45	1:50	19/12/94	P.C. SLAB
Blk D 3rd Storey	3	12:15	12:55	0:40	19/12/94	P.C. SLAB
Blk D 3rd Storey	3	13:50	14:30	0:40	19/12/94	P.C. SLAB
Blk D 3rd Storey	3	08:30	09:10	0:40	19/12/94	P.C. SLAB
Blk D 3rd Storey	3	14:10	15:00	0:50	19/12/94	P.C. SLAB
Blk D 3rd Storey	3	09:30	10:30	1:00	19/12/94	P.C. SLAB
Blk D 3rd Storey	3	10:40	11:15	0:35	20/12/94	P.C. SLAB
Blk D 3rd Storey	3	11:20	12:15	0:55	20/12/94	P.C. SLAB
Blk D 3rd Storey	1	12:00	13:00	1:00	20/12/94	P.C. SLAB
Blk D 3rd Storey	1	-	-	0:30	12/2/95	P.C. WALL
Blk D 3rd Storey	1	-	-	0:30	12/2/95	P.C. WALL
Blk D Roof	4	-	-	Overnight	11/12/94	R.C. ROOF BEAM
Blk D Roof	4	18:15	19:00	0:45	16/12/94	R.C. ROOF BEAM
Blk D Roof	4	17:55	18:15	0:20	16/12/94	R.C. ROOF BEAM
Blk D Roof	4	-	-	1:00	11/2/95	P.C. ROOF BEAM

188

Location	No of Pcs Delivered	Time In	Time Out	Unloading Time	Date of Delivery	Type of Elements
Blk E 1st Storey	5	-	-	1:15	25/10/94	P.C. COLUMN
Blk E 1st Storey	2	-	-	0:05	26/10/94	P.C. COLUMN
Blk E 1st Storey	5	-	-	1:30	27/10/94	P.C. COLUMN
Blk E 1st Storey	1	-	-	0:10	27/10/94	P.C. WALL
Blk E 1st Storey	1	-	-	0:30	27/10/94	P.C. WALL
Blk E 1st Storey	4	-	-	0:35	28/10/94	P.C. COLUMN
Blk E 2nd Storey	5	-	-	0:30	25/10/94	P.C. BEAM
Blk E 2nd Storey	4	-	-	0:30	27/10/94	P.C. BEAM
Blk E 2nd Storey	1	-	-	0:05	28/10/94	P.C. BEAM
Blk E 2nd Storey	4	-	-	0:15	5/11/94	P.C. BEAM
Blk E 2nd Storey	4	09:45	11:00	1:15	7/11/94	P.C. SLAB
Blk E 2nd Storey	3	11:05	11:45	0:40	7/11/94	P.C. SLAB
Blk E 2nd Storey	3	12:20	12:55	0:35	7/11/94	P.C. SLAB
Blk E 2nd Storey	3	13:00	13:30	0:30	7/11/94	P.C. SLAB
Blk E 2nd Storey	3	13:35	14:30	0:55	7/11/94	P.C. SLAB
Blk E 2nd Storey	1	14:35	15:10	0:35	7/11/94	P.C. BEAM
Blk E 2nd Storey	10	17:10	17:20	0:10	7/11/94	P.C. BEAM
Blk E 2nd Storey	1	17:20	18:30	1:10	7/11/94	P.C. PLANK
Blk E 2nd Storey	1	-	-	1:05	5/12/94	P.C. WALL
Blk E 2nd Storey	5	-	-	0:40	5/12/94	P.C. WALL
Blk E 3rd Storey	5	-	-	Overnight	3/12/94	P.C. BEAM
Blk E 3rd Storey	5	-	-	Overnight	3/12/94	P.C. BEAM
Blk E 3rd Storey	5	-	-	0:40	5/12/94	P.C. BEAM
Blk E 3rd Storey	4	09:35	10:15	0:40	10/12/94	P.C. SLAB
Blk E 3rd Storey	3	10:20	11:05	0:45	10/12/94	P.C. SLAB
Blk E 3rd Storey	3	12:10	12:40	0:30	10/12/94	P.C. SLAB
Blk E 3rd Storey	3	11:10	11:35	0:25	10/12/94	P.C. SLAB
Blk E 3rd Storey	4	13:25	14:25	1:00	10/12/94	P.C. SLAB
Blk E 3rd Storey	3	15:30	16:20	0:50	10/12/94	P.C. SLAB
Blk E 3rd Storey	10	16:30	17:20	0:50	10/12/94	P.C. PLANK

Location	No of Pcs Delivered	Time In	Time Out	Unloading Time	Date of Delivery	Type of Elements
Blk E 3rd Storey	1	-	-	Overnight	18/1/95	P.C. WALL
Blk E 3rd Storey	1	-	-	0:30	18/1/95	P.C. WALL
Blk E 4th Storey	2	-	-	Overnight	9/2/95	P.C. COLUMN
Blk E 4th Storey	5	-	-	0:30	11/2/95	P.C. COLUMN
Blk E Roof	5	-	-	Overnight	11/12/94	R.C. ROOF BEAM
Blk E Roof	7	-	-	Overnight	12/12/94	R.C. ROOF BEAM

190

Location	No of Pcs Delivered	Time In	Time Out	Unloading Time	Date of Delivery	Type of Elements
Blk F 1st Storey	8	09:05	09:45	0:40	16/9/94	P.C. SLAB
Blk F 1st Storey	8	09:45	10:25	0:40	16/9/94	P.C. SLAB
Blk F 1st Storey	7	11:25	11:50	0:25	16/9/94	P.C. SLAB
Blk F 1st Storey	7	12:15	12:45	0:30	16/9/94	P.C. SLAB
Blk F 1st Storey	5	-	-	0:30	6/11/94	P.C. COLUMN
Blk F 1st Storey	2	-	-	0:15	6/11/94	P.C. COLUMN
Blk F 1st Storey	5	-	-	1:00	16/11/94	P.C. COLUMN
Blk F 1st Storey	4	-	-	6:00	16/11/94	P.C. COLUMN
Blk F 1st Storey	1	-	-	0:40	20/11/94	P.C. WALL
Blk F 2nd Storey	2	-	-	0:15	6/11/94	P.C. BEAM
Blk F 2nd Storey	4	-	-	0:30	6/11/94	P.C. BEAM
Blk F 2nd Storey	4	-	-	0:30	20/11/94	P.C. BEAM
Blk F 2nd Storey	3	-	-	0:30	20/11/94	P.C. BEAM
Blk F 2nd Storey	3	-	-	0:30	20/11/94	P.C. BEAM
Blk F 2nd Storey	19	10:00	12:00	2:00	23/11/94	P.C. PLANK
Blk F 2nd Storey	1	-	-	Overnight	23/11/94	P.C. BEAM
Blk F 2nd Storey	2	-	-	Overnight	23/11/94	P.C. COLUMN
Blk F 2nd Storey	8	11:15	12:05	0:50	24/11/94	P.C. SLAB
Blk F 2nd Storey	8	13:25	14:10	0:45	24/11/94	P.C. SLAB
Blk F 2nd Storey	6	14:15	14:55	0:40	24/11/94	P.C. SLAB
Blk F 2nd Storey	4	-	-	0:10	29/11/94	P.C. PLANK
Blk F 2nd Storey	1	-	-	0:05	29/11/94	P.C. BEAM
Blk F 2nd Storey	1	-	-	0:30	20/12/94	P.C. WALL
Blk F 3rd Storey	3	-	-	1:30	20/12/94	P.C. BEAM
Blk F 3rd Storey	3	-	-	0:45	20/12/94	P.C. BEAM
Blk F 3rd Storey	3	-	-	2:05	20/12/94	P.C. BEAM
Blk F 3rd Storey	4	-	-	0:45	22/12/94	P.C. BEAM
Blk F 3rd Storey	3	-	-	1:25	22/12/94	P.C. BEAM
Blk F 3rd Storey	5	-	-	0:35	22/12/94	P.C. BEAM

Location	No of Pcs Delivered	Time In	Time Out	Unloading Time	Date of Delivery	Type of Elements
Blk F 3rd Storey	8	09:10	10:10	1:00	24/12/94	P.C. SLAB
Blk F 3rd Storey	8	10:10	10:45	0:35	24/12/94	P.C. SLAB
Blk F 3rd Storey	8	14:10	15:00	0:50	24/12/94	P.C. SLAB
Blk F 3rd Storey	5	14:00	14:30	0:30	27/12/94	P.C. SLAB
Blk F 3rd Storey	19	15:35	16:00	0:25	27/12/94	P.C. PLANK
Blk F 3rd Storey	1	17:25	17:30	0:05	27/12/94	P.C. PLANK
Blk F 3rd Storey	6	10:00	10:45	0:45	30/12/94	P.C. SLAB
Blk F 3rd Storey	8	10:50	11:25	0:35	30/12/94	P.C. SLAB
Blk F 3rd Storey	8	11:30	12:35	1:05	30/12/94	P.C. SLAB
Blk F 3rd Storey	8	12:40	13:10	0:30	30/12/94	P.C. SLAB
Blk F 3rd Storey	6	13:50	14:30	0:40	30/12/94	P.C. SLAB
Blk F 3rd Storey	1	10:35	10:50	0:15	31/12/94	P.C. SLAB
Blk F 3rd Storey	1	-	-	0:10	31/12/94	P.C. BEAM
Blk F 3rd Storey	1	-	-	0:20	17/1/95	P.C. WALL
Blk F 3rd Storey	1	-	-	0:05	17/1/95	P.C. WALL
Blk F 4th Storey	4	-	-	0:40	29/12/94	P.C. BEAM
Blk F 4th Storey	3	-	-	0:30	10/1/95	P.C. BEAM
Blk F 4th Storey	1	-	-	0:10	10/1/95	P.C. BEAM
Blk F 4th Storey	2	-	-	0:05	10/1/95	P.C. BEAM
Blk F 4th Storey	4	-	-	0:30	10/1/95	P.C. BEAM
Blk F 4th Storey	24	08:30	09:00	0:30	11/1/95	P.C. PLANK
Blk F 4th Storey	3	-	-	0:40	12/1/95	P.C. BEAM
Blk F 4th Storey	2	-	-	0:30	12/1/95	P.C. BEAM
Blk F 4th Storey	2	-	-	0:40	12/1/95	P.C. BEAM
Blk F 4th Storey	4	-	-	1:25	12/1/95	P.C. PLANK
Blk F 4th Storey	8	09:20	10:15	0:55	16/1/95	P.C. SLAB
Blk F 4th Storey	8	10:20	10:55	0:35	16/1/95	P.C. SLAB
Blk F 4th Storey	8	13:55	15:15	1:20	16/1/95	P.C. SLAB
Blk F 4th Storey	6	14:00	14:40	0:40	16/1/95	P.C. SLAB
Blk F 4th Storey	14	-	-	4:00	6/2/95	P.C. COLUMN
Blk F 4th Storey	5	-	-	Overnight	9/2/95	P.C. COLUMN

Location	No of Pcs Delivered	Time In	Time Out	Unloading Time	Date of Delivery	Type of Elements
Blk F 4th Storey	2	-	-	0:15	20/3/95	P.C. BEAM
Blk F 4th Storey	7	-	-	0:30	20/3/95	P.C. PLANK
Blk F Roof	5	-	-	1:30	10/2/95	P.C. ROOF BEAM
Blk F Roof	4	-	-	0:45	10/2/95	P.C. ROOF BEAM
Blk F Roof	2	-	-	0:30	11/2/95	P.C. ROOF BEAM
Blk F Roof	5	-	-	0:15	11/2/95	P.C. ROOF BEAM

Location	No of Pcs Delivered	Time In	Time Out	Unloading Time	Date of Delivery	Type of Elements
Blk G 1st Storey	4	-	-	0:20	14/11/94	P.C. COLUMN
Blk G 1st Storey	4	-	-	0:10	14/11/94	P.C. COLUMN
Blk G 1st Storey	5	-	-	0:25	14/11/94	P.C. COLUMN
Blk G 1st Storey	1	-	-	0:05	25/11/94	P.C. WALL
Blk G 1st Storey	1	-	-	Overnight	25/11/94	P.C. WALL
Blk G 1st Storey	1	-	-	0:25	26/11/94	P.C. WALL
Blk G 2nd Storey	5	-	-	3:00	25/11/94	P.C. BEAM
Blk G 2nd Storey	4	-	-	0:45	25/11/94	P.C. BEAM
Blk G 2nd Storey	5	-	-	0:25	26/11/94	P.C. BEAM
Blk G 2nd Storey	3	09:05	09:25	0:20	30/11/94	P.C. SLAB
Blk G 2nd Storey	3	10:25	10:45	0:20	30/11/94	P.C. SLAB
Blk G 2nd Storey	3	11:15	11:45	0:30	30/11/94	P.C. SLAB
Blk G 2nd Storey	3	15:55	16:30	0:35	30/11/94	P.C. SLAB
Blk G 2nd Storey	3	12:15	13:35	1:20	30/11/94	P.C. SLAB
Blk G 2nd Storey	3	14:40	15:10	0:30	30/11/94	P.C. SLAB
Blk G 2nd Storey	3	14:35	15:45	1:10	30/11/94	P.C. SLAB
Blk G 2nd Storey	4	12:15	12:50	0:35	30/11/94	P.C. SLAB
Blk G 2nd Storey	8	17:20	18:30	1:10	30/11/94	P.C. SLAB
Blk G 2nd Storey	1	-	-	0:15	3/1/95	P.C. WALL
Blk G 2nd Storey	1	-	-	0:10	3/1/95	P.C. WALL
Blk G 2nd Storey	1	-	-	0:10	4/1/95	P.C. WALL
Blk G 2nd Storey	1	-	-	1:00	4/1/95	P.C. WALL
Blk G 3rd Storey	4	-	-	0:20	3/1/95	P.C. BEAM
Blk G 3rd Storey	4	-	-	0:25	3/1/95	P.C. BEAM
Blk G 3rd Storey	5	-	-	0:30	4/1/95	P.C. BEAM
Blk G 3rd Storey	1	-	-	0:10	4/1/95	P.C. BEAM
Blk G 3rd Storey	8	09:05	09:45	0:40	5/1/95	P.C. PLANK
Blk G 3rd Storey	3	12:10	12:45	0:35	5/1/95	P.C. SLAB
Blk G 3rd Storey	3	12:50	13:30	0:40	5/1/95	P.C. SLAB
Blk G 3rd Storey	3	13:35	14:10	0:35	5/1/95	P.C. SLAB
Blk G 3rd Storey	3	14:00	15:00	1:00	5/1/95	P.C. SLAB

194

Location	No of Pcs Delivered	Time In	Time Out	Unloading Time	Date of Delivery	Type of Elements
Blk G 3rd Storey	3	14:15	15:10	0:55	5/1/95	P.C. SLAB
Blk G 3rd Storey	3	16:50	17:50	1:00	5/1/95	P.C. SLAB
Blk G 3rd Storey	3	17:50	18:50	1:00	5/1/95	P.C. SLAB
Blk G 3rd Storey	4	18:10	19:10	1:00	5/1/95	P.C. SLAB
Blk G 3rd Storey	1	-	-	0:30	19/1/95	P.C. WALL
Blk G 3rd Storey	1	-	-	0:10	19/1/95	P.C. WALL
Blk G 3rd Storey	1	-	-	0:10	19/1/95	P.C. WALL
Blk G 3rd Storey	1	-	-	0:10	19/1/95	P.C. WALL
Blk G 4th Storey	5	-	-	Overnight	22/1/95	P.C. BEAM
Blk G 4th Storey	4	-	-	Overnight	22/1/95	P.C. BEAM
Blk G 4th Storey	6	-	-	0:30	22/1/95	P.C. BEAM
Blk G 4th Storey	2	-	-	0:10	22/1/95	P.C. BEAM
Blk G 4th Storey	1	-	-	0:05	22/1/95	P.C. BEAM
Blk G 4th Storey	12	-	-	Overnight	25/1/95	P.C. PLANK
Blk G 4th Storey	3	-	-	0:35	27/1/95	P.C. SLAB
Blk G 4th Storey	3	-	-	0:30	27/1/95	P.C. SLAB
Blk G 4th Storey	3	-	-	0:15	27/1/95	P.C. SLAB
Blk G 4th Storey	3	-	-	0:30	27/1/95	P.C. SLAB
Blk G 4th Storey	3	-	-	0:15	27/1/95	P.C. SLAB
Blk G 4th Storey	3	-	-	0:30	27/1/95	P.C. SLAB
Blk G 4th Storey	3	-	-	0:30	27/1/95	P.C. SLAB
Blk G 4th Storey	4	-	-	0:45	27/1/95	P.C. SLAB
Blk G 4th Storey	13	-	-	0:30	21/2/95	P.C. COLUMN
Blk G 4th Storey	1	-	-	0:40	22/2/95	P.C. WALL
Blk G 4th Storey	1	-	-	0:10	22/2/95	P.C. WALL
Blk G 4th Storey	1	-	-	0:20	22/2/95	P.C. WALL
Blk G 4th Storey	1	-	-	0:30	22/2/95	P.C. WALL
Blk G Roof	2	-	-	Overnight	11/12/94	R.C. ROOF BEAM
Blk G Roof	5	-	-	Overnight	25/02/95	P.C. ROOF BEAM
Blk G Roof	4	-	-	Overnight	27/02/95	P.C. ROOF BEAM

195

Location	No of Pcs Delivered	Time In	Time Out	Unloading Time	Date of Delivery	Type of Elements
Blk H 1st Storey	8	08:25	08:55	0:30	23/9/94	P.C. SLAB
Blk H 1st Storey	8	09:40	10:05	0:25	23/9/94	P.C. SLAB
Blk H 1st Storey	8	10:20	10:45	0:25	23/9/94	P.C. SLAB
Blk H 1st Storey	6	11:10	11:30	0:20	23/9/94	P.C. SLAB
Blk H 1st Storey	8	10:20	10:40	0:20	1/10/94	P.C. SLAB
Blk H 1st Storey	4	-	-	0:30	18/11/94	P.C. COLUMN
Blk H 1st Storey	4	-	-	0:15	18/11/94	P.C. COLUMN
Blk H 1st Storey	3	-	-	1:00	18/11/94	P.C. COLUMN
Blk H 1st Storey	1	-	-	1:05	19/11/94	P.C. WALL
Blk H 1st Storey	1	-	-	0:20	29/11/94	P.C. WALL
Blk H 2nd Storey	3	-	-	0:30	20/11/94	P.C. BEAM
Blk H 2nd Storey	3	-	-	0:30	20/11/94	P.C. BEAM
Blk H 2nd Storey	4	-	-	0:30	20/11/94	P.C. BEAM
Blk H 2nd Storey	3	-	-	0:30	20/11/94	P.C. BEAM
Blk H 2nd Storey	5	-	-	0:45	20/11/94	P.C. BEAM
Blk H 2nd Storey	23	14:15	17:00	2:45	23/11/94	P.C. PLANK
Blk H 2nd Storey	4	-	-	0:30	26/11/94	P.C. BEAM
Blk H 2nd Storey	8	09:15	09:40	0:25	28/11/94	P.C. SLAB
Blk H 2nd Storey	8	10:35	11:15	0:40	28/11/94	P.C. SLAB
Blk H 2nd Storey	8	12:10	13:00	0:50	28/11/94	P.C. SLAB
Blk H 2nd Storey	7	13:05	13:35	0:30	28/11/94	P.C. SLAB
Blk H 2nd Storey	6	13:35	14:05	0:30	28/11/94	P.C. SLAB
Blk H 2nd Storey	1	15:45	16:00	0:15	28/11/94	P.C. SLAB
Blk H 2nd Storey	7	-	-	0:30	29/11/94	P.C. PLANK
Blk H 3rd Storey	1	-	-	0:10	21/12/94	P.C. WALL
Blk H 3rd Storey	2	-	-	0:25	21/12/94	P.C. BEAM
Blk H 3rd Storey	2	-	-	0:25	21/12/94	P.C. BEAM
Blk H 3rd Storey	3	-	-	1:45	21/12/94	P.C. BEAM
Blk H 3rd Storey	3	-	-	0:35	22/12/94	P.C. BEAM
Blk H 3rd Storey	4	-	-	0:10	22/12/94	P.C. BEAM
Blk H 3rd Storey	3	-	-	1:15	22/12/94	P.C. BEAM

Location	No of Pcs Delivered	Time In	Time Out	Unloading Time	Date of Delivery	Type of Elements
Blk H 3rd Storey	4	14:30	15:00	0:30	27/12/94	P.C. PLANK
Blk H 3rd Storey	17	17:30	18:00	0:30	27/12/94	P.C. PLANK
Blk H 3rd Storey	2	-	-	1:25	31/12/94	P.C. BEAM
Blk H 3rd Storey	1	-	-	0:10	31/12/94	P.C. BEAM
Blk H 3rd Storey	2	-	-	0:25	4/1/95	P.C. BEAM
Blk H 3rd Storey	1	-	-	0:10	9/1/95	P.C. SLAB
Blk H 3rd Storey	4	-	-	0:40	9/1/95	P.C. PLANK
Blk H 3rd Storey	1	-	-	0:45	20/1/95	P.C. WALL
Blk H 3rd Storey	4	-	-	0:50	29/12/94	P.C. BEAM
Blk H 4th Storey	2	-	-	0:20	10/1/95	P.C. BEAM
Blk H 4th Storey	3	-	-	0:25	10/1/95	P.C. BEAM
Blk H 4th Storey	3	-	-	0:15	17/1/95	P.C. BEAM
Blk H 4th Storey	2	-	-	1:00	17/1/95	P.C. BEAM
Blk H 4th Storey	5	-	-	0:45	17/1/95	P.C. BEAM
Blk H 4th Storey	21	-	-	Overnight	21/1/95	P.C. PLANK
Blk H 4th Storey	8	-	-	2:20	21/1/95	P.C. SLAB
Blk H 4th Storey	8	-	-	0:30	21/1/95	P.C. SLAB
Blk H 4th Storey	8	-	-	0:15	21/1/95	P.C. SLAB
Blk H 4th Storey	6	-	-	1:15	21/1/95	P.C. SLAB
Blk H 4th Storey	8	09:15	10:05	0:50	24/1/95	P.C. SLAB
Blk H 4th Storey	1	-	-	0:30	12/2/95	P.C. WALL
Blk H 4th Storey	1	-	-	0:30	12/2/95	P.C. WALL
Blk H 4th Storey	12	-	-	0:30	14/2/95	P.C. COLUMN
Blk H 4th Storey	8	-	-	0:25	17/02/95	P.C. COLUMN
Blk H 4th Storey	2	-	-	Overnight	4/3/95	P.C. COLUMN
Blk H 4th Storey	2	-	-	Overnight	4/3/95	P.C. BEAM
Blk H 4th Storey	2	-	-	Overnight	4/3/95	P.C. BEAM
Blk H 4th Storey	7	-	-	1:30	4/3/95	P.C. PLANK
Blk H 4th Storey	2	-	-	0:15	20/03/95	P.C. BEAM

Location	No of Pcs Delivered	Time In	Time Out	Unloading Time	Date of Delivery	Type of Elements
Blk H 4th Storey	4	-	-	0:25	27/03/95	P.C. BEAM
Blk H 4th Storey	7	-	-	0:20	27/03/95	P.C. PLANK
Blk H 4th Storey	2	-	-	0:05	1/4/95	P.C. COLUMN
Blk H 4th Storey	17	-	-	0:25	1/4/95	P.C. STAIR TREAD
Blk H Roof	5	-	-	0:30	16/2/95	P.C. ROOF BEAM
Blk H Roof	4	-	-	0:25	16/2/95	P.C. ROOF BEAM
Blk H Roof	4	-	-	0:15	17/02/95	P.C. ROOF BEAM
Blk H Roof	5	-	-	0:10	17/02/95	P.C. ROOF BEAM

Time computation for precast elements in PWD school project (processed format)

Location	No of Pcs Delivered	Unloading Time	Type of Elements	P.C. Slab Category			
				Unloading Time Per Slab	Process Time Wastage	Process Time Wastage (RPT)	Rounded RTP
Blk A 1st Storey	6	2:00	P.C. SLAB	0:20:00	0:17:30	30%	30%
Blk A 1st Storey	6	1:50	P.C. SLAB	0:18:20	0:15:50	28%	30%
Blk A 1st Storey	6	0:35	P.C. SLAB	0:05:50	0:03:20	6%	10%
Blk A 1st Storey	7	0:55	P.C. SLAB	0:07:51	0:05:21	9%	10%
Blk A 1st Storey	10	2:10	P.C. SLAB	0:13:00	0:10:30	18%	20%
Blk A 1st Storey	6	0:25	P.C. SLAB	0:04:10	0:01:40	3%	0%
Blk A 1st Storey	7	0:30	P.C. SLAB	0:04:17	0:01:47	3%	0%
Blk A 1st Storey	6	0:25	P.C. SLAB	0:04:10	0:01:40	3%	0%
Blk A 1st Storey	6	0:40	P.C. SLAB	0:06:40	0:04:10	7%	10%
Blk A 1st Storey	5	0:20	P.C. SLAB	0:04:00	0:01:30	3%	0%
Blk A 1st Storey	5	0:25	P.C. SLAB	0:05:00	0:02:30	4%	0%
Blk A 1st Storey	3	0:25	P.C. SLAB	0:08:20	0:05:50	10%	10%
Blk A 1st Storey	5	0:15	P.C. COLUMN				
Blk A 1st Storey	6	0:30	P.C. COLUMN				
Blk A 1st Storey	4	0:25	P.C. COLUMN				
Blk A 1st Storey	3	0:30	P.C. COLUMN				
Blk A 1st Storey	5	0:30	P.C. COLUMN				
Blk A 1st Storey	4	0:15	P.C. COLUMN				
Blk A 1st Storey	4	0:10	P.C. COLUMN				
Blk A 1st Storey	3	0:20	P.C. COLUMN				
Blk A 2nd Storey	2	0:15	P.C. COLUMN				
Blk A 2nd Storey	1	0:05	P.C. BEAM				
Blk A 2nd Storey	5	0:15	P.C. BEAM				
Blk A 2nd Storey	3	0:20	P.C. BEAM				
Blk A 2nd Storey	4	0:15	P.C. BEAM				
Blk A 2nd Storey	3	0:15	P.C. BEAM				
Blk A 2nd Storey	6	0:25	P.C. BEAM				
Blk A 2nd Storey	5	0:25	P.C. BEAM				
Blk A 2nd Storey	6	0:45	P.C. SLAB	0:07:30	0:05:00	9%	10%
Blk A 2nd Storey	6	0:30	P.C. SLAB	0:05:00	0:02:30	4%	0%
Blk A 2nd Storey	6	1:00	P.C. SLAB	0:10:00	0:07:30	13%	10%

Location	No of Pcs Delivered	Unloading Time	Type of Elements	P.C. Slab Category			
				Unloading Time Per Slab	Process Time Wastage	Process Time Wastage (RPT)	Rounded RTP
Blk A 2nd Storey	6	0:35	P.C. SLAB	0:05:50	0:03:20	6%	10%
Blk A 2nd Storey	6	0:35	P.C. SLAB	0:05:50	0:03:20	6%	10%
Blk A 2nd Storey	6	0:35	P.C. SLAB	0:05:50	0:03:20	6%	10%
Blk A 2nd Storey	4	0:25	P.C. SLAB	0:06:15	0:03:45	7%	10%
Blk A 2nd Storey	3	0:30	P.C. BEAM				
Blk A 2nd Storey	6	0:50	P.C. SLAB	0:08:20	0:05:50	10%	10%
Blk A 2nd Storey	6	1:10	P.C. SLAB	0:11:40	0:09:10	16%	20%
Blk A 2nd Storey	6	0:35	P.C. SLAB	0:05:50	0:03:20	6%	10%
Blk A 2nd Storey	6	0:55	P.C. SLAB	0:09:10	0:06:40	12%	10%
Blk A 2nd Storey	6	1:05	P.C. SLAB	0:10:50	0:08:20	14%	10%
Blk A 2nd Storey	6	0:35	P.C. SLAB	0:05:50	0:03:20	6%	10%
Blk A 2nd Storey	6	0:40	P.C. SLAB	0:06:40	0:04:10	7%	10%
Blk A 2nd Storey	8	3:05	P.C. SLAB	0:23:07	0:20:38	36%	40%
Blk A 3rd Storey	4	1:30	P.C. BEAM				
Blk A 3rd Storey	6	1:00	P.C. BEAM				
Blk A 3rd Storey	6	0:30	P.C. BEAM				
Blk A 3rd Storey	7	0:40	P.C. BEAM				
Blk A 3rd Storey	6	2:15	P.C. SLAB	0:22:30	0:20:00	35%	30%
Blk A 3rd Storey	6	2:50	P.C. SLAB	0:28:20	0:25:50	45%	40%
Blk A 3rd Storey	6	2:00	P.C. SLAB	0:20:00	0:17:30	30%	30%
Blk A 3rd Storey	6	1:10	P.C. SLAB	0:11:40	0:09:10	16%	20%
Blk A 3rd Storey	6	1:25	P.C. SLAB	0:14:10	0:11:40	20%	20%
Blk A 3rd Storey	6	2:35	P.C. SLAB	0:25:50	0:23:20	41%	40%
Blk A 3rd Storey	4	2:40	P.C. SLAB	0:40:00	0:37:30	65%	70%
Blk A 3rd Storey	6	1:10	P.C. SLAB	0:11:40	0:09:10	16%	20%
Blk A 3rd Storey	5	0:25	P.C. SLAB	0:05:00	0:02:30	4%	0%
Blk A 3rd Storey	5	0:35	P.C. SLAB	0:07:00	0:04:30	8%	10%
Blk A 3rd Storey	4	1:00	P.C. SLAB	0:15:00	0:12:30	22%	20%
Blk A 3rd Storey	6	1:40	P.C. SLAB	0:16:40	0:14:10	25%	20%
Blk A 3rd Storey	6	2:10	P.C. SLAB	0:21:40	0:19:10	33%	30%
Blk A 3rd Storey	6	0:50	P.C. SLAB	0:08:20	0:05:50	10%	10%

| | | | | P.C. Slab Category | | | |
Location	No of Pcs Delivered	Unloading Time	Type of Elements	Unloading Time Per Slab	Process Time Wastage	Process Time Wastage (RPT)	Rounded RTP
Blk A 3rd Storey	6	2:25	P.C. SLAB	0:24:10	0:21:40	38%	40%
Blk A 3rd Storey	6	2:30	P.C. SLAB	0:25:00	0:22:30	39%	40%
Blk A Roof	5	3:15	P.C. ROOF BEAM				
Blk A Roof	5	2:45	P.C. ROOF BEAM				
Blk A Roof	6	1:30	R.C. ROOF BEAM				

Location	No of Pcs Delivered	Unloading Time	Type of Elements	P.C. Slab Category			
				Unloading Time Per Slab	Process Time Wastage	Process Time Wastage (RPT)	Rounded RTP
Blk B 1st Storey	6	0:30	P.C. COLUMN				
Blk B 1st Storey	4	0:35	P.C. COLUMN				
Blk B 1st Storey	3	0:15	P.C. COLUMN				
Blk B 1st Storey	1	0:15	P.C. WALL				
Blk B 1st Storey	3	0:15	P.C. COLUMN				
Blk B 1st Storey	6	0:25	P.C. SLAB	0:04:10	0:01:40	3%	0%
Blk B 1st Storey	3	0:30	P.C. COLUMN				
Blk B 1st Storey	3	0:25	P.C. BEAM				
Blk B 2nd Storey	4	0:15	P.C. COLUMN				
Blk B 2nd Storey	2	0:10	P.C. BEAM				
Blk B 2nd Storey	3	0:20	P.C. BEAM				
Blk B 2nd Storey	5	0:30	P.C. SLAB	0:06:00	0:03:30	6%	10%
Blk B 2nd Storey	6	0:40	P.C. SLAB	0:06:40	0:04:10	7%	10%
Blk B 2nd Storey	5	0:25	P.C. SLAB	0:05:00	0:02:30	4%	0%
Blk B 2nd Storey	5	0:20	P.C. SLAB	0:04:00	0:01:30	3%	0%
Blk B 2nd Storey	3	0:25	P.C. SLAB	0:08:20	0:05:50	10%	10%
Blk B 2nd Storey	6	0:45	P.C. SLAB	0:07:30	0:05:00	9%	10%
Blk B 2nd Storey	5	0:40	P.C. SLAB	0:08:00	0:05:30	10%	10%
Blk B 2nd Storey	5	0:30	P.C. SLAB	0:06:00	0:03:30	6%	10%
Blk B 2nd Storey	5	0:30	P.C. SLAB	0:06:00	0:03:30	6%	10%
Blk B 2nd Storey	3	0:15	P.C. SLAB	0:05:00	0:02:30	4%	0%
Blk B 2nd Storey	1	0:05	P.C. BEAM				
Blk B 2nd Storey	4	0:15	P.C. BEAM				
Blk B 2nd Storey	6	0:45	P.C. SLAB	0:07:30	0:05:00	9%	10%
Blk B 2nd Storey	5	0:35	P.C. SLAB	0:07:00	0:04:30	8%	10%
Blk B 2nd Storey	5	0:20	P.C. SLAB	0:04:00	0:01:30	3%	0%
Blk B 2nd Storey	5	0:50	P.C. SLAB	0:10:00	0:07:30	13%	10%
Blk B 2nd Storey	6	0:25	P.C. SLAB	0:04:10	0:01:40	3%	0%
Blk B 2nd Storey	6	0:30	P.C. SLAB	0:05:00	0:02:30	4%	0%
Blk B Roof	4	1:00	P.C. ROOF BEAM				

Location	No of Pcs Delivered	Unloading Time	Type of Elements	P.C. Slab Category			
				Unloading Time Per Slab	Process Time Wastage	Process Time Wastage (RPT)	Rounded RTP
Blk B Roof	4	0:30	P.C. ROOF BEAM				

Location	No of Pcs Delivered	Unloading Time	Type of Elements	P.C. Slab Category			
				Unloading Time Per Slab	Process Time Wastage	Process Time Wastage (RPT)	Rounded RTP
Blk C 1st Storey	9	0:15	P.C. COLUMN				
Blk C 1st Storey	8	0:20	P.C. COLUMN				
Blk C 1st Storey	1	0:25	P.C. WALL				
Blk C 1st Storey	1	1:10	P.C. WALL				
Blk C 1st Storey	1	0:05	P.C. COLUMN				
Blk C 1st Storey	1	0:10	P.C. WALL				
Blk C 1st Storey	1	0:10	P.C. WALL				
Blk C 1st Storey	5	0:10	P.C. COLUMN				
Blk C 2nd Storey	6	0:20	P.C. BEAM				
Blk C 2nd Storey	2	1:25	P.C. BEAM				
Blk C 2nd Storey	3	0:30	P.C. BEAM				
Blk C 2nd Storey	4	0:20	P.C. BEAM				
Blk C 2nd Storey	8	0:45	P.C. SLAB	0:05:37	0:03:08	5%	10%
Blk C 2nd Storey	8	0:40	P.C. SLAB	0:05:00	0:02:30	4%	0%
Blk C 2nd Storey	8	0:40	P.C. SLAB	0:05:00	0:02:30	4%	0%
Blk C 2nd Storey	6	0:25	P.C. SLAB	0:04:10	0:01:40	3%	0%
Blk C 2nd Storey	5	0:20	P.C. COLUMN				
Blk C 2nd Storey	8	0:55	P.C. SLAB	0:06:52	0:04:23	8%	10%
Blk C 2nd Storey	8	0:40	P.C. SLAB	0:05:00	0:02:30	4%	0%
Blk C 2nd Storey	8	0:45	P.C. SLAB	0:05:37	0:03:08	5%	10%
Blk C 2nd Storey	1	0:15	P.C. WALL				
Blk C 2nd Storey	1	0:10	P.C. WALL				
Blk C 2nd Storey	1	5:00	P.C. WALL				
Blk C Roof	6	0:15	P.C. ROOF BEAM				
Blk C Roof	3	0:20	P.C. ROOF BEAM				
Blk C Roof	6	0:30	P.C. ROOF BEAM				

Location	No of Pcs Delivered	Unloading Time	Type of Elements	P.C. Slab Category			
				Unloading Time Per Slab	Process Time Wastage	Process Time Wastage (RPT)	Rounded RTP
Blk D 1st Storey	4	1:30	P.C. SLAB	0:22:30	0:20:00	35%	30%
Blk D 1st Storey	4	0:35	P.C. SLAB	0:08:45	0:06:15	11%	10%
Blk D 1st Storey	4	0:35	P.C. SLAB	0:08:45	0:06:15	11%	10%
Blk D 1st Storey	4	0:50	P.C. SLAB	0:12:30	0:10:00	17%	20%
Blk D 1st Storey	4	0:25	P.C. SLAB	0:06:15	0:03:45	7%	10%
Blk D 1st Storey	3	0:45	P.C. SLAB	0:15:00	0:12:30	22%	20%
Blk D 1st Storey	4	0:10	P.C. COLUMN				
Blk D 1st Storey	4	0:20	P.C. COLUMN				
Blk D 1st Storey	5	0:45	P.C. COLUMN				
Blk D 1st Storey	1	0:10	P.C. COLUMN				
Blk D 1st Storey	1	0:15	P.C. WALL				
Blk D 1st Storey	1	0:15	P.C. WALL				
Blk D 2nd Storey	6	0:35	P.C. BEAM				
Blk D 2nd Storey	4	0:35	P.C. BEAM				
Blk D 2nd Storey	3	0:15	P.C. BEAM				
Blk D 2nd Storey	2	0:15	P.C. BEAM				
Blk D 2nd Storey	4	0:55	P.C. SLAB	0:13:45	0:11:15	20%	20%
Blk D 2nd Storey	3	0:40	P.C. SLAB	0:13:20	0:10:50	19%	20%
Blk D 2nd Storey	3	0:30	P.C. SLAB	0:10:00	0:07:30	13%	10%
Blk D 2nd Storey	3	0:30	P.C. SLAB	0:10:00	0:07:30	13%	10%
Blk D 2nd Storey	3	0:45	P.C. SLAB	0:15:00	0:12:30	22%	20%
Blk D 2nd Storey	3	0:35	P.C. SLAB	0:11:40	0:09:10	16%	20%
Blk D 2nd Storey	3	0:40	P.C. SLAB	0:13:20	0:10:50	19%	20%
Blk D 2nd Storey	3	1:05	P.C. SLAB	0:21:40	0:19:10	33%	30%
Blk D 2nd Storey	1	0:10	P.C. BEAM				
Blk D 2nd Storey	12	0:25	P.C. PLANK				
Blk D 2nd Storey	1	0:15	P.C. WALL				
Blk D 2nd Storey	1	1:00	P.C. WALL				
Blk D 3rd Storey	5	0:35	P.C. BEAM				
Blk D 3rd Storey	5	0:20	P.C. BEAM				
Blk D 3rd Storey	5	0:20	P.C. BEAM				

Location	No of Pcs Delivered	Unloading Time	Type of Elements	P.C. Slab Category			
				Unloading Time Per Slab	Process Time Wastage	Process Time Wastage (RPT)	Rounded RTP
Blk D 3rd Storey	1	0:05	R.C. ROOF BEAM				
Blk D 3rd Storey	3	1:50	P.C. SLAB	0:36:40	0:34:10	59%	60%
Blk D 3rd Storey	3	0:40	P.C. SLAB	0:13:20	0:10:50	19%	20%
Blk D 3rd Storey	3	0:40	P.C. SLAB	0:13:20	0:10:50	19%	20%
Blk D 3rd Storey	3	0:40	P.C. SLAB	0:13:20	0:10:50	19%	20%
Blk D 3rd Storey	3	0:50	P.C. SLAB	0:16:40	0:14:10	25%	20%
Blk D 3rd Storey	3	1:00	P.C. SLAB	0:20:00	0:17:30	30%	30%
Blk D 3rd Storey	3	0:35	P.C. SLAB	0:11:40	0:09:10	16%	20%
Blk D 3rd Storey	3	0:55	P.C. SLAB	0:18:20	0:15:50	28%	30%
Blk D 3rd Storey	1	1:00	P.C. SLAB	1:00:00	0:57:30	100%	100%
Blk D 3rd Storey	1	0:30	P.C. WALL				
Blk D 3rd Storey	1	0:30	P.C. WALL				
Blk D Roof	4	Overnight	R.C. ROOF BEAM				
Blk D Roof	4	0:45	R.C. ROOF BEAM				
Blk D Roof	4	0:20	R.C. ROOF BEAM				
Blk D Roof	4	1:00	P.C. ROOF BEAM				

Location	No of Pcs Delivered	Unloading Time	Type of Elements	P.C. Slab Category			
				Unloading Time Per Slab	Process Time Wastage	Process Time Wastage (RPT)	Rounded RTP
Blk E 1st Storey	5	1:15	P.C. COLUMN				
Blk E 1st Storey	2	0:05	P.C. COLUMN				
Blk E 1st Storey	5	1:30	P.C. COLUMN				
Blk E 1st Storey	1	0:10	P.C. WALL				
Blk E 1st Storey	1	0:30	P.C. WALL				
Blk E 1st Storey	4	0:35	P.C. COLUMN				
Blk E 2nd Storey	5	0:30	P.C. BEAM				
Blk E 2nd Storey	4	0:30	P.C. BEAM				
Blk E 2nd Storey	1	0:05	P.C. BEAM				
Blk E 2nd Storey	4	0:15	P.C. BEAM				
Blk E 2nd Storey	4	1:15	P.C. SLAB	0:18:45	0:16:15	28%	30%
Blk E 2nd Storey	3	0:40	P.C. SLAB	0:13:20	0:10:50	19%	20%
Blk E 2nd Storey	3	0:35	P.C. SLAB	0:11:40	0:09:10	16%	20%
Blk E 2nd Storey	3	0:30	P.C. SLAB	0:10:00	0:07:30	13%	10%
Blk E 2nd Storey	3	0:55	P.C. SLAB	0:18:20	0:15:50	28%	30%
Blk E 2nd Storey	3	0:35	P.C. SLAB	0:11:40	0:09:10	16%	20%
Blk E 2nd Storey	1	0:10	P.C. BEAM				
Blk E 2nd Storey	10	1:10	P.C. PLANK				
Blk E 2nd Storey	1	1:05	P.C. WALL				
Blk E 2nd Storey	1	0:40	P.C. WALL				
Blk E 3rd Storey	5	Overnight	P.C. BEAM				
Blk E 3rd Storey	5	Overnight	P.C. BEAM				
Blk E 3rd Storey	5	0:40	P.C. BEAM				
Blk E 3rd Storey	4	0:40	P.C. SLAB	0:10:00	0:07:30	13%	10%
Blk E 3rd Storey	3	0:45	P.C. SLAB	0:15:00	0:12:30	22%	20%
Blk E 3rd Storey	3	0:30	P.C. SLAB	0:10:00	0:07:30	13%	10%
Blk E 3rd Storey	3	0:25	P.C. SLAB	0:08:20	0:05:50	10%	10%
Blk E 3rd Storey	4	1:00	P.C. SLAB	0:15:00	0:12:30	22%	20%
Blk E 3rd Storey	3	0:50	P.C. SLAB	0:16:40	0:14:10	25%	20%
Blk E 3rd Storey	10	0:50	P.C. PLANK				

Location	No of Pcs Delivered	Unloading Time	Type of Elements	Unloading Time Per Slab	P.C. Slab Category		
					Process Time Wastage	Process Time Wastage (RPT)	Rounded RTP
Blk E 3rd Storey	1	Overnight	P.C. WALL				
Blk E 3rd Storey	1	0:30	P.C. WALL				
Blk E 4th Storey	2	Overnight	P.C. COLUMN				
Blk E 4th Storey	5	0:30	P.C. COLUMN				
Blk E Roof	5	Overnight	R.C. ROOF BEAM				
Blk E Roof	7	Overnight	R.C. ROOF BEAM				

208

Location	No of Pcs Delivered	Unloading Time	Type of Elements	P.C. Slab Category			
				Unloading Time Per Slab	Process Time Wastage	Process Time Wastage (RPT)	Rounded RTP
Blk F 1st Storey	8	0:40	P.C. SLAB	0:05:00	0:02:30	4%	0%
Blk F 1st Storey	8	0:40	P.C. SLAB	0:05:00	0:02:30	4%	0%
Blk F 1st Storey	7	0:25	P.C. SLAB	0:03:34	0:01:04	2%	0%
Blk F 1st Storey	7	0:30	P.C. SLAB	0:04:17	0:01:47	3%	0%
Blk F 1st Storey	5	0:30	P.C. COLUMN				
Blk F 1st Storey	2	0:15	P.C. COLUMN				
Blk F 1st Storey	5	1:00	P.C. COLUMN				
Blk F 1st Storey	4	6:00	P.C. COLUMN				
Blk F 1st Storey	1	0:40	P.C. WALL				
Blk F 2nd Storey	2	0:15	P.C. BEAM				
Blk F 2nd Storey	4	0:30	P.C. BEAM				
Blk F 2nd Storey	4	0:30	P.C. BEAM				
Blk F 2nd Storey	3	0:30	P.C. BEAM				
Blk F 2nd Storey	3	0:30	P.C. BEAM				
Blk F 2nd Storey	19	2:00	P.C. PLANK				
Blk F 2nd Storey	1	Overnight	P.C. BEAM				
Blk F 2nd Storey	2	Overnight	P.C. COLUMN				
Blk F 2nd Storey	8	0:50	P.C. SLAB	0:06:15	0:03:45	7%	10%
Blk F 2nd Storey	8	0:45	P.C. SLAB	0:05:37	0:03:08	5%	10%
Blk F 2nd Storey	6	0:40	P.C. SLAB	0:06:40	0:04:10	7%	10%
Blk F 2nd Storey	4	0:10	P.C. PLANK				
Blk F 2nd Storey	1	0:05	P.C. BEAM				
Blk F 2nd Storey	1	0:30	P.C. WALL				
Blk F 2nd Storey	3	1:30	P.C. BEAM				
Blk F 3rd Storey	3	0:45	P.C. BEAM				
Blk F 3rd Storey	3	2:05	P.C. BEAM				
Blk F 3rd Storey	4	0:45	P.C. BEAM				
Blk F 3rd Storey	3	1:25	P.C. BEAM				
Blk F 3rd Storey	5	0:35	P.C. BEAM				

209

Location	No of Pcs Delivered	Unloading Time	Type of Elements	Unloading Time Per Slab	Process Time Wastage	Process Time Wastage (RPT)	Rounded RTP
				P.C. Slab Category			
Blk F 3rd Storey	8	1:00	P.C. SLAB	0:07:30	0:05:00	9%	10%
Blk F 3rd Storey	8	0:35	P.C. SLAB	0:04:23	0:01:53	3%	0%
Blk F 3rd Storey	8	0:50	P.C. SLAB	0:06:15	0:03:45	7%	10%
Blk F 3rd Storey	5	0:30	P.C. SLAB	0:06:00	0:03:30	6%	10%
Blk F 3rd Storey	19	0:25	P.C. PLANK				
Blk F 3rd Storey	1	0:05	P.C. PLANK				
Blk F 3rd Storey	6	0:45	P.C. SLAB	0:07:30	0:05:00	9%	10%
Blk F 3rd Storey	8	0:35	P.C. SLAB	0:04:22	0:01:53	3%	0%
Blk F 3rd Storey	8	1:05	P.C. SLAB	0:08:08	0:05:38	10%	10%
Blk F 3rd Storey	8	0:30	P.C. SLAB	0:03:45	0:01:15	2%	0%
Blk F 3rd Storey	6	0:40	P.C. SLAB	0:06:40	0:04:10	7%	10%
Blk F 3rd Storey	1	0:15	P.C. SLAB	0:15:00	0:12:30	22%	20%
Blk F 3rd Storey	1	0:10	P.C. BEAM				
Blk F 3rd Storey	1	0:20	P.C. WALL				
Blk F 3rd Storey	1	0:05	P.C. WALL				
Blk F 4th Storey	4	0:40	P.C. BEAM				
Blk F 4th Storey	3	0:30	P.C. BEAM				
Blk F 4th Storey	1	0:10	P.C. BEAM				
Blk F 4th Storey	2	0:05	P.C. BEAM				
Blk F 4th Storey	4	0:30	P.C. BEAM				
Blk F 4th Storey	24	0:30	P.C. PLANK				
Blk F 4th Storey	3	0:40	P.C. BEAM				
Blk F 4th Storey	2	0:30	P.C. BEAM				
Blk F 4th Storey	2	0:40	P.C. BEAM				
Blk F 4th Storey	4	1:25	P.C. PLANK				
Blk F 4th Storey	8	0:55	P.C. SLAB	0:06:52	0:04:23	8%	10%
Blk F 4th Storey	8	0:35	P.C. SLAB	0:04:22	0:01:53	3%	0%
Blk F 4th Storey	8	1:20	P.C. SLAB	0:10:00	0:07:30	13%	10%
Blk F 4th Storey	6	0:40	P.C. SLAB	0:06:40	0:04:10	7%	10%
Blk F 4th Storey	14	4:00	P.C. COLUMN				
Blk F 4th Storey	5	Overnight	P.C. COLUMN				

Location	No of Pcs Delivered	Unloading Time	Type of Elements	P.C. Slab Category			
				Unloading Time Per Slab	Process Time Wastage	Process Time Wastage (RPT)	Rounded RTP
Blk F 4th Storey	2	0:15	P.C. BEAM				
Blk F 4th Storey	7	0:30	P.C. PLANK				
Blk F Roof	5	1:30	P.C. ROOF BEAM				
Blk F Roof	4	0:45	P.C. ROOF BEAM				
Blk F Roof	2	0:30	P.C. ROOF BEAM				
Blk F Roof	5	0:15	P.C. ROOF BEAM				

211

Location	No of Pcs Delivered	Unloading Time	Type of Elements	P.C. Slab Category			
				Unloading Time Per Slab	Process Time Wastage	Process Time Wastage (RPT)	Rounded RTP
Blk G 1st Storey	4	0:20	P.C. COLUMN				
Blk G 1st Storey	4	0:10	P.C. COLUMN				
Blk G 1st Storey	5	0:25	P.C. COLUMN				
Blk G 1st Storey	1	0:05	P.C. WALL				
Blk G 1st Storey	1	Overnight	P.C. WALL				
Blk G 1st Storey	1	0:25	P.C. WALL				
Blk G 1st Storey	5	3:00	P.C. BEAM				
Blk G 2nd Storey	4	0:45	P.C. BEAM				
Blk G 2nd Storey	5	0:25	P.C. BEAM				
Blk G 2nd Storey	3	0:20	P.C. SLAB	0:06:40	0:04:10	7%	10%
Blk G 2nd Storey	3	0:20	P.C. SLAB	0:06:40	0:04:10	7%	10%
Blk G 2nd Storey	3	0:30	P.C. SLAB	0:10:00	0:07:30	13%	10%
Blk G 2nd Storey	3	0:35	P.C. SLAB	0:11:40	0:09:10	16%	20%
Blk G 2nd Storey	3	1:20	P.C. SLAB	0:26:40	0:24:10	42%	40%
Blk G 2nd Storey	3	0:30	P.C. SLAB	0:10:00	0:07:30	13%	10%
Blk G 2nd Storey	3	1:10	P.C. SLAB	0:23:20	0:20:50	36%	40%
Blk G 2nd Storey	4	0:35	P.C. SLAB	0:08:45	0:06:15	11%	10%
Blk G 2nd Storey	8	1:10	P.C. SLAB	0:08:45	0:06:15	11%	10%
Blk G 2nd Storey	1	0:15	P.C. WALL				
Blk G 2nd Storey	1	0:10	P.C. WALL				
Blk G 2nd Storey	1	0:10	P.C. WALL				
Blk G 2nd Storey	1	1:00	P.C. WALL				
Blk G 3rd Storey	4	0:20	P.C. BEAM				
Blk G 3rd Storey	4	0:25	P.C. BEAM				
Blk G 3rd Storey	5	0:30	P.C. BEAM				
Blk G 3rd Storey	1	0:10	P.C. BEAM				
Blk G 3rd Storey	8	0:40	P.C. PLANK				
Blk G 3rd Storey	3	0:35	P.C. SLAB	0:11:40	0:09:10	16%	20%
Blk G 3rd Storey	3	0:40	P.C. SLAB	0:13:20	0:10:50	19%	20%
Blk G 3rd Storey	3	0:35	P.C. SLAB	0:11:40	0:09:10	16%	20%
Blk G 3rd Storey	3	1:00	P.C. SLAB	0:20:00	0:17:30	30%	30%

Location	No of Pcs Delivered	Unloading Time	Type of Elements	P.C. Slab Category			
				Unloading Time Per Slab	Process Time Wastage	Process Time Wastage (RPT)	Rounded RTP
Blk G 3rd Storey	3	0:55	P.C. SLAB	0:18:20	0:15:50	28%	30%
Blk G 3rd Storey	3	1:00	P.C. SLAB	0:20:00	0:17:30	30%	30%
Blk G 3rd Storey	3	1:00	P.C. SLAB	0:20:00	0:17:30	30%	30%
Blk G 3rd Storey	4	1:00	P.C. SLAB	0:15:00	0:12:30	22%	20%
Blk G 3rd Storey	1	0:30	P.C. WALL				
Blk G 3rd Storey	1	0:10	P.C. WALL				
Blk G 3rd Storey	1	0:10	P.C. WALL				
Blk G 3rd Storey	1	0:10	P.C. WALL				
Blk G 4th Storey	5	Overnight	P.C. BEAM				
Blk G 4th Storey	4	Overnight	P.C. BEAM				
Blk G 4th Storey	6	0:30	P.C. BEAM				
Blk G 4th Storey	2	0:10	P.C. BEAM				
Blk G 4th Storey	1	0:05	P.C. BEAM				
Blk G 4th Storey	12	Overnight	P.C. PLANK				
Blk G 4th Storey	3	0:35	P.C. SLAB	0:11:40	0:09:10	16%	20%
Blk G 4th Storey	3	0:30	P.C. SLAB	0:10:00	0:07:30	13%	10%
Blk G 4th Storey	3	0:15	P.C. SLAB	0:05:00	0:02:30	4%	0%
Blk G 4th Storey	3	0:30	P.C. SLAB	0:10:00	0:07:30	13%	10%
Blk G 4th Storey	3	0:15	P.C. SLAB	0:05:00	0:02:30	4%	0%
Blk G 4th Storey	3	0:30	P.C. SLAB	0:10:00	0:07:30	13%	10%
Blk G 4th Storey	3	0:30	P.C. SLAB	0:10:00	0:07:30	13%	10%
Blk G 4th Storey	4	0:45	P.C. SLAB	0:11:15	0:08:45	15%	20%
Blk G 4th Storey	13	0:30	P.C. COLUMN				
Blk G 4th Storey	1	0:40	P.C. WALL				
Blk G 4th Storey	1	0:10	P.C. WALL				
Blk G 4th Storey	1	0:20	P.C. WALL				
Blk G 4th Storey	1	0:30	P.C. WALL				
Blk G Roof	2	Overnight	R.C. ROOF BEAM				
Blk G Roof	5	Overnight	P.C. ROOF BEAM				
Blk G Roof	4	Overnight	P.C. ROOF BEAM				

Location	No of Pcs Delivered	Unloading Time	Type of Elements	P.C. Slab Category			
				Unloading Time Per Slab	Process Time Wastage	Process Time Wastage (RPT)	Rounded RTP
Blk H 1st Storey	8	0:30	P.C. SLAB	0:03:45	0:01:15	2%	0%
Blk H 1st Storey	8	0:25	P.C. SLAB	0:03:08	0:00:38	1%	0%
Blk H 1st Storey	8	0:25	P.C. SLAB	0:03:07	0:00:38	1%	0%
Blk H 1st Storey	6	0:20	P.C. SLAB	0:03:20	0:00:50	1%	0%
Blk H 1st Storey	8	0:20	P.C. SLAB	0:02:30	0:00:00	0%	0%
Blk H 1st Storey	4	0:30	P.C. COLUMN				
Blk H 1st Storey	4	0:15	P.C. COLUMN				
Blk H 1st Storey	3	1:00	P.C. COLUMN				
Blk H 1st Storey	1	1:05	P.C. WALL				
Blk H 1st Storey	1	0:20	P.C. WALL				
Blk H 2nd Storey	3	0:30	P.C. BEAM				
Blk H 2nd Storey	3	0:30	P.C. BEAM				
Blk H 2nd Storey	4	0:30	P.C. BEAM				
Blk H 2nd Storey	3	0:30	P.C. BEAM				
Blk H 2nd Storey	5	0:45	P.C. PLANK				
Blk H 2nd Storey	23	2:45	P.C. BEAM				
Blk H 2nd Storey	4	0:30	P.C. BEAM				
Blk H 2nd Storey	8	0:25	P.C. SLAB	0:03:08	0:00:38	1%	0%
Blk H 2nd Storey	8	0:40	P.C. SLAB	0:05:00	0:02:30	4%	0%
Blk H 2nd Storey	8	0:50	P.C. SLAB	0:06:15	0:03:45	7%	10%
Blk H 2nd Storey	7	0:30	P.C. SLAB	0:04:17	0:01:47	3%	0%
Blk H 2nd Storey	6	0:30	P.C. SLAB	0:05:00	0:02:30	4%	0%
Blk H 2nd Storey	1	0:15	P.C. SLAB	0:15:00	0:12:30	22%	20%
Blk H 2nd Storey	7	0:30	P.C. PLANK				
Blk H 3rd Storey	1	0:10	P.C. WALL				
Blk H 3rd Storey	2	0:25	P.C. BEAM				
Blk H 3rd Storey	2	0:25	P.C. BEAM				
Blk H 3rd Storey	3	1:45	P.C. BEAM				
Blk H 3rd Storey	3	0:35	P.C. BEAM				
Blk H 3rd Storey	4	0:10	P.C. BEAM				
Blk H 3rd Storey	3	1:15	P.C. BEAM				

Location	No of Pcs Delivered	Unloading Time	Type of Elements	Unloading Time Per Slab	Process Time Wastage	Process Time Wastage (RPT)	Rounded RTP
Blk H 3rd Storey	4	0:30	P.C. PLANK				
Blk H 3rd Storey	17	0:30	P.C. PLANK				
Blk H 3rd Storey	2	1:25	P.C. BEAM				
Blk H 3rd Storey	1	0:10	P.C. BEAM				
Blk H 3rd Storey	2	0:25	P.C. BEAM				
Blk H 3rd Storey	1	0:10	P.C. SLAB	0:10:00	0:07:30	13%	10%
Blk H 3rd Storey	4	0:40	P.C. PLANK				
Blk H 3rd Storey	1	0:45	P.C. WALL				
Blk H 4th Storey	4	0:50	P.C. BEAM				
Blk H 4th Storey	2	0:20	P.C. BEAM				
Blk H 4th Storey	3	0:25	P.C. BEAM				
Blk H 4th Storey	3	0:15	P.C. BEAM				
Blk H 4th Storey	2	1:00	P.C. BEAM				
Blk H 4th Storey	5	0:45	P.C. BEAM				
Blk H 4th Storey	21	Overnight	P.C. PLANK				
Blk H 4th Storey	8	2:20	P.C. SLAB	0:17:30	0:15:00	26%	30%
Blk H 4th Storey	8	0:30	P.C. SLAB	0:03:45	0:01:15	2%	0%
Blk H 4th Storey	8	0:15	P.C. SLAB	Exceptional Timing			
Blk H 4th Storey	6	1:15	P.C. SLAB	0:12:30	0:10:00	17%	20%
Blk H 4th Storey	8	0:50	P.C. SLAB	0:06:15	0:03:45	7%	10%
Blk H 4th Storey	1	0:30	P.C. WALL				
Blk H 4th Storey	1	0:30	P.C. WALL				
Blk H 4th Storey	12	0:30	P.C. COLUMN				
Blk H 4th Storey	8	0:25	P.C. COLUMN				
Blk H 4th Storey	2	Overnight	P.C. COLUMN				
Blk H 4th Storey	2	Overnight	P.C. BEAM				
Blk H 4th Storey	2	Overnight	P.C. BEAM				
Blk H 4th Storey	7	1:30	P.C. PLANK				
Blk H 4th Storey	2	0:15	P.C. BEAM				

Location	No of Pcs Delivered	Unloading Time	Type of Elements	P.C. Slab Category			
				Unloading Time Per Slab	Process Time Wastage	Process Time Wastage (RPT)	Rounded RTP
Blk H 4th Storey	4	0:25	P.C. BEAM				
Blk H 4th Storey	7	0:20	P.C. PLANK				
Blk H 4th Storey	2	0:05	P.C. COLUMN				
Blk H 4th Storey	17	0:25	P.C. STAIR TREAD				
Blk H Roof	5	0:30	P.C. ROOF BEAM				
Blk H Roof	4	0:25	P.C. ROOF BEAM				
Blk H Roof	4	0:15	P.C. ROOF BEAM				
Blk H Roof	5	0:10	P.C. ROOF BEAM				

Location	No of Pcs Delivered	Unloading Time	Type of Elements	Unloading Time Per Slab	Process Time Wastage	Process Time Wastage (RPT)	Rounded RTP
Blk A 1st Storey	6	2:00	P.C. SLAB				
Blk A 1st Storey	6	1:50	P.C. SLAB				
Blk A 1st Storey	6	0:35	P.C. SLAB				
Blk A 1st Storey	7	0:55	P.C. SLAB				
Blk A 1st Storey	10	2:10	P.C. SLAB				
Blk A 1st Storey	6	0:25	P.C. SLAB				
Blk A 1st Storey	7	0:30	P.C. SLAB				
Blk A 1st Storey	6	0:25	P.C. SLAB				
Blk A 1st Storey	6	0:40	P.C. SLAB				
Blk A 1st Storey	5	0:20	P.C. SLAB				
Blk A 1st Storey	5	0:25	P.C. SLAB				
Blk A 1st Storey	3	0:25	P.C. SLAB				
Blk A 1st Storey	5	0:15	P.C. COLUMN	0:03:00	0:01:45	2%	0%
Blk A 1st Storey	6	0:30	P.C. COLUMN	0:05:00	0:03:45	4%	0%
Blk A 1st Storey	4	0:25	P.C. COLUMN	0:06:15	0:05:00	6%	10%
Blk A 1st Storey	3	0:30	P.C. COLUMN	0:10:00	0:08:45	10%	10%
Blk A 1st Storey	5	0:30	P.C. COLUMN	0:06:00	0:04:45	5%	10%
Blk A 1st Storey	4	0:15	P.C. COLUMN	0:03:45	0:02:30	3%	0%
Blk A 1st Storey	4	0:10	P.C. COLUMN	0:02:30	0:01:15	1%	0%
Blk A 1st Storey	3	0:20	P.C. COLUMN	0:06:40	0:05:25	6%	10%
Blk A 2nd Storey	2	0:15	P.C. COLUMN	0:07:30	0:06:15	7%	10%
Blk A 2nd Storey	1	0:05	P.C. BEAM	0:05:00	0:03:45	4%	0%
Blk A 2nd Storey	5	0:15	P.C. BEAM	0:03:00	0:01:45	2%	0%
Blk A 2nd Storey	3	0:20	P.C. BEAM	0:06:40	0:05:25	6%	10%
Blk A 2nd Storey	4	0:15	P.C. BEAM	0:03:45	0:02:30	3%	0%
Blk A 2nd Storey	3	0:15	P.C. BEAM	0:05:00	0:03:45	4%	0%
Blk A 2nd Storey	6	0:25	P.C. BEAM	0:04:10	0:02:55	3%	0%
Blk A 2nd Storey	5	0:25	P.C. BEAM	0:05:00	0:03:45	4%	0%
Blk A 2nd Storey	6	0:45	P.C. SLAB				
Blk A 2nd Storey	6	0:30	P.C. SLAB				
Blk A 2nd Storey	6	1:00	P.C. SLAB				

Location	No of Pcs Delivered	Unloading Time	Type of Elements	Unloading Time Per Slab	Process Time Wastage	Process Time Wastage (RPT)	Rounded RTP
				Other P.C. Element Category			
Blk A 2nd Storey	6	0:35	P.C. SLAB				
Blk A 2nd Storey	6	0:35	P.C. SLAB				
Blk A 2nd Storey	6	0:35	P.C. SLAB				
Blk A 2nd Storey	4	0:25	P.C. SLAB				
Blk A 2nd Storey	3	0:30	P.C. BEAM	0:10:00	0:08:45	10%	10%
Blk A 2nd Storey	6	0:50	P.C. SLAB				
Blk A 2nd Storey	6	1:10	P.C. SLAB				
Blk A 2nd Storey	6	0:35	P.C. SLAB				
Blk A 2nd Storey	6	0:55	P.C. SLAB				
Blk A 2nd Storey	6	1:05	P.C. SLAB				
Blk A 2nd Storey	6	0:35	P.C. SLAB				
Blk A 2nd Storey	6	0:40	P.C. SLAB				
Blk A 2nd Storey	8	3:05	P.C. SLAB				
Blk A 3rd Storey	4	1:30	P.C. BEAM	0:22:30	0:21:15	24%	20%
Blk A 3rd Storey	6	1:00	P.C. BEAM	0:10:00	0:08:45	10%	10%
Blk A 3rd Storey	6	0:30	P.C. BEAM	0:05:00	0:03:45	4%	0%
Blk A 3rd Storey	7	0:40	P.C. BEAM	0:05:43	0:04:28	5%	10%
Blk A 3rd Storey	6	2:15	P.C. SLAB				
Blk A 3rd Storey	6	2:50	P.C. SLAB				
Blk A 3rd Storey	6	2:00	P.C. SLAB				
Blk A 3rd Storey	6	1:10	P.C. SLAB				
Blk A 3rd Storey	6	1:25	P.C. SLAB				
Blk A 3rd Storey	6	2:35	P.C. SLAB				
Blk A 3rd Storey	4	2:40	P.C. SLAB				
Blk A 3rd Storey	6	1:10	P.C. SLAB				
Blk A-3rd Storey	5	0:25	P.C. SLAB				
Blk A 3rd Storey	5	0:35	P.C. SLAB				
Blk A 3rd Storey	4	1:00	P.C. SLAB				
Blk A 3rd Storey	6	1:40	P.C. SLAB				
Blk A 3rd Storey	6	2:10	P.C. SLAB				
Blk A 3rd Storey	6	0:50	P.C. SLAB				

218

Location	No of Pcs Delivered	Unloading Time	Type of Elements	Other P.C. Element Category			
				Unloading Time Per Slab	Process Time Wastage	Process Time Wastage (RPT)	Rounded RTP
Blk A 3rd Storey	6	2:25	P.C. SLAB				
Blk A 3rd Storey	6	2:30	P.C. SLAB				
Blk A Roof	5	3:15	P.C. ROOF BEAM	0:39:00	0:37:45	43%	40%
Blk A Roof	5	2:45	P.C. ROOF BEAM	0:33:00	0:31:45	36%	40%
Blk A Roof	6	1:30	R.C. ROOF BEAM	0:15:00	0:13:45	15%	20%

Location	No of Pcs Delivered	Unloading Time	Type of Elements	Other P.C. Element Category			
				Unloading Time Per Slab	Process Time Wastage	Process Time Wastage (RPT)	Rounded RTP
Blk B 1st Storey	6	0:30	P.C. COLUMN	0:05:00	0:03:45	4%	0%
Blk B 1st Storey	4	0:35	P.C. COLUMN	0:08:45	0:07:30	8%	10%
Blk B 1st Storey	3	0:15	P.C. COLUMN	0:05:00	0:03:45	4%	0%
Blk B 1st Storey	1	0:15	P.C. WALL	0:15:00	0:13:45	15%	20%
Blk B 1st Storey	3	0:15	P.C. COLUMN	0:05:00	0:03:45	4%	0%
Blk B 1st Storey	6	0:25	P.C. SLAB				
Blk B 1st Storey	3	0:30	P.C. COLUMN	0:10:00	0:08:45	10%	10%
Blk B 1st Storey	3	0:25	P.C. BEAM	0:08:20	0:07:05	8%	10%
Blk B 2nd Storey	4	0:15	P.C. COLUMN	0:03:45	0:02:30	3%	0%
Blk B 2nd Storey	2	0:10	P.C. BEAM	0:05:00	0:03:45	4%	0%
Blk B 2nd Storey	3	0:20	P.C. BEAM	0:06:40	0:05:25	6%	10%
Blk B 2nd Storey	5	0:30	P.C. SLAB				
Blk B 2nd Storey	6	0:40	P.C. SLAB				
Blk B 2nd Storey	5	0:25	P.C. SLAB				
Blk B 2nd Storey	5	0:20	P.C. SLAB				
Blk B 2nd Storey	3	0:25	P.C. SLAB				
Blk B 2nd Storey	6	0:45	P.C. SLAB				
Blk B 2nd Storey	5	0:40	P.C. SLAB				
Blk B 2nd Storey	5	0:30	P.C. SLAB				
Blk B 2nd Storey	5	0:30	P.C. SLAB				
Blk B 2nd Storey	3	0:15	P.C. SLAB				
Blk B 2nd Storey	1	0:05	P.C. BEAM	0:05:00	0:03:45	4%	0%
Blk B 2nd Storey	4	0:15	P.C. BEAM	0:03:45	0:02:30	3%	0%
Blk B 2nd Storey	6	0:45	P.C. SLAB				
Blk B 2nd Storey	5	0:35	P.C. SLAB				
Blk B 2nd Storey	5	0:20	P.C. SLAB				
Blk B 2nd Storey	5	0:50	P.C. SLAB				
Blk B 2nd Storey	6	0:25	P.C. SLAB				
Blk B 2nd Storey	6	0:30	P.C. SLAB				
Blk B Roof	4	1:00	P.C. ROOF BEAM	0:15:00	0:13:45	15%	20%

Location	No of Pcs Delivered	Unloading Time	Type of Elements	Other P.C. Element Category			
				Unloading Time Per Slab	Process Time Wastage	Process Time Wastage (RPT)	Rounded RTP
Blk B Roof	4	0:30	P.C. ROOF BEAM	0:07:30	0:06:15	7%	10%

Location	No of Pcs Delivered	Unloading Time	Type of Elements	Other P.C. Element Category			
				Unloading Time Per Slab	Process Time Wastage	Process Time Wastage (RPT)	Rounded RTP
Blk C 1st Storey	9	0:15	P.C. COLUMN	0:01:40	0:00:25	0%	0%
Blk C 1st Storey	8	0:20	P.C. COLUMN	0:02:30	0:01:15	1%	0%
Blk C 1st Storey	1	0:25	P.C. WALL	0:25:00	0:23:45	27%	30%
Blk C 1st Storey	1	1:10	P.C. WALL	1:10:00	1:08:45	77%	80%
Blk C 1st Storey	1	0:05	P.C. COLUMN	0:05:00	0:03:45	4%	0%
Blk C 1st Storey	1	0:10	P.C. WALL	0:10:00	0:08:45	10%	10%
Blk C 1st Storey	1	0:10	P.C. WALL	0:10:00	0:08:45	10%	10%
Blk C 1st Storey	5	0:10	P.C. COLUMN	0:02:00	0:00:45	1%	0%
Blk C 2nd Storey	6	0:20	P.C. BEAM	0:03:20	0:02:05	2%	0%
Blk C 2nd Storey	2	1:25	P.C. BEAM	0:42:30	0:41:15	46%	50%
Blk C 2nd Storey	3	0:30	P.C. BEAM	0:10:00	0:08:45	10%	10%
Blk C 2nd Storey	4	0:20	P.C. BEAM	0:05:00	0:03:45	4%	0%
Blk C 2nd Storey	8	0:45	P.C. SLAB				
Blk C 2nd Storey	8	0:40	P.C. SLAB				
Blk C 2nd Storey	8	0:40	P.C. SLAB				
Blk C 2nd Storey	6	0:25	P.C. SLAB				
Blk C 2nd Storey	5	0:20	P.C. COLUMN	0:04:00	0:02:45	3%	0%
Blk C 2nd Storey	8	0:55	P.C. SLAB				
Blk C 2nd Storey	8	0:40	P.C. SLAB				
Blk C 2nd Storey	8	0:45	P.C. SLAB				
Blk C 2nd Storey	1	0:15	P.C. WALL	0:15:00	0:13:45	15%	20%
Blk C 2nd Storey	1	0:10	P.C. WALL	0:10:00	0:08:45	10%	10%
Blk C 2nd Storey	1	5:00	P.C. WALL	Exceptional Timing			
Blk C Roof	6	0:15	P.C. ROOF BEAM	0:02:30	0:01:15	1%	0%
Blk C Roof	3	0:20	P.C. ROOF BEAM	0:06:40	0:05:25	6%	10%
Blk C Roof	6	0:30	P.C. ROOF BEAM	0:05:00	0:03:45	4%	0%

Location	No of Pcs Delivered	Unloading Time	Type of Elements	Other P.C. Element Category			
				Unloading Time Per Slab	Process Time Wastage	Process Time Wastage (RPT)	Rounded RTP
Blk D 1st Storey	4	1:30	P.C. SLAB				
Blk D 1st Storey	4	0:35	P.C. SLAB				
Blk D 1st Storey	4	0:35	P.C. SLAB				
Blk D 1st Storey	4	0:50	P.C. SLAB				
Blk D 1st Storey	4	0:25	P.C. SLAB				
Blk D 1st Storey	3	0:45	P.C. SLAB				
Blk D 1st Storey	4	0:10	P.C. COLUMN	0:02:30	0:01:15	1%	0%
Blk D 1st Storey	4	0:20	P.C. COLUMN	0:05:00	0:03:45	4%	0%
Blk D 1st Storey	5	0:45	P.C. COLUMN	0:09:00	0:07:45	9%	10%
Blk D 1st Storey	1	0:10	P.C. COLUMN	0:10:00	0:08:45	10%	10%
Blk D 1st Storey	1	0:15	P.C. WALL	0:15:00	0:13:45	15%	20%
Blk D 1st Storey	1	0:15	P.C. WALL	0:15:00	0:13:45	15%	20%
Blk D 1st Storey	6	0:35	P.C. BEAM	0:05:50	0:04:35	5%	10%
Blk D 2nd Storey	4	0:35	P.C. BEAM	0:08:45	0:07:30	8%	10%
Blk D 2nd Storey	3	0:15	P.C. BEAM	0:05:00	0:03:45	4%	0%
Blk D 2nd Storey	2	0:15	P.C. BEAM	0:07:30	0:06:15	7%	10%
Blk D 2nd Storey	4	0:55	P.C. SLAB				
Blk D 2nd Storey	3	0:40	P.C. SLAB				
Blk D 2nd Storey	3	0:30	P.C. SLAB				
Blk D 2nd Storey	3	0:45	P.C. SLAB				
Blk D 2nd Storey	3	0:35	P.C. SLAB				
Blk D 2nd Storey	3	0:40	P.C. SLAB				
Blk D 2nd Storey	3	1:05	P.C. SLAB				
Blk D 2nd Storey	1	0:10	P.C. BEAM	0:10:00	0:08:45	10%	10%
Blk D 2nd Storey	12	0:25	P.C. PLANK	0:02:05	0:00:50	1%	0%
Blk D 2nd Storey	1	0:15	P.C. WALL	0:15:00	0:13:45	15%	20%
Blk D 2nd Storey	1	1:00	P.C. WALL	1:00:00	0:58:45	66%	70%
Blk D 3rd Storey	5	0:35	P.C. BEAM	0:07:00	0:05:45	6%	10%
Blk D 3rd Storey	5	0:20	P.C. BEAM	0:04:00	0:02:45	3%	0%
Blk D 3rd Storey	5	0:20	P.C. BEAM	0:04:00	0:02:45	3%	0%

Location	No of Pcs Delivered	Unloading Time	Type of Elements	Other P.C. Element Category			
				Unloading Time Per Slab	Process Time Wastage	Process Time Wastage (RPT)	Rounded RTP
Blk D 3rd Storey	1	0:05	R.C. ROOF BEAM	0:05:00	0:03:45	4%	0%
Blk D 3rd Storey	3	1:50	P.C. SLAB				
Blk D 3rd Storey	3	0:40	P.C. SLAB				
Blk D 3rd Storey	3	0:40	P.C. SLAB				
Blk D 3rd Storey	3	0:40	P.C. SLAB				
Blk D 3rd Storey	3	0:50	P.C. SLAB				
Blk D 3rd Storey	3	1:00	P.C. SLAB				
Blk D 3rd Storey	3	0:35	P.C. SLAB				
Blk D 3rd Storey	3	0:55	P.C. SLAB				
Blk D 3rd Storey		1:00	P.C. SLAB				
Blk D 3rd Storey	1	0:30	P.C. WALL	0:30:00	0:28:45	32%	30%
Blk D 3rd Storey	1	0:30	P.C. WALL	0:30:00	0:28:45	32%	30%
Blk D Roof	4	Overnight	R.C. ROOF BEAM				
Blk D Roof	4	0:45	R.C. ROOF BEAM	0:11:15	0:10:00	11%	10%
Blk D Roof	4	0:20	R.C. ROOF BEAM	0:05:00	0:03:45	4%	0%
Blk D Roof	4	1:00	P.C. ROOF BEAM	0:15:00	0:13:45	15%	20%

Location	No of Pcs Delivered	Unloading Time	Type of Elements	Other P.C. Element Category			
				Unloading Time Per Slab	Process Time Wastage	Process Time Wastage (RPT)	Rounded RTP
Blk E 1st Storey	5	1:15	P.C. COLUMN	0:15:00	0:13:45	15%	20%
Blk E 1st Storey	2	0:05	P.C. COLUMN	0:02:30	0:01:15	1%	0%
Blk E 1st Storey	5	1:30	P.C. COLUMN	0:18:00	0:16:45	19%	20%
Blk E 1st Storey	1	0:10	P.C. WALL	0:10:00	0:08:45	10%	10%
Blk E 1st Storey	1	0:30	P.C. WALL	0:30:00	0:28:45	32%	30%
Blk E 1st Storey	4	0:35	P.C. COLUMN	0:08:45	0:07:30	8%	10%
Blk E 1st Storey	5	0:30	P.C. BEAM	0:06:00	0:04:45	5%	10%
Blk E 2nd Storey	4	0:30	P.C. BEAM	0:07:30	0:06:15	7%	10%
Blk E 2nd Storey	1	0:05	P.C. BEAM	0:05:00	0:03:45	4%	0%
Blk E 2nd Storey	4	0:15	P.C. BEAM	0:03:45	0:02:30	3%	0%
Blk E 2nd Storey	4	1:15	P.C. SLAB				
Blk E 2nd Storey	3	0:40	P.C. SLAB				
Blk E 2nd Storey	3	0:35	P.C. SLAB				
Blk E 2nd Storey	3	0:30	P.C. SLAB				
Blk E 2nd Storey	3	0:55	P.C. SLAB				
Blk E 2nd Storey	3	0:35	P.C. SLAB	0:10:00	0:08:45	10%	10%
Blk E 2nd Storey	1	0:10	P.C. BEAM	0:07:00	0:05:45	6%	10%
Blk E 2nd Storey	10	1:10	P.C. PLANK	1:05:00	1:03:45	72%	70%
Blk E 2nd Storey	1	1:05	P.C. WALL	0:40:00	0:38:45	44%	40%
Blk E 2nd Storey	1	0:40	P.C. WALL				
Blk E 3rd Storey	5	Overnight	P.C. BEAM				
Blk E 3rd Storey	5	Overnight	P.C. BEAM				
Blk E 3rd Storey	5	0:40	P.C. BEAM	0:08:00	0:06:45	8%	10%
Blk E 3rd Storey	4	0:40	P.C. SLAB				
Blk E 3rd Storey	3	0:45	P.C. SLAB				
Blk E 3rd Storey	3	0:30	P.C. SLAB				
Blk E 3rd Storey	3	0:25	P.C. SLAB				
Blk E 3rd Storey	4	1:00	P.C. SLAB				
Blk E 3rd Storey	3	0:50	P.C. SLAB	0:05:00	0:03:45	4%	0%
Blk E 3rd Storey	10	0:50	P.C. PLANK				

Location	No of Pcs Delivered	Unloading Time	Type of Elements	Other P.C. Element Category			
				Unloading Time Per Slab	Process Time Wastage	Process Time Wastage (RPT)	Rounded RTP
Blk E 3rd Storey	1	Overnight	P.C. WALL	0:30:00	0:28:45	32%	30%
Blk E 3rd Storey	1	0:30	P.C. WALL				
Blk E 4th Storey	2	Overnight	P.C. COLUMN	0:06:00	0:04:45	5%	10%
Blk E 4th Storey	5	0:30	P.C. COLUMN				
Blk E Roof	5	Overnight	R.C. ROOF BEAM				
Blk E Roof	7	Overnight	R.C. ROOF BEAM				

Location	No of Pcs Delivered	Unloading Time	Type of Elements	Other P.C. Element Category			
				Unloading Time Per Slab	Process Time Wastage	Process Time Wastage (RPT)	Rounded RTP
Blk F 1st Storey	8	0:40	P.C. SLAB				
Blk F 1st Storey	8	0:40	P.C. SLAB				
Blk F 1st Storey	7	0:25	P.C. SLAB				
Blk F 1st Storey	7	0:30	P.C. SLAB				
Blk F 1st Storey	5	0:30	P.C. COLUMN	0:06:00	0:04:45	5%	10%
Blk F 1st Storey	2	0:15	P.C. COLUMN	0:07:30	0:06:15	7%	10%
Blk F 1st Storey	5	1:00	P.C. COLUMN	0:12:00	0:10:45	12%	10%
Blk F 1st Storey	4	6:00	P.C. COLUMN	1:30:00	1:28:45	100%	100%
Blk F 1st Storey	1	0:40	P.C. WALL	0:40:00	0:38:45	44%	40%
Blk F 2nd Storey	2	0:15	P.C. BEAM	0:07:30	0:06:15	7%	10%
Blk F 2nd Storey	4	0:30	P.C. BEAM	0:07:30	0:06:15	7%	10%
Blk F 2nd Storey	4	0:30	P.C. BEAM	0:07:30	0:06:15	7%	10%
Blk F 2nd Storey	3	0:30	P.C. BEAM	0:10:00	0:08:45	10%	10%
Blk F 2nd Storey	3	0:30	P.C. BEAM	0:10:00	0:08:45	10%	10%
Blk F 2nd Storey	19	2:00	P.C. PLANK	0:06:19	0:05:04	6%	10%
Blk F 2nd Storey	1	Overnight	P.C. BEAM				
Blk F 2nd Storey	2	Overnight	P.C. COLUMN				
Blk F 2nd Storey	8	0:50	P.C. SLAB	0:06:15	0:05:00	6%	10%
Blk F 2nd Storey	8	0:45	P.C. SLAB	0:05:37	0:04:23	5%	0%
Blk F 2nd Storey	6	0:40	P.C. SLAB	0:06:40	0:05:25	6%	10%
Blk F 2nd Storey	4	0:10	P.C. PLANK	0:02:30	0:01:15	1%	0%
Blk F 2nd Storey	1	0:05	P.C. BEAM	0:05:00	0:03:45	4%	0%
Blk F 2nd Storey	1	0:30	P.C. WALL	0:30:00	0:28:45	32%	30%
Blk F 3rd Storey	3	1:30	P.C. BEAM	0:30:00	0:28:45	32%	30%
Blk F 3rd Storey	3	0:45	P.C. BEAM	0:15:00	0:13:45	15%	20%
Blk F 3rd Storey	3	2:05	P.C. BEAM	0:41:40	0:40:25	46%	50%
Blk F 3rd Storey	4	0:45	P.C. BEAM	0:11:15	0:10:00	11%	10%
Blk F 3rd Storey	3	1:25	P.C. BEAM	0:28:20	0:27:05	31%	30%
Blk F 3rd Storey	5	0:35	P.C. BEAM	0:07:00	0:05:45	6%	10%

Location	No of Pcs Delivered	Unloading Time	Type of Elements	Other P.C. Element Category			
				Unloading Time Per Slab	Process Time Wastage	Process Time Wastage (RPT)	Rounded RTP
Blk F 3rd Storey	8	1:00	P.C. SLAB				
Blk F 3rd Storey	8	0:35	P.C. SLAB				
Blk F 3rd Storey	8	0:50	P.C. SLAB				
Blk F 3rd Storey	5	0:30	P.C. SLAB				
Blk F 3rd Storey	19	0:25	P.C. PLANK	0:01:19	0:00:04	0%	0%
Blk F 3rd Storey	1	0:05	P.C. PLANK	0:05:00	0:03:45	4%	0%
Blk F 3rd Storey	6	0:45	P.C. SLAB				
Blk F 3rd Storey	8	0:35	P.C. SLAB				
Blk F 3rd Storey	8	1:05	P.C. SLAB				
Blk F 3rd Storey	8	0:30	P.C. SLAB				
Blk F 3rd Storey	6	0:40	P.C. SLAB				
Blk F 3rd Storey	1	0:15	P.C. SLAB				
Blk F 3rd Storey	1	0:10	P.C. BEAM	0:10:00	0:08:45	10%	10%
Blk F 3rd Storey	1	0:20	P.C. WALL	0:20:00	0:18:45	21%	20%
Blk F 3rd Storey	1	0:05	P.C. WALL	0:05:00	0:03:45	4%	0%
Blk F 4th Storey	4	0:40	P.C. BEAM	0:10:00	0:08:45	10%	10%
Blk F 4th Storey	3	0:30	P.C. BEAM	0:10:00	0:08:45	10%	10%
Blk F 4th Storey	1	0:10	P.C. BEAM	0:10:00	0:08:45	10%	10%
Blk F 4th Storey	2	0:05	P.C. BEAM	0:02:30	0:01:15	1%	0%
Blk F 4th Storey	4	0:30	P.C. BEAM	0:07:30	0:06:15	7%	10%
Blk F 4th Storey	24	0:30	P.C. PLANK	0:01:15	0:00:00	0%	0%
Blk F 4th Storey	3	0:40	P.C. BEAM	0:13:20	0:12:05	14%	10%
Blk F 4th Storey	2	0:30	P.C. BEAM	0:15:00	0:13:45	15%	20%
Blk F 4th Storey	2	0:40	P.C. BEAM	0:20:00	0:18:45	21%	20%
Blk F 4th Storey	4	1:25	P.C. PLANK	0:21:15	0:20:00	23%	20%
Blk F 4th Storey	8	0:55	P.C. SLAB				
Blk F 4th Storey	8	0:35	P.C. SLAB				
Blk F 4th Storey	8	1:20	P.C. SLAB				
Blk F 4th Storey	6	0:40	P.C. SLAB				
Blk F 4th Storey	14	4:00	P.C. COLUMN	0:17:09	0:15:54	18%	20%
Blk F 4th Storey	5	Overnight	P.C. COLUMN				

228

Location	No of Pcs Delivered	Unloading Time	Type of Elements	Other P.C. Element Category			
				Unloading Time Per Slab	Process Time Wastage	Process Time Wastage (RPT)	Rounded RTP
Blk F 4th Storey	2	0:15	P.C. BEAM	0:07:30	0:06:15	7%	10%
Blk F 4th Storey	7	0:30	P.C. PLANK	0:04:17	0:03:02	3%	0%
Blk F Roof	5	1:30	P.C. ROOF BEAM	0:18:00	0:16:45	19%	20%
Blk F Roof	4	0:45	P.C. ROOF BEAM	0:11:15	0:10:00	11%	10%
Blk F Roof	2	0:30	P.C. ROOF BEAM	0:15:00	0:13:45	15%	20%
Blk F Roof	5	0:15	P.C. ROOF BEAM	0:03:00	0:01:45	2%	0%

229

Location	No of Pcs Delivered	Unloading Time	Type of Elements	Other P.C. Element Category			
				Unloading Time Per Slab	Process Time Wastage	Process Time Wastage (RPT)	Rounded RTP
Blk G 1st Storey	4	0:20	P.C. COLUMN	0:05:00	0:03:45	4%	0%
Blk G 1st Storey	4	0:10	P.C. COLUMN	0:02:30	0:01:15	1%	0%
Blk G 1st Storey	5	0:25	P.C. COLUMN	0:05:00	0:03:45	4%	0%
Blk G 1st Storey	1	0:05	P.C. WALL	0:05:00	0:03:45	4%	0%
Blk G 1st Storey	1	Overnight	P.C. WALL				
Blk G 1st Storey	1	0:25	P.C. WALL	0:25:00	0:23:45	27%	30%
Blk G 2nd Storey	5	3:00	P.C. BEAM	0:36:00	0:34:45	39%	40%
Blk G 2nd Storey	4	0:45	P.C. BEAM	0:11:15	0:10:00	11%	10%
Blk G 2nd Storey	5	0:25	P.C. BEAM	0:05:00	0:03:45	4%	0%
Blk G 2nd Storey	3	0:20	P.C. SLAB				
Blk G 2nd Storey	3	0:20	P.C. SLAB				
Blk G 2nd Storey	3	0:30	P.C. SLAB				
Blk G 2nd Storey	3	0:35	P.C. SLAB				
Blk G 2nd Storey	3	1:20	P.C. SLAB				
Blk G 2nd Storey	3	0:30	P.C. SLAB				
Blk G 2nd Storey	3	1:10	P.C. SLAB				
Blk G 2nd Storey	4	0:35	P.C. SLAB				
Blk G 2nd Storey	8	1:10	P.C. SLAB				
Blk G 2nd Storey	1	0:15	P.C. WALL	0:15:00	0:13:45	15%	20%
Blk G 2nd Storey	1	0:10	P.C. WALL	0:10:00	0:08:45	10%	10%
Blk G 2nd Storey	1	0:10	P.C. WALL	0:10:00	0:08:45	10%	10%
Blk G 2nd Storey	1	1:00	P.C. WALL	1:00:00	0:58:45	66%	70%
Blk G 3rd Storey	4	0:20	P.C. BEAM	0:05:00	0:03:45	4%	0%
Blk G 3rd Storey	4	0:25	P.C. BEAM	0:06:15	0:05:00	6%	10%
Blk G 3rd Storey	5	0:30	P.C. BEAM	0:06:00	0:04:45	5%	10%
Blk G 3rd Storey	1	0:10	P.C. BEAM	0:10:00	0:08:45	10%	10%
Blk G 3rd Storey	8	0:40	P.C. PLANK	0:05:00	0:03:45	4%	0%
Blk G 3rd Storey	3	0:35	P.C. SLAB				
Blk G 3rd Storey	3	0:40	P.C. SLAB				
Blk G 3rd Storey	3	0:35	P.C. SLAB				
Blk G 3rd Storey	3	1:00	P.C. SLAB				

Location	No of Pcs Delivered	Unloading Time	Type of Elements	Other P.C. Element Category			
				Unloading Time Per Slab	Process Time Wastage	Process Time Wastage (RPT)	Rounded RTP
Blk G 3rd Storey	3	0:55	P.C. SLAB				
Blk G 3rd Storey	3	1:00	P.C. SLAB				
Blk G 3rd Storey	3	1:00	P.C. SLAB				
Blk G 3rd Storey	4	1:00	P.C. SLAB				
Blk G 3rd Storey	1	0:30	P.C. WALL	0:30:00	0:28:45	32%	30%
Blk G 3rd Storey	1	0:10	P.C. WALL	0:10:00	0:08:45	10%	10%
Blk G 3rd Storey	1	0:10	P.C. WALL	0:10:00	0:08:45	10%	10%
Blk G 3rd Storey	1	0:10	P.C. WALL	0:10:00	0:08:45	10%	10%
Blk G 4th Storey	5	Overnight	P.C. BEAM				
Blk G 4th Storey	4	Overnight	P.C. BEAM				
Blk G 4th Storey	6	0:30	P.C. BEAM	0:05:00	0:03:45	4%	0%
Blk G 4th Storey	2	0:10	P.C. BEAM	0:05:00	0:03:45	4%	0%
Blk G 4th Storey	1	0:05	P.C. BEAM	0:05:00	0:03:45	4%	0%
Blk G 4th Storey	12	Overnight	P.C. PLANK				
Blk G 4th Storey	3	0:35	P.C. SLAB				
Blk G 4th Storey	3	0:30	P.C. SLAB				
Blk G 4th Storey	3	0:15	P.C. SLAB				
Blk G 4th Storey	3	0:30	P.C. SLAB				
Blk G 4th Storey	3	0:15	P.C. SLAB				
Blk G 4th Storey	3	0:30	P.C. SLAB				
Blk G 4th Storey	3	0:30	P.C. SLAB				
Blk G 4th Storey	4	0:45	P.C. SLAB				
Blk G 4th Storey	13	0:30	P.C. COLUMN	0:02:18	0:01:03	1%	0%
Blk G 4th Storey	1	0:40	P.C. WALL	0:40:00	0:38:45	44%	40%
Blk G 4th Storey	1	0:10	P.C. WALL	0:10:00	0:08:45	10%	10%
Blk G 4th Storey	1	0:20	P.C. WALL	0:20:00	0:18:45	21%	20%
Blk G 4th Storey	1	0:30	P.C. WALL	0:30:00	0:28:45	32%	30%
Blk G Roof	2	Overnight	R.C. ROOF BEAM				
Blk G Roof	5	Overnight	P.C. ROOF BEAM				
Blk G Roof	4	Overnight	P.C. ROOF BEAM				

231

Location	No of Pcs Delivered	Unloading Time	Type of Elements	Other P.C. Element Category			
				Unloading Time Per Slab	Process Time Wastage	Process Time Wastage (RPT)	Rounded RTP
Blk H 1st Storey	8	0:30	P.C. SLAB				
Blk H 1st Storey	8	0:25	P.C. SLAB				
Blk H 1st Storey	8	0:25	P.C. SLAB				
Blk H 1st Storey	6	0:20	P.C. SLAB				
Blk H 1st Storey	8	0:20	P.C. SLAB				
Blk H 1st Storey	4	0:30	P.C. COLUMN	0:07:30	0:06:15	7%	10%
Blk H 1st Storey	4	0:15	P.C. COLUMN	0:03:45	0:02:30	3%	0%
Blk H 1st Storey	3	1:00	P.C. COLUMN	0:20:00	0:18:45	21%	20%
Blk H 1st Storey	1	1:05	P.C. WALL	1:05:00	1:03:45	72%	70%
Blk H 1st Storey	1	0:20	P.C. WALL	0:20:00	0:18:45	21%	20%
Blk H 2nd Storey	3	0:30	P.C. BEAM	0:10:00	0:08:45	10%	10%
Blk H 2nd Storey	3	0:30	P.C. BEAM	0:10:00	0:08:45	10%	10%
Blk H 2nd Storey	4	0:30	P.C. BEAM	0:07:30	0:06:15	7%	10%
Blk H 2nd Storey	3	0:30	P.C. BEAM	0:10:00	0:08:45	10%	10%
Blk H 2nd Storey	5	0:45	P.C. BEAM	0:09:00	0:07:45	9%	10%
Blk H 2nd Storey	23	2:45	P.C. PLANK	0:07:10	0:05:55	7%	10%
Blk H 2nd Storey	4	0:30	P.C. BEAM	0:07:30	0:06:15	7%	10%
Blk H 2nd Storey	8	0:25	P.C. SLAB				
Blk H 2nd Storey	8	0:40	P.C. SLAB				
Blk H 2nd Storey	8	0:50	P.C. SLAB				
Blk H 2nd Storey	7	0:30	P.C. SLAB				
Blk H 2nd Storey	6	0:30	P.C. SLAB				
Blk H 2nd Storey	1	0:15	P.C. SLAB				
Blk H 2nd Storey	7	0:30	P.C. PLANK	0:04:17	0:03:02	3%	0%
Blk H 2nd Storey	1	0:10	P.C. WALL	0:10:00	0:08:45	10%	10%
Blk H 3rd Storey	2	0:25	P.C. BEAM	0:12:30	0:11:15	13%	10%
Blk H 3rd Storey	2	0:25	P.C. BEAM	0:12:30	0:11:15	13%	10%
Blk H 3rd Storey	3	1:45	P.C. BEAM	0:35:00	0:33:45	38%	40%
Blk H 3rd Storey	3	0:35	P.C. BEAM	0:11:40	0:10:25	12%	10%
Blk H 3rd Storey	4	0:10	P.C. BEAM	0:02:30	0:01:15	1%	0%
Blk H 3rd Storey	3	1:15	P.C. BEAM	0:25:00	0:23:45	27%	30%

Location	No of Pcs Delivered	Unloading Time	Type of Elements	Other P.C. Element Category			
				Unloading Time Per Slab	Process Time Wastage	Process Time Wastage (RPT)	Rounded RPT
Blk H 3rd Storey	4	0:30	P.C. PLANK	0:07:30	0:06:15	7%	10%
Blk H 3rd Storey	17	0:30	P.C. PLANK	0:01:46	0:00:31	1%	0%
Blk H 3rd Storey	2	1:25	P.C. BEAM	0:42:30	0:41:15	46%	50%
Blk H 3rd Storey	1	0:10	P.C. BEAM	0:10:00	0:08:45	10%	10%
Blk H 3rd Storey	2	0:25	P.C. BEAM	0:12:30	0:11:15	13%	10%
Blk H 3rd Storey	1	0:10	P.C. SLAB				
Blk H 3rd Storey	4	0:40	P.C. PLANK	0:10:00	0:08:45	10%	10%
Blk H 3rd Storey	1	0:45	P.C. WALL	0:45:00	0:43:45	49%	50%
Blk H 4th Storey	4	0:50	P.C. BEAM	0:12:30	0:11:15	13%	10%
Blk H 4th Storey	2	0:20	P.C. BEAM	0:10:00	0:08:45	10%	10%
Blk H 4th Storey	3	0:25	P.C. BEAM	0:08:20	0:07:05	8%	10%
Blk H 4th Storey	3	0:15	P.C. BEAM	0:05:00	0:03:45	4%	0%
Blk H 4th Storey	2	1:00	P.C. BEAM	0:30:00	0:28:45	32%	30%
Blk H 4th Storey	5	0:45	P.C. BEAM	0:09:00	0:07:45	9%	10%
Blk H 4th Storey	21	Overnight	P.C. PLANK				
Blk H 4th Storey	8	2:20	P.C. SLAB				
Blk H 4th Storey	8	0:30	P.C. SLAB				
Blk H 4th Storey	8	0:15	P.C. SLAB	0:01:52	0:00:38	1%	0%
Blk H 4th Storey	6	1:15	P.C. SLAB				
Blk H 4th Storey	8	0:50	P.C. SLAB				
Blk H 4th Storey.	1	0:30	P.C. WALL	0:30:00	0:28:45	32%	30%
Blk H 4th Storey.	1	0:30	P.C. WALL	0:30:00	0:28:45	32%	30%
Blk H 4th Storey	12	0:30	P.C. COLUMN	0:02:30	0:01:15	1%	0%
Blk H 4th Storey	8	0:25	P.C. COLUMN	0:03:08	0:01:53	2%	0%
Blk H 4th Storey	2	Overnight	P.C. COLUMN				
Blk H 4th Storey	2	Overnight	P.C. BEAM				
Blk H 4th Storey	2	Overnight	P.C. BEAM				
Blk H 4th Storey	7	1:30	P.C. PLANK	0:12:51	0:11:36	13%	10%
Blk H 4th Storey	2	0:15	P.C. BEAM	0:07:30	0:06:15	7%	10%

Location	No of Pcs Delivered	Unloading Time	Type of Elements	Other P.C. Element Category			
				Unloading Time Per Slab	Process Time Wastage	Process Time Wastage (RPT)	Rounded RTP
Blk H 4th Storey	4	0:25	P.C. BEAM	0:06:15	0:05:00	6%	10%
Blk H 4th Storey	7	0:20	P.C. PLANK	0:02:51	0:01:36	2%	0%
Blk H 4th Storey	2	0:05	P.C. COLUMN	0:02:30	0:01:15	1%	0%
Blk H 4th Storey	17	0:25	P.C. STAIR TREAD	0:01:28	0:00:13	0%	0%
Blk H Roof	5	0:30	P.C. ROOF BEAM	0:06:00	0:04:45	5%	10%
Blk H Roof	4	0:25	P.C. ROOF BEAM	0:06:15	0:05:00	6%	10%
Blk H Roof	4	0:15	P.C. ROOF BEAM	0:03:45	0:02:30	3%	0%
Blk H Roof	5	0:10	P.C. ROOF BEAM	0:02:00	0:00:45	1%	0%

234

APPENDIX 4

Product Development Assistance Scheme (PDAS)

Eligibility

1   Singapore companies with 31 per cent or more local shareholding.

General criteria

1   Product must be of high technical standard and conform to sound design practice.

2   Product development team must demonstrate indepth knowledge of technical and commercial aspects of product / process.

3   Development work must be carried out in Singapore by local engineers or designers.

4   Foreign experts or local consultants can be engaged to supervise the project.

5   Product / process must be marketable and not a one-off project.

Amount of grant

1   Grant equals to 50 per cent of approved, direct development costs, including manpower, equipment, materials and utilities.

2   No ceiling on amount of grant.

3   Support available for feasibility studies.

Disbursement of funds

1   Disbursed in two stages on a reimbursement basis. First disbursement of 50 per cent of actual cost incurred up to maximum of 50 per cent of grant. Second disbursement on completion of project.

(Source: Construction Industry Development Board, Singapore)

Bibliography

Aggarwal, S.C. (1985), 'MRP, JIT, OPT, FMS? Making sense of production operation systems', *Harvard Business Review*, September-October 1985, pp. 8-16.

Akintoye, A. (1995), 'Just-In-Time application and implementation for building material management', *Construction Management and Economics* Vol. 13 No. 2, pp. 105-113.

Anderson, J.C., et.al. (1982), *Material requirement planning systems: The state of the art,* Fourt Quarter.

Ansari, A. and Modarress, B. (1990), *Just-In-Time Purchasing*, The Free Press, New York.

Ball, M. (1988), *Rebuilding Construction*, Routledge, London.

Baxendale, A.T. (1985), 'Site production efficiency', *Building Technology and Management,* October 1985.

Bishop, D. (1975), *Productivity in the construction industry*, in Turin, D.A. (Ed) *Aspects of the economics of construction*, Godwin, London, pp. 58-96.

Bell, L.C. and Stukhart, G. (1986), 'Attributes of materials management systems', *Journal of Construction Engineering and Management,* ASCE, Vol. 112 No. 1, pp. 14-21.

Chandler, I.E. (1978), *Materials management on building sites*, Construction Press, Lancaster, UK.

Chartered Institute of Building (1980), *Materials Control and Waste in Building,* HMSO, UK.

Cheetham, D.W. and Hall, A.D. (1984), 'The key to productivity improvements through the use of hand held power tools', in *Proceedings of the 1st CIB W65 International Symposium on Organisation and Management*, University of Waterloo, Ontario, Vol. 2, pp. 517-555.

Christian, A.J. (1987), 'The impact of microcomputers and artificial intelligence on productivity', in *Proceedings of the 5th CIB W65 International Symposium on The Organisation and Management of Construction*, Vol. 2, 'Productivity and Human Factors in Construction', Lansley, P.R. and Harlow, D.A. (Eds), E & FN Spon, London, pp. 710-715.

CIDB (1992), *Construction Productivity Taskforce Report*, Construction Industry Development Board, Singapore.

CIDB (1992), *CONQUAS. The CIDB Construction Quality Assessment System*, Construction Industry Development Board, Singapore.

Dale, B.G and Plunkett, J.J. (1990), *Managing Quality*, Phillip Alan, London.

Dale, S. (1986), *JIT and its impact on the supplier claim*, in Mortimer, J. (Ed) *Just-In-Time: An executive briefing*, IFS (Publishers) Ltd, Bedford, UK.

Economic Planning Committee, The (1991), *The strategic economic plan. Towards a developed nation*, Ministry of Trade and Industry, Singapore.

Feigenbaum, A.V. (1983), *Total Quality Control*, McGraw-Hill, New York.

Grimm, C.T and Wagner, N.K. (1974), 'Weather effects on mason productivity', *Journal of the Construction Division*, ASCE, Vol. 100 No. CO3, September 1974.

Hall, R.W. (1983), *Zero Inventories*, Homewood, IL: Dow Jones - Irwin.

Hay, E.J. (1988), *The Just-In-Time Breakthrough - Implementing the new manufacturing basics*, John Wiley & Sons, New York.

Henderson, B.D. (1986), 'The logic of kanban', *Journal of Business Strategy*, Vol. 6, Winter 1986, pp. 6-12.

Hernandez, A. (1989), *Just-In-Time manufacturing - A practical approach*, Prentice-Hall, Englewood Cliffs, New Jersey.

Hutchins, D. (1988), *Just-In-Time*, Gower Technical Press.

Institute of Building (1979), *Try Reducing Waste*, IOB Site Control Guide, UK.

Juran, J.M. (Ed) (1974), *Quality control handbook*, McGraw-Hill, New York.

Kangari, R. and Halpin, D.W. (1989), 'Potential robotics utilisation in construction', *Journal of Construction Engineering and Management*, ASCE, Vol. 115 No. 1, March 1989, pp. 126-143.

Lascelles, D.M. and Dale, B.G. (1990), 'Product quality improvement through supplier development', in *Managing Quality,* Dale, B.G. and Plunkett, J.J. (Eds), Phillip Allan, UK.

Lewis, T.M. (1987), 'Is productivity a problem?', *In Proceedings of the 5th CIB W65 International Symposium on The Organisation and Management of Construction*, Vol. 2, 'Productivity and Human Factors in Construction', Lansley, P.R. and Harlow, P.A. (Eds), E & FN Spon, London, pp. 778-787.

Lim, L.Y. and Low, S.P. (1992), *Just-In-Time productivity for construction*, SNP Publishers Pte Ltd, Singapore.

Low, S.P. (1991), 'Improving productivity in the construction industry', *Southeast Asia Building,* p. 30.

Low, S.P. (1992), 'The Just-In-Time concept to improving manufacturing productivity: Is it applicable to the construction industry?', *Construction Papers Series*, The Chartered Institute of Building, UK.

Low, S.P. (1992a), 'Productivity issues in construction procurement methods', *The Surveyor,* Vol. 27 No. 3, Institution of Surveyors, Malaysia, pp. 58-63.

Low, S.P. (1992b), 'Management: sizing up the best', *The Chartered Builder,* Vol. 4 No. 10, p. 14.

Low, S.P. (1992c), 'Improving construction productivity: lessons from the manufacturing industry', *Southeast Asia Building,* pp. 41-46.

Low, S.P. (1992d), 'Raising construction productivity in Singapore', *Stock Exchange of Singapore Journal,* Vol. 20 No. 12, pp. 28-32.

Low, S. P. (1993), 'The application of quantitative methods for Just-In-Time Construction', *Unibeam,* Vol. 22, Building and Estate Management Society, National University of Singapore, pp. 37-51.

Low, S.P. (1993a) 'Just-In-Time productivity for building management: The design-and-build perspective', *The Building Journal,* pp. 24-30.

Low, S.P. (1994), 'Managing confined construction sites using the Just-In-Time concept', *Building Technology and Management Journal,* Vol. 20, pp. 23-29.

Low, S.P. and Chan, Y.M. (1996), 'The application of Just-In-Time principles to process layout for precast concrete production', *Singapore Management Review,* Vol. 18 No. 2, pp. 16-20.

Low, S.P. and Tan. K.L. (1996), 'Quantifying JIT productivity for construction: Three case studies', in *Proceedings of the Second International Congress on Construction: Productivity in Construction - International Experiences,* Raffles City Convention Centre, Singapore, 5-6 November 1996, pp. 104-110.

Lubben, R.T. (1988), *Just-In-Time Manufacturing: An aggressive manufacturing strategy,* McGraw-Hill, New York.

Macbeth, D.K., Baxter, L.F., Ferguson, N. and George, C. (1988), 'Buyer-Vendor relationships with Just-In-Time: Lessons from US multinationals', *Industrial Engineering,* September 1988, pp. 38-41.

Malcolm, R., et. al. (1987), 'Measurement of factors affecting labour productivity on construction site', *In Proceedings of the 5th CIB W65 International Symposium on The Organisation and Management of Construction,* Vol. 2, 'Productivity and Human Factors in Construction', Lansley, P.R. and Harlow, P.A. (Eds), E & FN Spon, London, pp. 669-680.

Maloney, W.F. (1983), 'Productivity improvement: The influence of labour', *Journal of Construction Engineering and Management,* Vol. 109 No. 3, September 1983.

Monden, Y. (1983), *Toyota Production System: A practical approach to production management,* Institute of Industrial Engineering, Norcoss, Georgia.

Mortimer, J. (Ed) (1986), *Just-In-Time: An executive briefing,* IFS (Publications) Ltd, Bedford, UK.

Neo, R. B. (1995), 'Accounting for waste in construction' *In Proceedings of the First International Conference on Construction Project Management* organised by the Centre for Advanced Construction Studies, Nanyang Technological University, January 1995, pp. 399-406.

O'Grady, P.J. (1988), *Putting the Just-In-Time philosophy into practice: A strategy for production managers,* Kogan Page Ltd.

Oglesby, C.H., Parker, H.W. and Howell, G.A. (1989), *Productivity improvement in construction,* McGraw-Hill Book Co., New York.

Orlicky, J. (1975), *Material Requirements Planning*, McGraw-Hill.

Ouchi, W. (1981), *Theory Z*, Addison-Wesley, Reading, Massachusetts.

Rosenfeld, Y., Warszawski, A. amd Laufer, A. (1991), 'Quality circles in temporary organisations: Lessons from construction projects', *International Journal of Project Management*, Vol. 9 No. 1, February 1991, pp. 21-27.

Schmenner, R.W. (1990), *Production / Operations Management*, 4th Edn., Macmillan Inc.

Schonberger, R.J. (1982), *Japanese manufacturing techniques - none hidden lessons in simplicity*, The Free Press, New York.

Schonberger, R.J. (1986), *World Class Manufacturing,* The Free Press, New York.

Schroeder, R.G. (1989), *Operations management decision making in the operations function*, McGraw-Hill, Inc.

Sepehri, M. (1986), *Just-In-Time, Not Just In Japan*, APICS.

Shingo, S. (1982), *Study of Toyota Production System from industrial engineering view point*, Japan Management Association, Tokyo.

Skoyles, E. R. (1976), *Material wastage - A misuse of resources*, Building Research Establishment, UK.

Skoyles, E. R. (1978), *Site accounting for materials,* Building Research Establishment, UK.

Skoyles, E.R. and Skoyles, J.R. (1987), *Waste prevention on site*, Mitchell Publishing Co., London.

Sozen, Z. and Giritli, H. (1987), 'Equipment policy as one of the factors affecting construction productivity. A comparative study', in *Proceedings of the 5th CIB W65 International Symposium on The Organisation and Management of Construction*, Vol. 2, 'Productivity and Human Factors in Construction', Lansley, P.R. and Harlow, D.A. (Eds), E & FN Spon, London, pp. 691-696.

Stendel, H.J. and Desruelle, P. (1992), *Manufacturing in the nineties*, Van Nostrand Reinhold, New York.

Strassman, P.A. (1985), *Information pay-off*, The Free Press, New York.

Sugimori, Y., Kusunoki, F., Cho, F. and Uchikawa, S. (1971), 'Toyota production system and kanban materialisation of just-in-time and respect-for-human system', *International Journal of Production Research*, Vol. 15 No. 6, pp. 553-564.

Sugimori, Y., Kusunoki, F., Cho, F. and Uchikawa, S. (1986), 'Toyota production and kanban system - The materialisation of just-in-time system', in Mortimer, J. (Ed) *Just-In-Time - An executive briefing*, IFS (Publications) Ltd, Bedford, UK.

Suite, W.H.E. (1987), 'Measurements of productivity in the construction sector', in *Proceedings of the 5th CIB W65 International Symposium on The Organisation and Management of Construction*, Vol. 2, 'Productivity and Human Factors in Construction', Lansley, P.R. and Harlow, D.A. (Eds), E & FN Spon, London, pp. 856-867.

Sumanth, D.J. (1984), *Productivity engineering and management*, McGraw-Hill Book Co.

Sunday Times (1996), 'Builders must upgrade or die', *The Sunday Times,* Singapore, 17 November 1996, p. 3.

239

Thomas, B. (1987), *Applicability of Just-In-Time techniques in the administrative area,* unpublished PhD thesis, University of Nebraska.

Thomas, H.R., Mathews, C.T. and Ward, J.G. (1986), 'Learning curve models of construction productivity', *Journal of Construction Engineering and Management,* ASCE, Vol. 122 No. 2, June 1986, pp. 245-258.

Vollman, E., Berry, L. and Whybark, D. (1984), *Manufacturing planning and control systems,* Dow Jones-Irwin.

Voss, C.A. (1987), *Just-In-Time Manufacture,* IFS (Publications) Ltd, Bedford, UK.

Voss, C.A. and Clutterbuck, D. (1989), *Just-In-Time: A global status report,* IFS (Publications) Ltd, Bedford, UK.

Voss, C.A. and Harrison, A. (1987), 'Strategies for implementing JIT', in Voss, C.A. (Ed) *Just-In-Time Manufacturing,* IFS (Publications) Ltd, Bedford, UK.

Voss, C.A. and Robinson, S.J (1987), 'Application of just-in-time manufacturing techniques in the United Kingdom', *International Journal of Operations & Production Management,* Vol. 7 No. 4, pp. 46-52.

Wallace, T. (1985), *MRP II: Making it happen,* Oliver Wight Publications.

Wantuck, K.A. (1989), *Just-In-Time for America: A common sense production strategy,* The Forum Ltd, Milwaukee, WI.

240